CHINA RETURNS

CHINA RETURNS

Klaus Mehnert

Translated from the German

E. P. DUTTON & CO., INC. | NEW YORK | 1972

All quotations from the Little Red Book (*Quotations from Chairman Mao Tse-tung*) are taken from the Peking translation. (Foreign Languages Press, second edition 1967).

Contents

PART III   BACKGROUND

PART IV   DOCUMENTS

Preface

China in the spring of 1971 was in many ways as little known to the rest of the world as the surface of the moon. With the onset of the Cultural Revolution five years before, the frontiers of that vast nation had been closed off so completely that there seemed to be about as many astronauts going to the moon as there were foreign observers getting into China.

It was my good fortune, just before the advent of "ping-pong politics," to spend a little over a month traveling through fourteen of China's twenty-nine provinces. The experience of being a visitor to China was hardly a novelty for me: my acquaintance with that country dates back no less than forty-two years, beginning with a visit I made there in 1929, following a year as an exchange student in California. Then in 1936, after Goebbels had ordered the three German newspapers for whom I was a Moscow correspondent not to continue publishing my dispatches, I left the Soviet Union for America—once again traveling by way of China. My third and most protracted visit came during the Second World War. I was still a German citizen, and when it became clear to me that the United States would soon be at war with Germany, I left my teaching post at the University of Hawaii and went to China. This time I stayed five years. Most of my stay was in Shanghai, where I taught in several universities and edited a periodical, *The Twentieth Century*. I returned to Europe in 1946. In 1957 I went back to China for a month as a journalist and radio commentator; I arrived in Shanghai by ship and left by train, traveling home through Mongolia and the Soviet Union. All these experiences, not to mention numerous visits to Hong Kong and Taiwan, formed the background for my visit in the spring of 1971. A stay of just over a month is, of course, hardly time to allow for more than a quick glance—but that compression of time does serve to allow impressions of a peculiar intensity.

Besides my years in China, I have spent five years of my life studying and working in the Soviet Union, and five more in the United States. My interest in Russia is natural enough: I was born in Moscow. My parents were German, and they left Russia at the outbreak of the First World War. During my university days I studied Russian history, and I returned whenever the opportunity presented itself, first as a student and later as a journalist. Since I speak the language without a foreign accent, I was often able to vanish into the crowd and to make friends of all sorts as I traveled through the country. My first book about the U.S.S.R. was *Youth in Soviet Russia* (1932); then came *Soviet Man* (1960), and *Peking and Moscow* (1963).

No less important were the five years I spent in America, teaching European, Russian, and Pacific history at the Universities of California and of Hawaii. Of first importance is the Berkeley girl I married, and who shared my roving life until her death in 1955. I have also visited the United States on numerous other occasions, lecturing at universities, taking part in scholarly conferences, teaching a semester at Berkeley, and doing research at Stanford and Harvard.

I have it on reliable authority that I am the only observer of world affairs who spent considerable time in all three of the great centers of power—China, Russia, and the United States—during the crucial year of 1971.

But although I have quite inevitably drawn on my past experiences in China, as well as on my familiarity with Russian communism, this book is concerned with China after the Cultural Revolution. By the time I arrived, the upheaval that had shaken the country appeared to be over: a huge effort of will and activity seemed to have brought both the economy and the social structure back into working order.

When I entered China, nothing was further from my mind than the thought of writing a book. I knew perfectly well that since the height of the Cultural Revolution in 1967, almost no one had been granted permission to travel around the country. So I hardly hoped for more than to be allowed to visit Canton and Shanghai, besides Peking. As it turned out, just about all the requests I listed were to be granted—with two exceptions, which will be duly noted and which are of some interest in themselves.

Of course I saw only what my hosts wanted me to see. But I was not led about blindfolded. Every waking minute I was taking in impressions. And years of study and investigation can be confirmed or shaken by what one sees and hears on the spot. Even a Mao quotation one knows by heart becomes something quite different when it comes from the mouth of a rock-laden peasant in one of China's distant provinces. And the political role of Mao's wife, which has been so much discussed by foreign China-watchers (including myself), takes on a very different meaning when one is face to face with her enormous cultural influence.

After leaving China, I became acutely aware of what a difference in perspective can do to the way one sees things. Experts in Hong Kong or Europe would ask questions to which I had scarcely given a thought while I was in China ("Where is Chen Po-ta? What has become of Kang Sheng?") Yet these same experts, I found, would barely listen when I tried to explain the results of my painstaking research into the finances of a tea brigade.

In this book I have followed what seems to me the sound journalistic principle of separating report from commentary. The first section records what I saw and heard. The second presents the thoughts that were stimulated by these impressions, and offers some conclusions. Can one offer conclusions after a visit of just over a month? I am convinced that we not only can but must have the courage to formulate opinions—and then to revise them if they prove incorrect. In this section I have drawn on the work of numerous others—whose names are duly noted—as well as some studies of my own: *Mao's Second Revolution* (1966) and *Peking and the New Left* (1969). The third section fills in the background with information on developments connected with the Cultural Revolution. Finally, part four gives a small sampling from the masses of directives, homilies, theorizing, and cultural propaganda that are now pouring from the presses of the Chinese People's Republic. It allows the reader to have a first-hand impression of the style of these things, and some of the atmosphere surrounding them.

As unfamiliar as the surface of the moon? Perhaps. But how much more important it is for us in the West to understand China's people, at this point in history, than it is to know what it looks like on the moon.

11

This visit was made possible by

Prince Norodom Sihanouk of Cambodia, who requested my visa

Premier Chou En-lai, who granted it

Li Ching-ping and Tao Hsiang-chen, my tireless travel companions

The hundreds of Chinese citizens who took the time to answer my questions

To you all, my thanks

PART I: REPORTING

The reports that follow were written in first draft during my trip, while the impressions were still fresh—either in the evening at my hotel or, some of them, on trains, with my typewriter perched on my knees. I finally retained only those notes that seemed to have political or immediate factual relevance; I left out what might be called tourist impressions. So the material has been organized according to my experiences, rather than according to themes or issues. In this way the reader can share the various stages of my journey and, in a sense, listen to my questions and their answers, so as to judge for himself how I came to various conclusions or interpretations: my understanding of the wage systems, for instance. He can see for himself how certain things became clearer to me as my journey progressed.

1: The Visa

My most recent trip to China has a long earlier history. Fifteen years ago I had received a letter bearing an unusual stamp. It came from Phnom Penh and carried the signature of the head of state of Cambodia, Prince Norodom Sihanouk. He wrote that his attention had been drawn to my then recent book *Asia, Moscow and Ourselves,* which contained, he said, an objective and factually correct account of Cambodia: and he invited me to visit him on my next trip to Indochina.

A year later I met him for the first time; after that we saw each other often, in Europe as well as in Asia. There grew between us a personal friendship which survived the Cambodian coup d'etat in the spring of 1970, and the Prince's departure for Peking.

Getting a visa for my previous visits to China had never been a particular problem, even in 1957, during the era of the Hundred Flowers. There had never been a long wait. But then things changed. China went through a major upheaval—the "Great Leap Forward," the ensuing economic crisis, and the internal struggle between the "two ways"—those of Mao and of his opponents. Then came the Great Proletarian Cultural Revolution, and I suppose the authorities in Peking did not welcome curious visitors, particularly those having some previous acquaintance with their country. But I never grew discouraged, and from time to time I would optimistically send in another request. For some time these were without result.

In 1969, as the situation in China returned to normal after the end of the Cultural Revolution, I received the first answer to my request for a visa. It was a refusal, but the tone seemed friendly and the no did not sound definitive; so in 1970 I harked back to this earlier request.

In the middle of January, 1971, I received a telegram from Peking, asking me to visit the embassy of the People's Republic of China in Paris. There I learned that Prince Sihanouk had interceded for me with the authorities. Prince Sihanouk is a distinguished visitor in Peking, so it is not extraordinary that his request that one of his friends be given a visa was granted. What did surprise me, as it did the foreign colony of Peking, was my being permitted to take a lengthy trip throughout the land, which for years had been closed to most foreigners.

So at the end of the winter semester I flew to East Asia, and on the sixth of March, 1971, I entered China—more than a month before the start of "ping-pong diplomacy."

One of the main reasons for my exceptional good fortune must have been that the Chinese leaders were eager to have the rest of the world better informed about China after her very swift return to the arena of world politics, and the best way of achieving this was through a few informed Western observers. It is possible that this official decision crossed some desk at the foreign ministry in Peking just as Prince Sihanouk was putting in his request for his friend. It may even have been the same desk on which my many previous requests had landed, or possibly transcripts of radio broadcasts I had made favoring diplomatic relations between Bonn and Peking may have wound up there. One thing is certain—that at some time in the course of winter 1970–71 a basic decision must have been made to allow the doors of China to swing open a little, and I just happened to be the first visitor to pass through them.

I do not know whether a friendly gesture toward Bonn was indicated by the generous decision to allow me a journey through fourteen provinces of China. Someone who knows China well said to me in Peking: "The Chinese engage in long-range politics; they may be irritated that the Germans go on pretending China does not exist, but they never forget that, outside of Russia, you are the strongest nation in Europe."

However it may have come about, I went to the Chinese Travel Service in Hong Kong, where for the equivalent of about fifty dollars I bought a ticket, including the sleeping car. I was on my way.

2: The First 1,200 Miles

When the hotel porter woke me at six o'clock I felt like an astronaut for whom the countdown had begun. In just four hours I would cross the border into China, and I had much to do. Before the China Travel Service handed over my ticket, I had signed my agreement to a paper stating that people sometimes slipped things into the baggage of voyagers from Hong Kong to the People's Republic of China; thus each traveler would be held responsible for bringing in only his own effects. I was determined to take not the slightest chance at this last moment before reaching the goal I had anticipated for so long. Whatever might have been the true import of the warning I had signed, for me an important part of the countdown was now a thorough inspection of my luggage.

At eight o'clock my taxi deposited me at the station just beside the harbor, where I was to check into a special room reserved for travelers to China. It was not difficult to find, since a few other Europeans were already standing before the door. They examined me as curiously as I examined them. By the time the door opened there were twelve of us.

At 8:25 the gates were opened, and immediately a stream of pushing, burden-carrying Chinese swept our little band onto the platform. Most of them, of course, were only going to one of the seven stations this side of the border. In the first-class carriage were the twelve of us, joined by a horde of blond English schoolgirls on an excursion to the nearby Temple of a Thousand Buddhas.

Pretty Chinese children from an English language school made their way through the train collecting money for a hospital. I put a coin into their box and was given a button—the last one not bearing the head of Mao that I was to see for the next four weeks. From time to time the man from the China Travel Service, in his blue uniform and white cap, would look in on the compartment to make sure his flock was complete.

A typical south China landscape rolled by our windows: rice fields, villages, pagodas, and a dense human swarm. When we reached the end of the line and clambered out of our train, I could already see the famous covered bridge, about a hundred yards away—the bridge across the border. A red flag fluttered in the breeze. At that precise moment the public address system went into action and began to drone the solemn rhythms of "The East Is Red."

Formalities on the British side took only a few minutes. I just had time enough to exchange a few words with the soldier in charge, who sat on a folding chair, all blond and pink and bored, glancing occasionally at the wares the street vendors exhibited at the entrance to the bridge. A little old woman, offering a great hodgepodge of wares, waved me to her side and then pointed with a huge grin at her stock of toilet paper. She must know what she's doing, I thought, and bought a roll. Later I was to be grateful for the hint.

And now there appeared a man wearing a Mao button; his suit and cap were gray. In very good English he asked us to follow him. So we walked across the famous bridge. The formalities on this side, in the customs house, took about two and a half hours. It was like being on a quirky escalator that was taking the twelve of us out of one world and into another. Each of the rooms through which we passed contained armchairs with white covers, pictures of Mao, and quotations from Mao.

In the first of these rooms we had to fill out forms about our luggage. Then we were called up one by one and led into separate customs booths. My customs man only looked briefly at my visa and then waved me through. Next came health formalities, followed by currency registration and exchange (I had brought German marks and Hong Kong dollars). Then came a fairly long walk leading to an especially splendid waiting room. Here the Mao quotations were composed of big wooden letters mounted on dark red velvet.

In the course of all this the twelve of us had come to know each other. Half of the group were diplomats: a chargé d'affaires from a European country, returning with his wife from home leave; another young man employed by a Western embassy in Peking, also with his wife; and two couriers, a man and a woman, easy to recognize by their big pouches. Of the rest, one was a lady who had come to spend several weeks at one of the embassies with a daughter who worked there, and two were French lady tourists. Finally, there was the head of a French business concern, accompanied by a colleague, and I brought the number to twelve. . . .

At about noon, in yet another room, we were served a Chinese luncheon. Then we were taken back into the waiting room with the Mao quotations on velvet. Girls in white aprons, wearing their hair in two short braids—as they did almost everywhere—brought us tea. They knew a few scraps of English, and giggled at us in a friendly fashion. I should probably say now, in fact, that almost everyone I met from the border on was extremely friendly. However it may have been during the Cultural Revolution—and a number of travelers reported extremely aggressive attitudes—the barometer was now set firmly on good cheer. When I asked whether I might have permission to photograph the famous bridge across the border, I was told, "Why, certainly!" A short time before, the answer would have been just as "certainly" to the contrary.

The trip from the border to Canton, the biggest and most important city in south China, took two hours. The twelve of us were all by ourselves in a big, very comfortable train carriage with sixty upholstered seats. I spent the trip looking eagerly out of the window at the hilly landscape. As always, I was impressed by the careful construction of the rice terraces and their irrigation systems; running between them were narrow paths, on which I could see people in dark cotton suits and big hats walking with small quick steps, carrying their loads on swaying bamboo poles. Children sat dozing on the backs of water buffaloes. Here and there on the sides of the hills I could still make out some ancient graves. A new product of the years 1969–70 was the sight of many caves dug into the sides of the hills—air raid shelters which the Chinese have dug by the hundreds of thousands to shield themselves against possible Soviet attack.

We arrived in Canton. I had barely gotten my coat on when I was asked, in German, whether I was the visitor from West Germany. The man had the usual Chinese difficulties with the "r" in my name, but no doubt about it, he meant me. He is about thirty-five, works for the China Travel Service, and his name is Chang. His German is fluent; he learned it in school, he tells me. As I start to reach for my luggage, it turns out that his people have already taken it away, unnoticed by me. I barely have time to say goodbye to my eleven companions, and here I am with Mr. Chang and my luggage in a car of vaguely English provenance.

Clearing the way with our horn, we make it to the other side of Canton. The architecture of my hotel is pure People's Democratic style, the kind one sees all over Eastern Europe. The lobby has been arranged to great effect: you go from the bright light in the street to the murky interior, and straight ahead of you is an enormous red curtain forming the backdrop for a huge plaster statue of Chairman Mao. I go up to my room, which is large and rather stiffly decorated, get rid of my luggage, and go back down to the car.

Canton today is a city of over two million inhabitants, but it has not changed much since the 1920s and 1930s, when a whole network of new streets was cut into its innards. A series of parks has made it more agreeable, and the slums, including the floating ones on the Pearl River, have disappeared.

The streets become more and more crowded; more and more people are returning from work, many of them on bicycles. Troops of school children, each with a little red flag, appear and stand in rows on both sides of the street to separate the bicycles from the cars in the center. But however eagerly the children brandish their flags, the whole thoroughfare is soon crowded with bicycles. This predominance of the two-wheeler is my first strong impression of change in the city.

I am eager for a look, once more, at Shamian Island in the middle of the Pearl River. Today it is part of the city; it once lay beyond the walls. Over a hundred years ago the English and French took possession of what was then just a sandbank, and began to transform it into a kind of miniature Europe. It still retains much of its old character today: it is full of villas that stand on straight, tree-lined streets, and there is a pretty promenade along the banks of the river. Once the Chinese accepted this bit of Europe quite cheerfully; but today, as my companion's remarks make clear, it inflames their national pride. Mr. Chang is eager to show me the new China, particularly the great halls where twice a year the city's famous fairs are held; the modern hotels, and the government buildings of the province; to say nothing of the new factories just outside the city limits.

In the evening we arrived at the station a few minutes before the train was due to leave. To my surprise I discovered I had been allotted a four-person compartment with "soft seats," which included pillows, bed linen, and a rug. As I was to discover later, I was the only non-Chinese on the entire train.

I was surrounded by small courtesies. The young conductor in charge of the "soft" car kept bringing me tea and hot water. The man in charge of the dining car saw to it that I had a seat by a window, and as soon as he had discovered that I was fond of Chinese cooking, urged his chef to outdo himself; which produced, among other things, an excellent fish in a sweet-and-sour sauce. The only thing lacking was the excellent amber-colored wine which the Chinese drink slightly warmed—an omission that seemed to pain him more than it did me. There was hot water to be had, in little beakerlike mugs with lids to guard against the dust, in the other, often overcrowded carriages.

At each station long lines of people came out of the train, to stand waiting for the women who sold flat cakes and an occasional orange. I barely glimpsed my companions in the "soft" car. They must have spent the time behind closed doors in their compartments, scarcely appearing even at the stations. There were large numbers of men in the green uniform of the military; but since all insignia of rank were abolished in 1965, the officers can no longer be distinguished from their men except perhaps by the stronger lines of their features and their slightly greater age.

In the compartment next to mine there was a young Chinese diplomat. He was thirty-one years old, and his career seemed to me incredibly close to the norm: twelve years of school, six years of university education, then a few years in the foreign ministry (although he had been sent abroad, he had not yet held a foreign post). No military service, nor physical labor in a village. His

21

wife, however, as part of the "Intellectual Youth to the Countryside" movement, had been sent to one of the provinces, he couldn't say for how long. Their two-year-old child is with its grandmother in Peking; he lives alone.

I had already grown used to the constant drone of the loudspeakers, which most visitors to China seem to find so intensely annoying. There are, I discovered, buttons to turn the thing off, only they're hard to find—mine was hidden underneath the small table. But even if you do manage to turn it off, you still get your share from the corridor and the neighboring compartments: editorials, political speeches, news, music; some of it from the radio, some of it from records that are played in the train's central transmission compartment.

During the first night we crossed Kwangtung Province, and then Hunan Province, Mao's home. Toward morning we reached Changsha, the capital of Hunan. Our ten-minute stopover kept me from visiting the sacred sites of this city, most notably the training school for teachers that Mao attended from 1913 to 1918, and which is responsible for the greater part of his classical education, as well as for his emotional development. It was in Changsha that he married the daughter of his favorite teacher, who was executed a decade later by Chiang Kai-shek's government.

Our train now crossed a hilly section of the country, passing thousands upon thousands of rice terraces. Many of the reservoirs, built to secure a regular flow of water throughout the year, appeared to be new. From time to time I saw small factories, but I could not make out what they produced. At about two in the afternoon we approached the city of Wuhan, which used to be three separate cities. The Yangtze River gives it access to the sea, and the flags of many nations were once to be seen along its quays.

I was particularly eager to see the bridge across the Yangtze that had been built here with Russian help in 1957. It is renowned less for its beauty than for its length (almost a mile) and its height (about 230 feet). There isn't a Chinese alive who will not declare that the other bridge across the Yangtze, near the city of Nanking, built without foreign help in 1960, after Russian aid was withdrawn, is much better and more beautiful.

The view from the bridge is splendid, down across the wide brown river with its many junks and boats. Broad stretches devoted to industry, with several high blast furnaces, were to be seen, but no tall buildings. Many of the houses seem to be in bad condition; often the roofs we looked down upon seemed in need of repair. As always, there were large crowds of people in the streets, and once again crowds of bicycles but few cars.

Now the landscape slowly became harsher. The gentle hills grew to mountains, which we passed under by way of a long tunnel. When I awoke the second morning I looked out upon a snowy landscape. The temperature had grown noticeably cooler in the train as well. Now we no longer had far to go: punctually at eight-thirty in the morning we arrived in Peking.

3: Return to Peking

The scene in Peking that morning was one of bustling activity. Trains were arriving simultaneously on many of the station's platforms. There were no porters, and I was glad I had remained true to my principle never to take more luggage than I could carry by myself. I had to walk half a mile or more: down the platform, through a tunnel, and across a huge lobby. The Chinese carried their things on the traditional bamboo poles, except for the numerous soldiers with neatly packed knapsacks on their backs.

Peking has a new central station, built in the Mao style just a few years ago. A sizeable section of town was torn down to make room for it and for the huge square in front of it. Running along the opposite side of this square is the new east-west axis. On this same thoroughfare is the Hotel Peking, to which a car now brought me, and a short distance farther on is the Gate of Heavenly Peace, the famous reviewing stand in front of what was once the entrance to the old Imperial Palace, where the national leaders appear during major parades. The oldest part of the hotel had been in existence at the time of my first visit forty-two years before; it is now used for other purposes. The new hotel, built next to it in the 1950s, also contains huge gala and meeting rooms.

I deposited my bags and went right out again to take my first walk across the famous parade ground. The Gate of Heavenly Peace is an impressive monument, entirely harmonious in both its form and colors. In the afternoon light it glowed a vivid crimson against the background of the blue northern sky. Not far away, lying behind the wall in the southwestern section of the old Imperial Palace grounds, are Chairman Mao's quarters.

This huge open space, to which many houses were sacrificed, is usually empty of people; but on holidays and demonstration days it is filled with crowds of hundreds of thousands, sometimes even millions, of human beings. Two enormous new buildings, the museum and the Hall of the People, face the square on the east and west. They are not everyone's taste: built in the ponderous People's-Democracy style, they are monuments to power rather than harmony. They are neither continuations of traditional Chinese art forms nor are they a breakthrough to something new. In other domains there are signs of strong new impulses, but in architecture today's China has not yet seen fit to include these new ideas. In the center of the open space is the Monument for the Dead of the Movement, which I did find most impressive. It reminded me of the steles of classical antiquity, raised here to a monumental level.

A few steps beyond the Peking Hotel, at right angles to the east-west axis, lay Peking's main shopping street, the Wang fuching. To the Americans and Europeans who once lived in Peking, or who came to visit, it was known as Morrison Street, and every rickshaw coolie understood what you meant when you said this name. Today hardly anyone remembers, and a foreigner must ask for it by the old Chinese name, which everyone still uses although several years ago it was officially renamed "The People's Street" because *The People's Daily,* China's most important newspaper, has its offices there.

Forty-two years ago Morrison Street was my idea of a Chinese street—stores and restaurants, a swarming tide of people, countless rickshaws and horse-drawn carts, and a marvelous bazaar which for me contained all the wonders of the Far East; little shops with all sorts of fabulous materials and lacquerware, vendors of precious stones both real and fake, even tellers of fairy stories, magicians, and sword-swallowers.

I noticed the first of the great changes in 1957: on the west side of the street, not far from the bazaar, a six-story department store had gone up. I now went straight to it, just as I had then. The selection of things on sale had grown markedly larger, and the pushing crowd seemed less intense. The place has lost its monopoly position, since today "The People's Street" contains a number of stores offering similar merchandise. In fact, even the bazaar has become a kind of one-story department store. For me its new, starkly utilitarian character was a disappointment, but for the people of Peking it is obviously a welcome advance, since the whole huge area is filled with wide roofed-over streets lined with shops.

In 1957 I had been in Peking in midsummer, and had found that I needed a couple of light sports shirts. When I went to this same department store, it was explained to me that I had to have a permit. In order to get this permit I had to place a request with the foreign ministry. A few days later I received my permit to buy two shirts, and eventually I got the shirts—which, incidentally, wore very well.

So, just for information's sake, I thought I'd see how it goes with shirts in Peking in 1971. Accordingly, I made my way to the same department store, and again I met with an obstacle; cotton fabrics still required a permit (purchases of up to eight yards per person per year, at about .75 yuan a yard, were allowable). But this time I was told that foreigners could easily buy such things without a permit in the "friendship store" around the corner. And in fact I got my shirts there—white, no-iron, long-sleeved, for eleven yuan apiece, or the equivalent of about $4.40. For the equivalent of less than two dollars I picked up a handsome blue cotton tie to go with them.

My most unproductive visits were to the bookstores. There is a special bookstore for foreigners, consisting of two huge rooms with high shelves all around, but they sold nothing except the works of Chairman Mao in two dozen languages, or brochures containing his or Lin Piao's speeches on current political themes—these too in dozens of languages. In short, I found nothing I didn't already have. The secondhand bookstore a few houses down was better supplied, although here too what I found was mainly textbooks, the greater part of them in Russian.

In the course of the next few weeks I took notes on the prices of a whole series of items and later I noticed that in different cities and regions of the country those prices hardly varied.

Clothing. Cotton suits in dark blue or other dark colors, which everyone wears and which can be obtained only with a permit, cost upwards of 15 yuan (about $6.00). A padded jacket, the universal winter garment, costs 12 yuan and up, and the same lined with camel's hair rather than cotton is 42 yuan; a woolen jacket is 57.70 yuan, the same with matching trousers 87.72 yuan. Canvas shoes with rubber soles, the most popular footgear, cost upwards of 3 yuan; leather shoes are 10 yuan and up. It seemed to me that socks were quite expensive by comparison with other prices—2.50 to 3 yuan.

Food (prices by the pound unless otherwise indicated). Rice costs from .11 to .16 yuan (the equivalent of 4 to 6 cents in American money); cooking oil is .68 yuan. At the butcher's, pork costs .90 yuan, mutton .59, spareribs .86, sausage 1.09, ham 1.32 to 2.50 yuan. At fruitstands, apples are .36 yuan and tangerines .45 yuan. At drink stands, a glass of milk is .14 yuan, a cup of coffee (I didn't taste it) .10 yuan. A medium-sized can of beef is 1.45, a can of fish is 1.20; mushrooms are one yuan a can, peas 1.80 yuan, jam is 1.45 yuan, pineapple 2.45. Among alcoholic drinks, Maotai, the most popular brandy (and the strongest, said to be 60 proof) costs 4.20 yuan (about $1.70) for a .6 liter bottle; it is thus incomparably cheaper to get drunk in China than in its great neighbor to the west, which is in the throes of an anti-alcoholism campaign and has accordingly set the price of vodka at approximately $4.00 for a .6 liter bottle.

Restaurants are cheap. Even meals in the dining car of the trains generally came to between 1.50 and 2.50 yuan (from 60 cents to $1.00) for an excellent Chinese meal, with rice wine costing one yuan more. Prices for food in the hotels where I stayed were about the same. At a simple public eating place you can get a plate of rice and vegetables for as little as .10 yuan.

Other consumer products. Chinese-made transistor radios, which may be seen in great quantities in the country as well as in the city, cost about 20 yuan (about $8.00) and up; a modest-sized television set costs 430 yuan, a sewing machine 145, a bicycle 120 to 150, and a motor for that bicycle 130; a motorcycle is 600 to 670 yuan, a wrist watch 100 to 120. And finally stationery, a not unimportant item for anyone like me: a hundred sheets of typewriter paper cost .34 yuan, a notebook about the size of a postcard .08 yuan.

During my trip to Yenan, my typewriter ribbon finally disintegrated. Since I was not prepared for a long trip through China, I had not brought along a spare. But when I gave a small piece of the old ribbon to our travel director in Sian, he made it a point of pride to help me out: and indeed he appeared half an hour later proudly bearing exactly the right ribbon, which cost me 2.75 yuan. I have typed the better part of this book with that ribbon.

One of the cheapest things of all in China, for the Chinese, is the roof over one's head, and usually it is not much more than that—generally just one room in which several people live packed together, but which costs no more than 2 to 3.50 yuan per month.

Of course, prices are meaningful only when they can be related to a payscale. I was assured in various parts of the country that the average city salary was about 60 yuan a month, or about $24.00 at the official rate of exchange.

From a personal point of view, my stay in Peking was a disappointment; with a few exceptions its famous monuments were closed to the public. I could not visit Coal Hill, with its view over the city—or the Forbidden City where the emperor lived until 1911 (it was opened a few weeks later for the ping-pong teams and a few diplomats for the first time since the beginning of the Cultural Revolution), or the network of parks with their lakes, castles, and pagodas, or the Temple of Confucius, or the Hall of Classics—or anything much except the Temple of Heaven and the Summer Palace. Of these, more later.

Nor was I able, by the way, to see the capital's latest achievement, the subway, although I asked to see it. And I never managed to find a foreigner living in Peking who had seen it, even though it was officially opened on October 1, 1969; people had gotten into the habit of making ironic remarks about whether it existed at all. But in the meantime it has been shown to a number of foreigners.

One day my driver, Mr. Tsao, took me into the mountains. The road we took went north and then veered to the northwest, almost as the crow flies, running almost parallel with the railway to Inner Mongolia that was opened in 1909. Once the first suburbs have been left behind, you drive through a mixed agrarian and industrial landscape. Several large factory complexes, some of them new since 1957, are visible along both sides of the road. They are situated at some distance from the road, with fields and villages between. The villages had changed far less than I expected. The gateways were new; they were like small triumphal arches, decorated with quotations and pictures of Chairman Mao. Equally new were the administration buildings and storage depots, as well as what were obviously small factories or workshops. The peasants' houses, for the most part, looked just as I remembered them. In some villages I saw one-story houses that looked new.

The fields were alive with rows of workers wearing the familiar padded jackets, many women among them (you could make them out from a distance by the kerchiefs on their heads). It was fertilizing time. Load upon load of manure, which had lain carefully stacked all winter, was being spread over the fields. Here and there it was carried on a horse-drawn cart, but the usual vehicle was a high-wheeled barrow pushed by a man or a woman. In China natural fertilizer has always been very important, and is carefully gathered. Our road was heavily traveled (there were some trucks and buses, but many horse-drawn and mule-drawn carts), and I kept seeing men on bicycles with baskets attached hurrying from one pile to the next, gathering manure for their villages. The road was well-paved, and was usually wide enough for three-or even four-lane traffic. Near the factories there was heavy traffic; later we drove without any delay or hindrance.

The city of Peking lies nestled in a plain, bounded on the west and the north by mountains. From the road one has a clear view of these mountains, since there are no intervening foothills. At the northwestern edge of this plain lies Nankow. The mountains that rise directly behind it are cut by the South Pass, which leads through the Great Wall to Mongolia.

Nankow was once a small town, and derived its importance solely from traffic through the pass; in those days it was filled with camels and carts. But it has grown considerably; many factories are now to be seen, and today a broad road has replaced the steep caravan pass.

But where the mountains begin we are abruptly set back by a decade. The road narrows, and the few houses seem as dateless as the mules and horses that draw the carts. Only the camels have been replaced by trucks. Several of these were making their careful way up the icy, winding road. When two of them meet, they have to pass in first gear.

Then, at last, there it was: the Great Wall! We reached the top of the pass, and I got out to walk through one of its massive gates. The sharp wind from Mongolia struck my face like a blow, and all but knocked me over.

Back at my hotel in Peking, the porter gave me an envelope with an expression appropriate to the delivery of a state document. And from a certain point of view, it was nothing less. It bore the arms of the People's Republic of China and contained an invitation to a banquet. The signature read Chou En-lai, Prime Minister.

4: Chou En-lai's Banquet

The banquet, given in the Great Hall of the People, was to honor Prince Sihanouk on the first anniversary of his new government, formed in Peking after the coup d'etat in Cambodia.

With the official invitation came the message that if I chose I might film the occasion; Radio Peking was prepared to put a camera crew at my disposal. I accepted this offer with thanks, and an hour later the television people arrived at my hotel to discuss details. I explained to them that I was interested mainly in the general atmosphere of the banquet, and its principal actors—the hosts as well as their Cambodian guests. I asked the crew to concentrate on the members of the Politbureau, and if at all possible to take them when they weren't wearing solemn faces for the photographers, but while they were eating or talking. The men nodded with complete understanding, and followed my wishes exactly.

Two weeks later I received a second invitation to the Great Hall of the People. This time the host was the Central Committee of the Chinese Communist Party. The occasion was a visit from highly placed guests from North Vietnam (including Party chief Le Duan), South Vietnam, and Laos. This second reception had an almost identical character, with roughly the same cast of characters. The Great Hall of the People covers an area of approximately five square acres. The entrance for guests is on the north side. A wide staircase leads to its marble-floored and many-columned foyer, which alone has a capacity of several thousand people. Here you find the cloakrooms. Then you go up a second red-carpeted staircase to the main floor. As you do so, you discover before you an enormous painting of sunrise over the mountains, dated 1959. It carries a line from one of Chairman Mao's poems: "How beautiful is the landscape of our homeland." I was to discover color reproductions of this painting adorning the walls of countless rooms in official buildings.

Directly above the foyer is the famous gala hall, well known from many press photographs. When I entered that evening, the stage along its south side was already festooned with microphones. Just below the stage, a long table was set with twenty-two places, all of them facing the room, so that everyone might see the Chinese leaders and their honored guests. On the opposite side of the table were a number of upholstered stools—for the interpreters, as it turned out.

I had come a bit early, with my interpreter, in order to take a look at the place cards on the table of honor. With the exception of Mao and of Lin Piao, who hardly ever goes out, the entire top rank of the Chinese leadership was on hand, or at least all those who were appearing publicly at the time (thus there was no sign of Chen

Po-ta or Kang Sheng, two members of the Politbureau who had taken a particularly radical position during the Cultural Revolution.

Thirty-four tables were set up in the room; I found my place at table number six. The place card to my left carried the name of Kang Mao-chao, the ambassador from the Chinese People's Republic to the government of Prince Sihanouk; after the Cambodian coup d'etat he had followed the Prince to Peking. The place to my right was assigned to one of the chief editorialists of the Peking *People's Daily,* the Chinese equivalent of the Russian *Pravda.* Two other members of my table were the Minister of Transport, Yang Hsieh, and the general in charge of sports in China, which fall under the jurisdiction of the army.

While I was making my rounds, the room had been filling up. There were about four hundred people in all, many of them in uniform, and these as a rule kept their caps on throughout the banquet. Many Cambodians were present, and among the foreigners I could see representatives of those countries that had recognized the legitimacy of Sihanouk's government (a total of twenty-four at that time), as well as others that, although they maintained their missions in Phnom Penh, were overtly friendly to Sihanouk; France was one of these.

A military band seated on the north side of the room, began playing, and as the guests stood respectfully, the dignitaries entered, led by Chou En-lai with Sihanouk. No sooner were they seated at the table of honor than they had to stand again, as six national anthems were played one after another: the Chinese, the Cambodian, the North Korean, the North Vietnamese, the South Vietnamese (Liberation Army), and the Laotian.

This gave me a chance to have a good look at the principal figures of the evening. (About Prince Sihanouk I shall have more to say later.) It was my third encounter with Chou En-lai: I had met him first at the Geneva Conference of 1954, and again during my stay in Peking in 1957, when I met him at a reception in the Peking Hotel on the Polish national holiday. He now looks older than when I had last seen him, and small wonder: the Great Leap Forward in 1958 and the various strains of the past thirteen years must have been harder on him than on most Chinese; yet he looks no older than befits his seventy-two years. He wore a gray suit with the usual high-collared Mao jacket. His face, compared with those of the more peasantlike military men at his table, seemed more finely chiseled and intellectual. He sometimes looked as though his thoughts were far, far away. His work load must be prodigious. It would appear that on three separate occasions questions concerning my visit were brought to him personally, which gives an idea of the enormous amount of detail this man concerns himself with. No flame burns in his eyes; his gaze is intelligent, even wise, and—perhaps this is just my imagination—he seems to me a bit detached. This is no tribune of the people, but a statesman, surely one of the ablest and most significant of our time. The address he gave later on during the banquet was free of rhetorical flourishes: he read it, he did not speak it freely. At the end of every paragraph he raised and increased his tone as a matter of routine, a signal for the audience to begin clapping.

Besides Chou En-lai, ten other members of the Politbureau (or their substitutes) were at the head table. Only one was a true civilian—Yao Wen-yuan, the man who has made a more rapid political rise than any other in the country these past years, thanks to his pen and his absolute fidelity to the party line. Hindsight tells us that already in the 1950s his writings were very much in evidence; and already at that time, incidentally, he was a harsh critic of any ideological deviation.

But Yao's true rise began in November, 1965, with an editorial in one of the Shanghai newspapers which at first seemed rather academic, a literary-historical polemic. Then, a few months later, it became apparent that this had been the starting signal for the Cultural Revolution. He, Mao's wife, and a few others became the core of the Cultural Revolution.

Yao's articles have indicated a series of turning points in recent phases of politics, such as the workers' takeover of education in the summer of 1968. He is also one of the Party secretaries at Shanghai, China's largest city. In a much reproduced photograph of the Party Congress in 1969, he was shown as the ninth man after Mao to cast his ballot. His unusually rapid ascent in the Party hierarchy— he is today the youngest full member of the Politbureau—gave rise to a rumor outside China that he is Mao's son-in-law; in China this is denied.

A quick look at Yao showed me none of the traits I recognized as those of an intellectual; in fact, it was most instructive to see the new type of intellectual of the Mao school alongside the old-style intellectual, Kuo Mo-jo, now aged eighty, who was also seated at the table of honor. A graduate of the Imperial University of Tokyo with a doctor's degree, he is a historian, an honored literary figure, president of the Academy of Sciences in Peking since its founding in 1959, and vice-president since 1954 of the National People's Congress—the only intellectual of the old school among the first rank of leadership, although he is not a member of the Politbureau.

Besides Chou En-lai and Yao, two members of the Politbureau at the high table were in civilian dress. Yet one of these, Marshal Yeh Chien-ying, a man with hard, disciplined features, has been a soldier since his early youth (and a member of the Party since 1924); today he is head of the powerful Military Committee of the Central Committee of the Party. The other, Li Hsien-nien, also began his active life as a soldier, although he later shifted to administrative and economic functions. He has been Finance Minister since 1954—so he has surely held this office longer than any other living man. Besides this he is Deputy Prime Minister, and lately he has also exercised the functions of a foreign minister on various occasions.

The most highly placed among the soldiers on active duty was Huang Yung-sheng, Army Chief of Staff since 1968. He too, like Yao Wen-yuan, looked different from what I had imagined him to be. According to his official biography, he was born in 1968 and came up from the ranks, without the benefit of much formal schooling. He looks like a true staff officer. During most of the banquet he sat grave and withdrawn in his place of honor next to the lively Prince; only once during the entire evening did I see him smile —and then it was a surprisingly boyish smile, at Sihanouk's wife, the charming Princess Monique.

The three other military members of the Politbureau were Deputy Chief of Staff Wu Fa-hsien (air force, ex-political commissar), Li Tso-peng (navy) and Chiu Hui-tso (chief of logistics) and the

generals Li Teh-sheng and Chi Teng-kuei (military and administrative chief of the provinces of Honan and Anhwei), and Wang
Tung-hsing, who in the 1950s used to be Mao's personal bodyguard
and later took on special assignments in the security service.

Thus the military element was dominant at this table—as it is
throughout the Politbureau, as well as in the central offices in the
provinces.

The menu consisted of several cold hors d'oeuvres, followed by
many hot main dishes, among them a particular delicacy, fish man-
darin style, and an exquisite vegetable I had never seen before, which
was identified for me as "heart of mustard." Dessert was "rice with
seven treasures" (raisins and other sweets), plus fruit. We were
served small glasses of a sweet red wine and of the potent Maotai.

The Chinese were never heavy drinkers, and now they drink
even less than before. So it came about that despite being a very
moderate drinker indeed, I suddenly acquired the reputation of
having an extraordinary capacity for alcohol. Ambassador Kang,
who had shared a table with me at a dinner once before, informed
everybody about this "amazing capacity," and so there was no help
for it but to uphold my new reputation. At every toast, while the
others at my table just sipped at their red wine, I was urged on
with cheerful calls of, "Kanpei, kanpei! (Bottoms up!)" I then
had to drink a whole glassful of Maotai and hold the glass upside
down over the table in the Chinese fashion, to prove that it was
truly empty.

Conversation with the ambassador was very easy for me; we
had a large number of mutual friends in Phnom Penh as well as in
Belgrade, where he had been chargé d'affaires. From him I learned
that the Foreign Ministry had its own Seventh of May School in
the southern province of Kiangsi, where he hoped to go as a student
one day.

The journalist at my table was uncharacteristically silent for a
man of the profession. The sporting general was visibly disappointed
by my meager information about ping-pong, since I didn't even
know the name of the German city where the world championship
matches in this sport had been played a few years before. If he was
aware of the coming ping-pong diplomacy, he gave no sign of it.

I had no trouble in talking to the Transport Minister, given my recent experiences on his trains.

Halfway through the meal, Chou En-lai and Sihanouk addressed the gathering. The Prince's quietly efficient staff had prepared Chinese, French, and English versions of his speeches. In addition, an interpreter translated both speeches paragraph by paragraph—Chou's into French, the Prince's into Chinese. As on previous occasions, Chou En-lai gave his full support to "the only legal head of state of Cambodia." It was good, he said, that the Prince was continuing the fight for his people from Peking. He mentioned a song whose words and music the Prince had composed in the 1960s, "Nostalgia for China," showing that even then he had felt close ties with China. Chou said the song was now popular throughout the land (as I subsequently found to be true). And, indeed, the military band played it a little later that evening—a somewhat melancholy but very charming melody containing both Cambodian and Chinese elements, and very pleasant to the Western ear.

The prince spoke with his usual élan. He thanked China for her invaluable help and then described the situation in Cambodia, quoting the Western press, as he generally does, to prove that the Cambodian guerrillas were fighting successfully against the Lon Nol troops and the South Vietnamese.

At exactly 10:15, hosts and guests arose. The guests of honor were the first to leave the hall, then the others followed. We stepped into the cold, clear night of early spring. Before the Gate of Heavenly Peace, the quiet square lay empty.

5: The Only Foreigner

Wherever I went—with the exception of Peking and Shanghai—I had the same experience: I was always the only foreigner. In Nanking I once went to the zoo. I wanted to see people at their leisure. The chief attractions of this zoo are a Himalayan giant panda and an entertaining swarm of monkeys. But that afternoon no one bothered about the animals, since they had me to look at.

It was funny to see people turn away from the cages as soon as I approached, to stare at a sight they found stranger than the antics of monkeys.

I traveled about three thousand miles, by train and car, throughout China without seeing a single foreigner. Things had been different even in 1957. At that time thousands of Soviet advisers and their families were living scattered across the land, and I was continually meeting them on trains and at hotels. And certainly foreigners were not uncommon in the days before the founding of the People's Republic. Then there had been thousands of businessmen traveling in the country at all times, bringing products of every kind to the "four hundred million customers," including "oil for the lamps of China" —to quote the titles of two best sellers at the time. Generations of European and American missionaries lived in the farthest reaches of the land, often surrounded by large families.

In a day of tourist hordes on the move, there is no such thing as an inaccessible country—except China. And in China I stood out as oddly as someone coiffed like Yul Brynner alongside the Beatles, or a nude at a formal dinner. I was particularly aware of this in Shanghai. There, Nanking Road has always been and is today the street in China with the biggest and best stores. From early morning until late at night it is jammed with people. . . .

Shanghai was once a cosmopolitan city. The Huang Pu, which flows into the Yangtze, served as a port for ships from all over the world, and the sailors from these ships were often seen in the city. There was also a foreign colony of about fifty thousand people, over half of them White Russians who had fled to China and settled there, mostly in Harbin and Shanghai. There was then a French Concession where the streets had French names (I had lived on the Avenue Joffre), and the international colony had many foreign schools, hospitals, theaters, movie houses, clubs, banks, even radio stations and newspapers—and, of course, countless shops.

At that time there wouldn't have been a city in the world where a foreigner was less remarkable: no one stared at you, certainly not on Nanking Road or on the lovely street along the Huang Pu, known as the Bund.

All this is changed. People followed me in droves along the Bund, with children pressing to the front of the crowd for a better look at the foreigner, and I saw several frightened children reach for their mothers' hands for protection. Twice I was asked whether people could take my photograph (they could). Wherever I went on Nanking Road, I was soon surrounded by a curious crowd who forgot about their own purchases as they watched me make mine. At one point, as I made my way through one of the big department stores taking notes on the prices, I saw exhibited just the pair of shoes I had been looking for. The price: 18.70 yuan. I asked for a pair in my size.

My Chinese companions tried to dissuade me. "If you want to buy a pair of shoes," they said, "why don't you go to the Friendship Store? It's intended specially for foreigners. There you can buy a pair of shoes in peace and quiet, instead of trying to make your way through this pushing crowd. Besides, they carry special export-quality merchandise."

Not to be deterred, I said: "But I'm not interested in export shoes. I want shoes from a department store, like the ones you buy for yourselves. Besides, I think these look very good; I can't see that they would in any way disgrace your shoe industry."

So they let me proceed. A pair in my size was brought, and I looked around for a place to sit down so I could try them on. The only nearby bench was occupied by Chinese customers, but as soon as they understood the reason for my searching glance they all sprang up and joined the crowd of the curious who already surrounded me. Now here was something really sensational! A European! Buying shoes in a Chinese department store! And trying them on! And then, to top it off, keeping them on and walking out in them! (They fit perfectly, and I have worn them a great deal since.) Just because Shanghai had once been a city so populated by foreigners, I was especially conscious of how sensational a foreigner appears there today.

I undertook another errand at that same department store. In the industrial exhibition in Shanghai (more about that later) I had seen a small motor, costing 130 yuan, that could easily be attached to a bicycle.

"Was that just for display, or are they for sale?" I asked.

"Yes, you can buy those little motors for bikes at that price."

"Where?" I asked.

"In any big department store."

I now insisted on seeing one. Machines were down in the basement, I was told. And sure enough, I found a whole row of bicycles and the little motors marked at 130 yuan apiece.

"Do people buy them?" I asked.

"Very few up till now, but they haven't been on sale very long."

I asked my companions if they had ever seen anyone in the streets with such a motor attached to his bicycle. They shook their heads.

"And when somebody buys such a motor for his bike, where does he get the gas for it?" I continued.

Those about me were all at a loss for an answer. They knew where gas could be bought for official cars, but no one had ever seen a public gas station and no one knew anyone to ask, since no one among their acquaintances had a private car or a private motorcycle. Then someone had an idea:

"Once a year I take my bike apart and wash down all the parts with kerosene before I put them back together. I know a store where you can buy a bottle of kerosene. They might be able to supply gas for a motor like this."

Motorization is obviously not China's problem.

In 1941, when I left America and went to Shanghai, I stayed in a hotel room for the first few days, until I could find an apartment. The hotel was on the Bund. Thirty years later, as things turned out, the Chinese Travel Service booked me at the same place, now called the Freedom Hotel. It is still the hotel for foreigners, but since there are hardly any of those around, it is nearly empty. There is a restaurant on the eighth floor, and apart from that only one floor was occupied—though the word is an exaggeration, since besides myself and my two Chinese companions, the fifty-odd rooms on that floor contained only about a dozen guests.

Among them was a stranded Greek sailor, who had broken his leg and been in a hospital for a while, and who was now waiting for his ship to come back. He was lonely and colossally bored, and at each meal he told me about his misfortunes. To pass the time, he had decided to take some pictures. No sooner had he ventured forth with his camera than a furious crowd wrenched the gadget from his hands, tore out the film, and led him to the nearest police station. It had taken him two hours to get out again. No more photo!" he declared emphatically. And there was nothing to do in Shanghai. "Many girls," he explained, "but nothing . . ." Quite clear what he meant by nothing.

In a land where every foreigner is a rare and exciting phenomenon, the meaning of the question "Could you move around as you wished in China?" gets lost. . . . No foreigner can take a step in China without being followed by a hundred or even a thousand pairs of eyes. Any of the hundreds of thousands of foreign tourists in the Soviet Union, for example, can decide whether or not to stand out by his dress or manner. In China there is no choice: you can't avoid sticking out like a sore thumb.

But whereas in Russia people respond to you quite differently—some coolly, some by trying to buy your shirts or Beatle records or to change your money—in China you soon become aware of an almost monolithic solidarity vis-à-vis the stranger—not an unfriendly one, as during the years of the Cultural Revolution, but a kind of spontaneous reaction: watch out, there goes a foreigner!

Under these circumstances it would be pure illusion to suppose that one can merge into the surroundings and take the pulse of the Chinese masses, whereas in the Soviet Union this is quite possible. And so any attempt to escape the Travel Service is pointless. Without Chinese companions I would have seemed still more of an oddity, and would have had to justify my presence wherever I went—whereas it was, of course, much easier for my companions to do this for me.

During my trip I sometimes had as many as five or six companions with me, and always at least two: my interpreter, Li Ching-ping, and a young diplomat, Tao Hsiang-chen.

The first to arrive had been Mr. Li. "I'm from the Travel Service and I am your interpreter," he said by way of introduction. Even though he lived in Peking, he moved onto the same floor of my hotel so he could be at my disposal day and night. A day later

Mr. Tao moved in with him; he had been a history teacher but was now an attaché at the foreign ministry. Mr. Li spoke very good English and Mr. Tao spoke rather good German.

Had I chosen my traveling companions myself, I could not have found two who were pleasanter or more congenial. For the time we were together, both of them attuned themselves completely to me and to my work habits. They both quickly understood that I regarded each minute of the day as unique and precious, that I wanted to see as much as was humanly possible in a short period, that I preferred walking to riding in a car, and that after each outing I liked to sit down at my typewriter for a few hours. At these moments they would withdraw quietly, to reappear for our next appointment, or at times occasionally in between, when I called on them, to consult with me and help me fill in some gap of memory.

Mr. Li translated every question I asked him to put to the people I met, even when it went visibly against his grain, as when I asked, "Are you a member of the Communist Party? For how long?"—or when I asked a woman her age. But Mr. Li never refused or hesitated; he must have understood that my seemingly tactless questions were motivated solely by a zeal for the facts.

Both my companions were cultivated men; both had an idea of the world beyond China even though they had never traveled, and their deeply grounded knowledge of Mao Tse-tung's thought stood me in very good stead, as did Mr. Tao's historical knowledge. Finally, both of them were confident enough not to bombard me with propaganda; they understood that I had come to their country to see with my own eyes, not to be converted. They never thought in terms of an eight-hour day; they were always on the job. Had they been fussy or bureaucratic, I would have seen and heard only half as much as I did.

I had agreed with the Travel Service on an overall price that included my travel expenses and my lodging. This was fine with me, since it meant that I did not need to negotiate trip by trip and meal by meal. It also meant that Mr. Li had to keep detailed accounts, and by the end of the trip he had devised an entire system of bookkeeping. I called my method of payment the Tachai system.

In the village of Tachai—I shall go into detail about this later—
every peasant receives a set daily wage, and in return it is taken
for granted that he will do his best. I said in effect that I agreed
to pay a specified sum, for which I assumed that I would be provided with the best possible conditions for the observations I wished
to make. This worked out extremely well. (Of course my trip was
not by invitation of the Chinese government; I was paying for it.)

When I arrived in Peking, the one thing I knew for sure was that
I would meet with Prince Sihanouk and interview him for a television
broadcast. Would I be required to go straight home after that?
Would I be able to stay a few days longer? Would I be allowed
to leave the city of Peking? Would I be allowed a few brief ex-
cursions into nearby areas, or perhaps a few trips into other provinces?

Just to be on the safe side, as soon as I arrived in Peking I presented the Travel Service with a list of requests, representing the
maximum of what I hoped for. My list was blandly accepted, but
without offering a clue as to what I could expect.

From the beginning there were abrupt and dismaying changes
in my schedule. One day Mr. Li said, "We are leaving for Nanking,
and then we shall go on to Shanghai and Hangchow." Delighted, I
packed my things and phoned to cancel a dinner engagement. The
same afternoon Mr. Li reappeared to say that we would not be going
after all. Even though he was surely aware of my disappointment, he offered no explanation (perhaps because he had none
to give). As we went about our sightseeing during the next three
days, I kept wondering what reason there could have been for this
change of plans—until I suddenly received the invitation to my first
banquet in the Great Hall of the People. Then I undersood that
the change had been made so that I could attend the banquet.
(We made the projected trip later.)

By my calculation, literally hundreds of people were mobilized
to help me. The amount of care expended on a single traveler, and
my privileged position as perhaps the first swallow of a coming
summer, were particularly evident to me in Tachai. I arrived just
as the intensive springtime preparation of the land was beginning

(on that day, as on most others, there were thousands of visitors from all over China, come to "learn from Tachai"; and they all had to be taken care of). Yet from just after four in the morning until long past midnight the two deputy chairmen of the revoluntionary committee were constantly at my side.

There are only two cities in China where foreigners are not an astounding rarity: Canton, where every year two huge fairs bring people from many lands, and Peking, with its colony of diplomats. But the diplomats have always led a kind of ghetto existence— especially during the time of the Cultural Revolution. In the old legation quarter of Peking, as today in the suburb of Sanlitun, you enter another world. As each new embassy arrives, it is assigned a compound there, surrounded by high walls and with a Chinese sentry at the gate. Living and working quarters are generally under the same roof.

I am grateful to each of the foreign diplomats I visited, for there were among them many thoughtful observers who had drawn some interesting conclusions. I learned, for example, that as one effect of the Cultural Revolution, their relations with the Chinese had grown somewhat more intimate. Conversations with them had become freer; some Chinese officials had even accepted invitations to dinner, although they came only in groups, not individually. Since the spring of 1971, a number of diplomats and their wives have been allowed to travel outside the capital.

One of the effects of the restricted community life in Sanlitun is that every bit of news circulates with the speed of light—far more quickly than in a village without the institution of the cocktail party. So everyone there seemed to have exact information of all my doings. I had told nobody I was coming, but by the time I arrived in Peking everybody knew all about me—thanks to the travelers who had entered China at the same time I did, and who had preceded me by plane to Peking. Some of the diplomats were more than a little envious that a short-term visitor was getting to see more than they, who had lived in China a long time. But they didn't seem to hold this against me, and interpreted my good fortune as a symptom of further relaxation which would shortly work in their favor. They were right.

I met no diplomats from the East, and encountered only a few Eastern journalists, all of them at the Prime Minister's first banquet. By the way, the Soviet Union is one of the few nations to have its embassy within the old city walls. It occupies a spacious and lovely compound in the northeast section, which in former days housed the Russian Orthodox church and a mission connected with it. During the heyday of their friendship with the People's Republic, the Russians had erected a stately embassy building there. During the Cultural Revolution, however, there were massive anti-Soviet demonstrations before the gates of this building, and for several days its inhabitants were cut off from the rest of the world. At that time the street that led to the embassy was renamed: it is now the "Street of Anti-Revisionism."

The diplomats I saw most often were the Italian chargé d'affaires and the Chilean ambassador, both of whom were still without permanent residences and lived, as I did, in the Peking Hotel. Even in this, the capital's main hotel for foreigners, visitors were few. In the restaurant I noticed a tableful of Cubans, another of North Koreans, and two Albanians.

The world press is notably underrepresented in this world capital. Apart from the Communist countries, only five countries have permanent press representatives in Peking: West Germany, France, Yugoslavia, Japan, and Canada. Whenever some Chinese would complain to me about the inaccurate image of China presented by the world press, I would say, "It's your own fault. Why do you let in so few journalists?"

Still more meager than the picture of China given to the outside is Chinese knowledge of the rest of the world. The press and radio concern themselves almost entirely with domestic events. An event like the Twenty-fourth Party Congress in Moscow is almost totally unknown in China. Outside a tiny circle of Peking sophisticates, I did not meet one Chinese who knew it had taken place. But in fact this event concerned China at least as much as it did the West, whose press every day carried detailed accounts of what was taking place.

Since the radio receiver in my room was not very good (I once caught a few scraps of Russian, and then gave up on it), during

43

the time I was in China my only news of the outside world was what I heard in Sanlitun or the Peking Hotel. Although there are stacks of periodicals and brochures on every floor of each hotel (with a sign reading, "Please help yourself"), these are concerned entirely with Chinese events—just as the weekly *Peking Review,* which is published in several languages, is of course devoted to Chinese affairs. The other periodicals, often magnificently illustrated, concentrate on China, with almost no world news. The one foreign newspaper I saw the whole time I was in China was in the hotel in Shanghai—an ancient issue of the Albanian journal *Zeri i Popullit.*

Except for the fathers of Marxism, my two countrymen Marx and Engels, and Lenin and Stalin, only one man from the Western world is mentioned often and with respect in China. This is the Canadian Communist Norman Bethune, who came to Yenan in 1938 and served with the Red Army as a surgeon. He died a year later of blood poisoning contracted during an operation. An obituary that Mao wrote at the time became part of the "Three Continually Read Articles." At the People's Park in Canton I saw an exhibition devoted entirely to Bethune. Such foreign names as Nixon, Khrushchev, or Nehru seem more like pejorative catchwords than references to actual people. Thus, so long after the end of the Cultural Revolution, I found the Chinese still living in a world of their own.

6: Learn from Tachai!

Few women in the world can be familiar to so many hundreds of millions of people as Sung Li-ying and Kuo Feng-lien, with whom I spent one long and very full day. Yet their names are hardly known at all outside the Chinese sphere of influence. But let me tell the story of that day from the beginning.

It started when the porter woke me shortly before four A.M. When, a short while later, I stood with my two companions on the windy platform of the station in Yangchuan, I was still heavy with

44

sleep. As we got off the train, a little group hurried out of the semidarkness to greet us. They were led by a middle-aged woman with a dark red kerchief on her head. She was about five feet tall, and looked graceful even in her heavy padded suit. The hand she extended to me was slender but strong. One of the men with her wore an army uniform, including the cap with the red star. Two cars awaited us. When the drivers sounded their horns, the station gates swung open. It was still dark as we turned down one of those long, gray-walled streets, so usual in Chinese towns, with the houses hidden behind them.

Yangchuan, with three hundred thousand inhabitants the third largest city in the province of Shansi, is located in the midst of an area rich in coal and mineral deposits. Riding through its suburbs, we passed many factories. The paved, tree-lined road rose slowly at first, then more steeply. We passed through dark villages, where our headlights revealed walls, trees, and gates; then we were in open countryside. As far as the headlights reached it was all loess, yellowish-brown loam crossed by gorges and ravines. Once we passed a truck; otherwise we saw only mule-drawn carts, most of them loaded with great chunks of coal that gleamed in the headlights. From Yangchuan to Tachai was about twenty-five miles.

Now suddenly I realized why the woman's face had seemed so familiar to me: this was Sung Li-ying, deputy chairman of the Revolutionary Committee of Tachai, whose photograph had appeared in countless reports of the model village. While we were still in the car, Mrs. Sung began plying me with information about the village. When the Japanese occupation ended in 1945, it had consisted of a landlord, four rich peasant families and about seventy poor ones. In the course of the years, after the landlord's estate had been broken up, the poor peasants organized themselves into increasingly active collectives, which in the end joined together to form one "Agrarian Production Collective of the Higher Type." The driving force in these developments was Chen Yung-kui, who came from among the ranks of the poor peasants.

In the summer of 1958, during the weeks known as the Great Leap Forward, Tachai joined with its neighboring villages to form a People's Commune. The village was now a production brigade, one

45

of twenty-one within the People's Commune. (Generally speaking, what was known before as a village is now called a brigade.) The Tachai brigade is composed of eighty-three families, totaling 420 persons, of whom 150 are full-time workers. They have 100 beasts of burden, 150 pigs, 400 sheep, and 796 mu of arable land (fifteen mu equal one acre). They also have several thousand fruit and nut trees.

Mrs. Sung told me that the harvests following the Great Leap Forward had not been good because of weather conditions. In 1962 things improved; but in August, 1963, came a natural catastrophe, the major event in the communal life of Tachai. Seven days of storm and downpour destroyed almost all the carefully built terraces, and leveled the village except for a few houses. Later I walked the fields, looked at photographs and films, and got a clearer idea of what things had been like at that time.

The village council sat in the midst of the rubble of its possessions and discussed the future. Some people were in favor of accepting the help offered by the state and by other brigades. Others, led by Chen, recalled the words of Chairman Mao, that it was necessary to solve one's problems with one's own strength and without depending on help from the outside. (Here Mrs. Sung quoted from memory the first sentences of the twenty-first chapter of the Little Red Book.) This second line of thought carried the day, and so there came about Tachai's famous "Three Refusals": the brigade decided not to accept money, food, or materials from the outside. As it turned out, within a very short time the villagers had overcome the effects of the catastrophe, and in 1964 they received two forms of recognition for their achievement. In March, Mao exhorted the Chinese, "In agriculture, learn from Tachai!" And on December 26, 1964, his own birthday, he received Chen in Peking.

In the ensuing conflict between the "two ways," those of Mao on the one hand and Liu Shao-chi on the other (see Part III), the brigade, resisting criticism from within as well as attacks from without, placed itself squarely on the side of Mao. And it followed this line even more stringently during the Cultural Revolution (which hit its full stride after August, 1966). Finally Tachai, joined by those who thought as its people did, took over the political leadership of the entire county to which it belonged. On February 1, 1967, a county revolutionary committee was formed with Chen, who already headed the brigade revolutionary committee of Tachai, as its chairman. He has since become a full member of the Party's Central Committee. Since that time not only the brigade but the entire county has made rapid strides, and today the "spirit of Tachai" is famous throughout China.

It was still dark as we drove through a red gate covered with Chinese characters. We were offered beds for a rest in the guest house until daylight. When we appeared for an ample Chinese breakfast an hour and a half later, we were again greeted by the same party who had met us at the train. With them was another woman, twenty-six-year-old Kuo Feng-lien. Like Mrs. Sung, she was a vice-chaiman of the revolutionary committee; also, it turned out, she was secretary of the local Youth League and political instructor of the village militia. She is in her way a Chinese village beauty, more robust than Mrs. Sung, with an even-featured, healthy-looking face and a firm handshake. She wears the usual short braids, is very well-informed and articulate. Beside her Madame Sung seemed even slimmer. Later I was to meet Mrs. Kuo's year-old son and one of Mrs. Sung's four children, a girl of twenty-two who had inherited her mother's graceful features. At the time, Mrs. Kuo's husband was in the army. Mrs. Sung's husband worked in the village. Others who took an active part in our conversation included the man in uniform, who turned out to be on a visit from the capital of the province, and a stocky man who was a member of the county's revolutionary committee. But the two women clearly took precedence.

Chen, the party secretary and chairman of the revolutionary committee, was away on an extended trip through several provinces, and had asked his two seconds-in-command to attend to my visit.

After breakfast we went to look at the fields. The day was cloudless, and the yellow tint of the bare loess in early spring seemed particularly vivid against the pale blue sky.

A narrow path leading from the edge of the village rose steeply to a place offering a splendid panoramic view. Tachai is situated at the foot of a ridge known as Tiger Mountain (a name it shares with a Peking opera, of which more later). Seven deep ravines cut through the loess, leading down from the mountain to the plain through the territory of the brigade; the village nestles at the foot of the largest of these ravines. Now all was dry, but in the rainy season raging torrents pour down over the terraces and through the ravines, just as they did during the catastrophe of August, 1963.

That evening I saw a film showing the effect of the floods. The flat terraces had been washed away; only steep slopes were left. Large numbers even of the deep caves in the walls of the canyons, where people had lived, had been destroyed, when supporting walls thirty to sixty feet high gave way under the enormous pressure of the water, and were hurled into the ravine.

Later I was shown photographs of the ravines as they appeared before and after the catastrophe. Originally they had been deep but narrow, broadening only now and then, and were strewn with pebbles and somewhat larger stones left behind by the annual rainy season. After 1963 the people of the village widened these ravines by toppling the loess walls on both sides into the canyons; using the soil gained in this manner, together with rough stones from the river bottom, they were able to build new and much broader terraces within the ravine. This also adds to the safety of the village: in times of heavy rain the water travels in a broader channel, and no longer rushes at such vast speed through a narrow canyon. (The new village, though built on the site of the old one, looks entirely different: it now consists of long, low buildings, made of heavy stone that can resist any flood.)

Since it was early spring—field work, in the raw climate here, began somewhat later—most members of the brigade were at work building supportive walls or terraces. Rocks for the walls were being hewn and transported by means of the usual bamboo shoulder carriers. Concrete was being mixed and poured between the stones; soil was being piled in heaps. Men with pickaxes were at work along the almost vertical walls of the ravines: the stones they loosened thundered to the valley floor, shattering along the way, and were gathered into baskets by other workers, who carried them on their bamboo poles with small, agile steps to where the terraces were being built.

From my own vantage point, the differences between the two kinds of terraces that are found by the millions in China's loess areas were quite evident. One kind is built inside the ravines; the other kind is built on the backs of the hills that divide them. Within the ravines the terraces run in an arc at right angles to the stream bed, in the same manner as a dam, and to some degree they serve the same purpose. Along the brow of the hill the terraces do just the opposite: they follow the contour of the slope. Of the retaining walls, about half are built of heavy field stones, mostly hewn into square blocks. The rest are constructed of big clay bricks, which gradually harden into a solid mass. The clay walls do not resist the water as well as the stone walls do, and they need more frequent repairs. So one project in the village is eventually to replace all the clay walls with stone.

The experience of the Chinese in building terraces goes back thousands of years, and they have developed many ways to control the ravages of flooding. For example, the supporting walls of the terraces are built a bit higher than the terraces themselves; in the event of sudden floods they can serve as little dams, holding some of the water and giving it time to seep into the ground. Storage caves, to catch the overflow, are carefully excavated underground, and there are troughs to be used for irrigation in times of drought.

A few machines have found their way to Tachai. I saw small bulldozers busy distributing the soil along the terraces, and a few mini-tractors, the kind that are pushed instead of ridden. One of the village's heavy investments was the acquisition of water pumps; they cost three hundred yuan apiece. Farther on two electrically-powered aerial tramways had been built; looking much like ski lifts, they were used to carry stones or soil or manure up to the terraces. While I watched, one of them was in the process of carrying manure up to a mountain terrace, and my companions' pride in their machinery was unmistakable as they pointed out to me a mule caravan doing the same job for a neighboring brigade on the other side of the valley.

Halfway up Tiger Mountain I was shown a ten-foot-deep, man-made pond with radiating canals, which serve for irrigation. I saw a stable for horses, a pigsty, and a round two-story granary, built of stone and just completed. Finally, I looked into a few old caves that had once been dwellings but were now used to store pigfeed, and the brigade's school and hospital.

I was surprised to see how closely the villagers had followed the shape of their old cave dwellings when they built their new houses: the long exterior walls have the look of cliffs with openings for doors and windows cut into them. Compared with the roomy "caves" of Yenan, where Mao and his friends lived in the early days of the revolution, those in Tachai are small and have narrow openings. Once you have passed through the door you have the feeling you are truly in a cave, since there are no openings apart from those facing the street. To the left as you go in, there is always a *kang,* a broad, built-in bed that can be heated from below. A narrow table, a few chairs, and possibly a sewing machine (as at Mrs. Sung's, for instance), and along the far wall five-foot-high earthenware jars containing various kinds of grain—such is the property owned by individuals, the only private property. Stored in smaller crocks were noodles and peas. The walls were crowded with photographs, many of them of Chairman Mao: in one room, whose owner obviously collected portraits of Mao as a hobby, I saw more than sixty of them. There were many group pictures taken within the brigade, as well as photographs of relatives. The walls of some of the rooms were entirely covered with pictures.

Each family was entitled to one "cave." Mrs. Kuo, carrying her small son in her arms, took me to visit several of them. I asked whether at the time of the Great Leap Forward, when the commune was founded, there were segregated domitories for men and women, and everyone answered with an emphatic no. Such things had never existed in Tachai, I was told, nor in any other brigade they knew of. Each family had always lived separately.

Having seen no stove in any of the houses, I asked to be shown the communal dining hall. General amazement: there was no such thing. At the time of the Great Leap Forward it had been tried but it hadn't worked; each family now cooked for itself. It was better that way; there were no fights.

"And where is it done?"

I was led to a series of kitchens near but a bit apart from the houses. Besides cooking utensils, they had room for storage.

Here and there I saw chickens cackling in front of a house.

"Are those private property?"

"Yes."

"Are there other animals that are private property? Pigs? Goats?"

"No."

"What about gardens?"

"No, we abolished private garden plots a long time ago. This brigade stopped having them in 1963, and little by little the other brigades in our people's commune did the same. Today in this county there are no more privately owned garden plots as there are in most other parts of China."

"Are people in Tachai forbidden to have them?"

"No, but our members work so intensively for the brigade that they have neither the time nor the energy for agricultural work of their own."

Everybody was very proud of the three well-run shops in the village; and justly so, since shops were formerly unknown in out-of-the-way Chinese villages. One shop sells clothing and shoes; another is what in the West would be called a general store—it offers a variety of things, from fruit to small electrical appliances; the third sells books and stationery. Above the village is the hospital, once the residence of the landlord, and now enlarged with three new buildings.

It occurred to me to ask my two lady companions about the attitude here concerning birth control. During my visit in 1957 I had witnessed an information campaign. Yes, they said, anyone could get birth control information, and abortion was legal and free of charge.

"Have women you know in the village made use of these facilities?"

"Of course. Many of them."

The meals to which I was invited consisted, Chinese fashion, of many different courses, and with very few exceptions the produce used had been raised by the brigade itself: wheat, corn, vegetables, eggs, and meat. The usual desserts were fruit grown on their own trees, and candied walnuts. No alcoholic beverages appeared on the table.

Meals provided the best opportunity to ask about things that interested me. One of these was the matter of wages. I had come to understand that among the leadership at Tachai, with their passionate "engagement" for Mao, the matter was of small importance; but I was eager for specific information. One of my reasons for asking was that in wages, too, the methods used at Tachai had set a standard for the rest of the country. Before going to China, I had read widely in an effort to understand the system, but I felt I hadn't really grasped the essentials, since Chinese books and periodicals seem to shy away from concrete facts and figures. But I believe I now understand how these things are regulated in Tachai.

The custom until 1963 was to pay in accordance with the work done each day; this system is still followed today in the Soviet kolkhoz. Norms had been established for each activity (field work, pig care, etc.), and each worker received a certain number of points every day for his work. Those who more than filled their quota got more points, and those who were under the quota got fewer. After the 1963 catastrophe, in the heat of enthusiasm for rebuilding the village, the people decided, I was told, that this system was far too complicated and time-consuming; furthermore, they believed everyone could be trusted to do the very best he could according to his ability. So a new system was worked out.

There are ten categories of payment. A strong man at the height of his powers is in the first category, which means he gets ten points for every working day, no matter how much work he actually does. A woman has less strength than a man, so she gets fewer points. An unmarried woman gets seven; a married woman who has to care for her family gets six and a half. But there are exceptions. A single woman who has grown lazy can sink to the pay scale of a married woman; but the pay can also be adjusted upwards. One of the hardest workers in the village, called Comrade Iron Shoulders for his ability in carrying great weights, receives ten and a half points a day; Chen, the active and noted chairman of the revolutionary committee, receives the maximum of eleven. The two ladies who were my hostesses each received six and a half, since they are both married.

"In my country," I said, "we battled a hundred years for women to have equal pay for equal work. Don't you find it an injustice to be paid so much less?"

"But a married woman devotes much of her working energy to her family," they answered. "Those are individual chores. Should the collective have to pay for work not done in the service of the collective?"

There is a logic to this. But so far as the unmarried women were concerned—and I saw them doing work of the heaviest kind in the fields—my hostesses would not be budged from their explanation that, since they aren't as strong as men, they aren't worth as much to the community.

Once a year there is an assembly at which everyone's pay category is set. The procedure begins with everyone suggesting his or her own place on the scale of points; then this is discussed, and finally it is decided whether the figure should be higher or lower than the worker's own estimate. This decision remains in force until the following year.

Several times I heard a mention of "political consciousness" being taken into consideration when the point scale is established; and I was to hear of this frequently during the weeks to follow. Naturally, I wanted to know what it really meant.

"There are objective criteria," I said, "as to whether someone is weak or strong, whether he's devoting his entire energies to the brigade or whether some are siphoned off to his family. But how does one measure political consciousness?"

There are several criteria, I was told: you can measure political concern by the amount of time devoted to Mao studies; by attendance at the brigade's meetings; by the arrangement of one's personal life (in other words, there is a moral criterion); and also by a person's eagerness to work, as well as the quality of the work itself. Unfortunately, I never got a chance to sit in on one of the meetings that determine a worker's pay scale, either in Tachai or anywhere else, so these explanations are the extent of my information.

53

Another question interested me: "What is it like," I asked, "when one is as famous as you are in Tachai—aren't you sometimes tempted to rest on your laurels? Or perhaps not you, but the rank and file workers in the village?"

"Of course," I was told, "everyone is subject to temptations. For example, we had long discussions about whether the agricultural area should be further enlarged, which would mean a lot of very hard work. Naturally we had begun by terracing the nearest hillsides and ravines; any more that are built from now on would call for a very much greater expenditure of energy. As it is, we have several thousand arable terraces, whose care takes up the brigade's entire energy. But after long discussions we did decide to build further."

I was given yet another example: one of the central merchandising organizations had wanted to reward the people of Tachai for their effort by sending a better quality of goods to their shops than to others in the county. "Believe it or not," Mrs. Kuo went on in a tone of amazement, "there were people who were glad about this, and who immediately began to buy things, not only for themselves but for others!"

"Aha, the beginnings of consumer mentality?" I asked; but nobody quite understood what I was talking about.

The Party committee recognized immediately that here was a dangerous case of decreased vigilance, which could open the door to bourgeois attitudes and all sorts of corruption. Some even suspected the sly hand of the class enemy, an intrigue by that arch fiend Liu Shao-chi. So they put the question to the brigade meeting, and these practices came to an end.

We returned to the question of wages. Every working point is equal to fifteen fen (there are a hundred fen in one yuan). Thus a strong man earns about 1.50 yuan a day, a married woman a little under one yuan, and so on. In Tachai, married women work on an average of something under three hundred days a year for the brigade, men somewhat over three hundred days. If we take three hundred days as an average, a strong man earns around 450 yuan a year, while Mrs. Sung and Mrs. Kuo earn roughly 300 yuan each. This money serves to buy food and the reserves that are stored in the crocks in their houses, along with other daily necessities. But their other needs are small, I was told, and they even managed to put aside some of their money as savings.

"Savings?" I asked. "Where do you put them?"

"There is a branch of the Bank of China in the brigade, and we deposit them there."

"Does the bank pay interest?"

Everyone nodded.

"What is the interest rate?" I asked.

Perplexed silence. They discussed the question for a while, one of them maintaining that it was 4 per cent, others disagreeing. In the end they conceded, quite shamefacedly, that they really didn't know. This little episode proved to me more clearly than anything else I saw or was told that—at least so far as these Tachai activists are concerned—money has lost its primary importance, and that the true reward for their effort is that they are honored and emulated throughout the country. I know that on a Russian kolkhoz anyone, above all those in positions of leadership, would have told me instantly that the state bank there pays an interest rate of 3 per cent.

I asked the women how much they had been able to save. Mrs. Sung said there were 750 yuan on deposit for her whole family. Young Mrs. Kuo had 400 yuan.

"That's for you and your husband together?" I asked her.

She laughed gaily. "No, I told my husband that I agree with Chairman Mao: Everyone must stand on his own feet!"

But I was still not finished. "You've saved some money. You have a better place to live and some grain reserves stored away. But throughout the eight years that have seen the rise of Tachai, your salary has stayed almost the same. During this same period, thanks to your extraordinary efforts, there has been a great increase in the value of Tachai, with its new terraces and irrigation works, its orchard and its noodle factory and all the other things. I saw that with my own eyes as we made our rounds. Don't you think there's something wrong with this discrepancy between your achievement and your rewards for it?"

"But this is our own venture! If the village is worth more than before, if we produce more than before, we all profit! It's a better place for all of us! Besides, we don't work just for ourselves . . ."

"What do you work for, then?" I prompted.

". . . we work for the honor of Chairman Mao and our socialist state." I was to hear these words over and over as I traveled—or sometimes the phrase would be "for our Chinese fatherland."

We returned to more prosaic matters. The brigade's income is derived mainly from its sales to the state. In 1970 the harvest amounted to 730,000 Chinese pounds, or jin (a jin equals half a kilo, or a little over one pound avoirdupois) of various grain crops, mostly corn. Of this total they sold 240,000 jin to the state. The remaining 490,000 pounds were used for their own food, for next year's seed, and as a general reserve ("in the event of war or natural catastrophe," they added, quoting a recent directive of Mao as they showed me their full reserve bins). The state pays eight fen for a pound of corn, and fourteen fen for a pound of wheat. Thus, taking an average of ten fen per pound, the brigade had earned 24,000 yuan from the government for the sale of grain in 1970. There had also been a considerable income from the sale of other produce to the state: pigs, apples, and nuts, as well as noodles made in the brigade factory from its own flour; besides all this, there had been sales of food to members of the brigade.

So far as the expenses of the brigade were concerned, salaries were by far the highest item. In 1970 the average per capita income in Tachai came to 140 yuan. Thus 420 residents were paid a total of around 59,000 yuan. Other expenses were for implements, electricity, gasoline, etc.

It is well known that Mao (as compared with Stalin) places a very light burden on the peasants. In Tachai, I was told, the brigade had formerly had to deliver grain to the state free of charge in proportion to its arable land and labor force—an amount that came at the end to eighty thousand pounds. But since 1963 the state had paid for every pound of grain the brigade had sold to it, and furthermore had collected no taxes.

Tachai built its own school; the state pays teachers' salaries and operating expenses. The school is a long, low stone building. The discipline is exemplary. A class would leap to its feet whenever the foreign visitor appeared at the door, clap their hands and gaze with unabashed curiosity at this peculiar bird. The teachers I saw were young, and all were happy to tell me in detail about the subjects covered in their classes, and also about themselves. As you leave the classroom they applaud you again, and you applaud them in turn. Of course the first-graders were particularly charming, and these had a lovely, interesting teacher. You have scarcely come in and greeted them before they have begun the "Song of the Helmsman" in their piping little voices, and they go on to other songs about Chairman Mao, with whose help the revolution is continuing. I found the kindergarten children playing out of doors, and they stopped to sing "The East Is Red" for me. Finally, I saw a nursery for the little ones, watched over by two older women.

When I asked whether as part of the movement known as "Down to the Villages and up into the Mountains," young people from the cities had come to Tachai too, the answer was an emphatic no. There had been many applications, but these had been refused. For the village of Tachai the worst was over; it was better for the young people to go to places that really needed them.

I saw proof of Tachai's fame as we made our rounds of the village. Once I observed what must have been eight hundred or a thousand people, moving in a blue column over Tachai's hills with red flags in their hands.

"What's happening over there?" I asked curiously, eager to go and take a picture.

"Those are our guests," was the unflustered answer. "We have as many as five thousand visitors a day, coming from all the provinces of China to learn from us."

Indeed, I could see that this was by no means an unusual occurrence, since we met with such columns of people at intervals all day long. When I asked any of them where they came from, I heard the names of many of China's provinces, some of them thousands of miles away. Many of the visitors had walked long distances. Some carried bedrolls on their backs, others had left them stacked down in the village. Some had come by bus. I was told that altogether, since Mao had declared Tachai a model village in 1964, it had been visited by about four and a half million people.

Tachai's success was strong enough even to overcome the traditional enmity between it and one of the neighboring villages. Whereas Tachai was inhabited mainly by the Kuo clan, the people of Wuchiaping were mainly of the Wang clan. At first the two had joined in a common effort. But there had been difficulties; peasants from Wuchiaping, which was relatively well-to-do, insisted that they shouldn't have to be linked into one cooperative with a poor mountain village. The evil genius of Liu Shao-chi had been at work there, I was told. And the two villages had split apart.

But then came Tachai's rapid ascent to honor and economic success. The neighbors watched with envious eyes, and even declared that Tachai had given out false production figures. They went so far as to call for an investigation—a futile venture, of course—and one that was carried out by the Provincial Party Committee, which was then controlled by followers of Liu Shao-chi. The people of Wuchiaping actually threw rocks onto the road leading to Tachai so as to block the way. Yet the rise of Tachai proved irresistible. Liu's faction lost its following in its own village and was removed from power. Even in Wuchiaping, the spirit of Tachai had triumphed!

Tachai set the pace. At an exhibition of regional improvements I saw tableaux, models, photographs, and drawings concerning the entire area, where the spirit of Tachai has spread to all the other brigades and communes.

The most spectacularly successful activity in the county has been in taming the great rivers. Usually they were dry for most of the year, changing abruptly for several weeks into savage torrents that swept all before them. For this reason the people of the area had not previously cultivated the wide valleys, since a day would inevitably come when the floods would undo their work. But for the last few years they had been diverting the course of rivers, and transforming old stream beds as well as flatlands into fertile fields. They had built stone dams many miles long, which at the time of my visit stood on dry land but which kept the river under control during the rainy season. By these methods they had gained thirty thousand mu of arable land at very low cost—through the use of abundant and cheap labor. Thirty thousand mu comes to about forty times the previous total of arable land in the area of Tachai. At my request, I was taken across one of these erstwhile flood plains. Along the middle of the broad valley ran two parallel walls of gray stone, about one hundred yards apart; and on either side, for as far as the eye could see, lay carefully tilled fields. It may very well be that at some time before in the long history of China, when a strong dynasty could ensure safety from invasion, there had been such dams here; but for the present generation they are completely new, and there is pride and enjoyment in the honor and privilege brought by these achievements.

Tachai has likewise set the pace for the construction of terraces. Tens of thousands of terraces in the area have been improved, repaired, or rebuilt for greater safety and higher yield in the face of drought and flood.

One of the "lessons of Tachai" is that the leadership must remain close to the people. I saw photographs of the Party secretary busy working hard in the fields, or deep in conversation with "the masses" —an old peasant woman, a group of children, a shepherd to whom he had personally brought a warm blanket to shield him from the cold night on the mountain.

Strong emphasis was laid on the help given by the army, the only help that had been accepted from outside. One day a group of soldiers arrived and dug the man-made lake mentioned earlier. Above all, however, what they had brought was the right spirit. For the people of the Tachai brigade performed their duties like soldiers, not in order to gain work points (soldiers' pay, they said, is likewise not totally geared to achievement) but to fulfill the directives of Chairman Mao.

At the exhibition I saw displays concerning the possibility of war and the need to be prepared for it. There were pictures of peasants at work with a stack of guns at the edge of the field, of brigade storerooms filled with food reserves, and of a popular demonstration against revisionists such as Liu Shao-chi and the leaders of the Soviet Union. As I was taking my leave of the people in charge of the exhibition, I said I hoped the county of Hsiyang would be able to carry on their construction in peace. Vehemently, the director of the exhibition replied that this was not China's decision. China was not an aggressor, China would never be the first to use an atom bomb, but if attacked she would annihilate her opponent.

The train back to Peking left Yangchuan at around one in the morning. I managed to persuade Mrs. Kuo that she must not accompany me but must stay with her baby. Mrs. Sung, however, was not to be dissuaded. The last thing I saw from the window of my train was an illuminated sign: IN AGRICULTURE LEARN FROM TACHAI!

I stretched out on my seat and asked myself what it was that China could learn from Tachai. Now that I had been there, the answer seemed quite clear: work, work, and more work—to the brink of exhaustion; not for financial gain (the workers of Tachai really regard the money they earn as a kind of allowance) but for "the honor of Chairman Mao and our socialist fatherland."

7: The Seventh of May Cadre Schools

We were driving northeast, and the farther we got from Peking, the worse the road became. The car moved ponderously through the mud, and twice I thought we were stuck for good. But finally we saw a red gateway rising in the distance. Across the arch I could read "Long live the Seventh of May Directive of Chairman Mao." The supporting pillars were inscribed with the first lines of the well-known song about Mao the helmsman. We drove through a newly planted grove, and then I could see, on a slight rise, a group of gray houses where the reception committee stood holding their Little Red Books.

We were taken into a simply furnished room and served the customary tea. On the walls, along with pictures of Mao, were two maps, one of China and the other of the world—a rarity. Two large posters covered with writing contained Mao's directive of May 7, 1966, and his speech of October 4, 1968. I did not need to have them read to me, since I already knew them as the two basic documents of the Cultural Revolution (see Part IV).

The Seventh of May Directive was an edict against specialization, proclaiming (to simplify a bit) that to be a rider one must be at home in any kind of saddle. The declaration of October 4, 1968, called upon the cadres—that is, officials of all sorts, managers, officials, the bureaucracy in general—to engage in physical labor. Over the years, I had read stacks of material from Peking about the Seventh of May schools, as well as analyses by Western specialists, but I had never been able to gain a clear picture of these institutions. Let me, then, simply describe what I saw.

While we drank our first cup of tea, several of the founders of the school told me its history. Two days after the Seventh of May Directive, the first Seventh of May School had been founded in the far northern province of Heilungkiang (Amur). Its goal had been to bring the cadres of the province back to work with their hands and to the simple life, so that they would become "closer to the masses." At first this school was an experiment, one among many that go on constantly all over China, and in the most diverse fields. But then two things happened.

As my hosts explained it, "On October 5, 1968, we read in the *People's Daily* a speech by Chairman Mao on the necessity of physical labor for cadres, and at the same time we read a long report on the experiences of the first Seventh of May School in the province of Heilungkiang. In an editorial in the same paper all cadres, excepting only the old and the sick, were urged to engage in physical activity for extended periods of time. This advice was especially directed at the young officials, who were in danger of becoming rulers at faraway desks, turning into bureaucrats and lofty gentlemen. It was they in particular, said the editorial, who should follow the example of the Heilungkiang school in order not to lose their proletarian and revolutionary spirit."

And so some of those who were now my hosts, and who were then cadres in East Peking, had (quite spontaneously, they said) called a meeting and decided to found a school for cadres in East Peking modeled on the one in Heilungkiang. They had found for it the place where we now sat, in sandy and infertile terrain just under twenty miles from Peking. A few weeks later, large numbers of the officials of East Peking had moved here. The "students" are mostly members of the city administration. There are also many teachers, some of them quite young. Many large enterprises and supraregional administrations, such as the various ministries, had later founded such schools of their own.

"Shouldn't they be called after the Fourth of October rather than the Seventh of May?" I asked.

My hosts admitted that the Fourth of October declaration was what had led to establishing these schools throughout the country; but they had all been modeled to some degree on the Heilungkiang school, and since that had been named for the Seventh of May directive, this was the name that had been kept.

My hosts continued the story: At first they had lived in a village under the most primitive conditions, together with the peasants. They had slept with them in the kangs, those big Chinese beds, and worked in the fields along with the peasants. Then the cadres had built a brick factory, and after that they began to build their own houses and dig their own wells. The commune to which the village belonged gave them what had been a cemetery for their buildings and a large sandy area for their fields. Thus a reclamation program began. The school is not a member of the commune but it has neighborly relations with the nearest brigade of the commune; they help each other out, extend mutual invitations, and join in evenings of Mao study. The students began by leveling the ground, carrying away two hills in the process, and built irrigation ditches. In 1969 they gathered their first harvest; beginning in 1970, with their second harvest, the school has provided its own rice, vegetables, and meat. A year ago its members had built a small metalwork factory.

I asked how big the school was. "At the moment, there are 1,255 men and women, about evenly divided between the sexes. About a thousand more people are graduates of the school. At this point about five hundred of the people here are cadres and about seven hundred are teachers or people working in various cultural fields—librarians, for example."

I stopped asking questions, since I wanted to gather my own direct impressions of the lives and work of the "students." (They are called that even though they are all adults, and for simplicity's sake I have adopted the term.)

First we went to look at a place where the students had dug a canal from a neighboring stream. From the canal the water was pumped electrically into a second canal at a higher level, which distributed water to the school's fields. The man in the pumphouse told me, not without pride, that nearly everything in the whole system had been built by the students with their own hands.

"How long have you been here?" I asked him.

"Two years."

"And what were you before?"

"I was in the East Peking finance department."

To everyone I talked with at the school, I put these same two questions. Some of those I met had been here since the school's beginning, and it seemed to me that their activities had changed from an educational course to an occupation. Others had arrived only a few months before. Many of the teachers were women. Among the culture cadres I met a school administrator and a librarian, among the city officials I met a factory manager, the East Peking commissioner for local industries, a woman health official, a factory manager, and two leaders of the Communist Youth League.

On our way to the pump station we heard the loud clang of hammering on metal from some nearby buildings. This was the factory at work. It produces containers that look much like a Western garbage can, with strong iron handles. Almost every stage of the process is laboriously carried on by hand. In room after room, men and women stood or squatted hammering, drilling, and boring. The finished product is stacked in a half-enclosed shed, for shipment to be sold in Peking.

"What about pay?" I asked.

"We don't pay the students anything, but their former salaries continue; many of them have dependent children."

"Do couples come here together?"

"No."

"Then how do they see each other?"

"Instead of one free day every week, we have two free days every two weeks, so that the students can go home for the weekend by bus."

"Do some of the people here get married?"

"Yes, there's a couple who met here in residence now."

63

We went to see the kitchen. The sight was one I shall never forget: eight or nine men in white smocks, most of them with glasses and the unmistakable traits of the intellectual, stood around a large table. In front of them rose a mountain of dough, out of which they were fashioning the famous Peking-style dumplings. They would lay these onto big wooden grills which were then plunged into hot water, several layers at a time. The chef, who also had the look of an intellectual, talked of what was taking place in his kitchens. "I was a cadre in the East Peking transport administration." He went on, "Our students have discovered a method of getting more heat from less coal. We'd like to show it to you."

We went down a few steps to the furnace room. Three men stood there, each one looking through a glass window, placed at about eye level, into the part of the furnace that was under his supervision. About five feet behind these windows, a small heap of glowing red coals lay on a gridiron, heating the bottom of the furnace. It was ventilated by a current of air from below. The trick was to add coal in the smallest possible quantities, so that it burned almost without leaving ash or any waste at all. For this purpose each of the men held a little shovel that had a very long handle, but was no broader than the palm of your hand; at exactly the right moment, which he could determine as he looked through his window, he would add a tiny quantity of new coal to the fire (to say he shoveled it in would be inaccurate, given the minute quantities). The three men were so intent on their work that I did not dare disturb them with questions. The one nearest me, once again, appeared to be a typical intellectual; I imagined he might have been principal of a school.

In the school's bookstore there were, of course, the works of Chairman Mao and all kinds of brochures, as well as the *People's Daily*. There were also various homemade newspapers, in which some of the Seventh of May schools reported on their various experiences.

Next we went to visit the dormitories, one-story buildings like all the others at the school. Here, each room was entered directly from the street, by its own door, and there were no doors from one room to another. There was space in each room for between eight and twelve people. The homemade cots consisted of boards on brick feet, with thin mattresses; they stood in narrow ranks, each one very neatly made up with carefully folded blankets and a pillow on top. There was a table, also homemade. The floor was of packed clay. Heat came from a small oven. Quotations and pictures of Mao were on the walls. A bookshelf held a bust of Mao and his works. Everything was very clean.

"What do you do about laundry? Is there a common laundry for the school?"

Heads were shaken. "Of course not, everybody washes his own things."

"Is there a washroom?"

"No, you have to go to the pump. Of course, we could have built a laundry, but the purpose of the school is for everyone to learn to do everything. It's the same with the cooking; we all take turns at it."

Another said: "The cadres used to be able to go to restaurants and eat well without having the slightest notion of how things looked in the kitchen. Now they're learning to prepare all kinds of food."

To my surprise, we were suddenly in a kindergarten where about twenty children were being looked after by three women. Then I realized that, of course, some of the students were mothers, and these were their children. On their biweekly visits to town, they take the children along so their fathers have a chance to see them.

The latrines were primitive, to say the least: walls of shoulder height, allowing you to see the heads of those inside, surrounded two open squares placed side by side—one for women, one for men—containing holes in the ground without partitions between, roofed on one side for use in bad weather. In short, here too the facilities were communal and as simple as possible.

Nearby was a small infirmary and a pharmacy; the latter dispensed Western and herbal medicines prepared from plants gathered by members of the school.

Returning to the car that had brought us, we drove down bad roads to visit the field cultivated by the school. Groups of students were harrowing the ground and spreading manure. Half a mile away, another group was busy breaking the ground. About fifty men and women were in the process of carrying away what was left of a hill, filling up some of the nearby sandy hollows with the clay and earth they had removed. About half of these, mostly women and older men, were trundling wheelbarrows, which the others were loading them with soil. A distance of about two hundred feet separated the hill from the hollows, and the students covered it at a rapid pace, often at a trot. From time to time all the "students" would break into a kind of spoken chorus of Mao sayings, without ever halting the rhythm of their work. This was led from the top of the hill by a sort of cheerleader, a robust young woman in a red jacket who was a student like the others.

A little farther on I saw a chicken coop and a pigsty, and after that the school's great pride: a round storage depot, filled to the top with rice the students had grown and harvested themselves.

I ate my noon meal with the reception committee, in the room where we had had our tea that morning. I was given to understand that two special dishes had been prepared in my honor: sliced sweet potatoes baked with sugar, and roasted peanuts. Otherwise, I was told, the meal was exactly what was being served that day in the dining hall: the pear-shaped dumplings I had seen being made, rice, chopped pork served in a brown sauce, a sort of corn-bread, a minced vegetable I couldn't identify, a mixture of scrambled eggs and steamed vegetables, and a cabbage soup containing small meatballs.

When I arrived I had been asked whether I would stay to see an amateur performance that afternoon. Of course I said yes. As the meal ended, people began running to and fro outside the reception room. Chairs and musical instruments were brought up. Then we were invited to come and take our places. Rows of chairs had been set up across the street, about fifty feet from an intersection. The front seats had been reserved for the foreign guest and the reception committee; most of the others were already occupied by students. To the left, on our side of the intersection, was an orchestra composed of Chinese instruments. The intersection, I soon found out, served as the stage, which could thus be entered from either left or right. The only piece of stage property was a round portrait of Mao, about three feet across, fastened to a stick and held in such a way that all you saw of the holder was his legs (from time to time someone else relieved him).

Now a lively, graceful little person—she turned out to be a teacher—leaped to the "stage" and began to recite a Mao quotation in the tones of an actress, emphasizing certain words with movements of her body, particularly her head and arms. At the end, she pointed silently to the portrait of Mao. Then she disappeared "offstage."

Next the music began. It was played by twenty-four young people of both sexes, all of them wearing blue suits, white kerchiefs around their necks and big straw hats fastened to their backs by a cord. With great verve, they struck up a dance tune that was meant to express joie de vivre and loyalty to Chairman Mao.

In the scenes that followed, various stages in the history of the school were depicted in dance and mime: the building of the houses; the leveling of the land; how the students had learned from the peasants (with a peasant telling his absorbed audience about the hard times before the revolution); sowing and reaping. One particularly impressive, quasi-acrobatic scene illustrated the saying of Mao that one had to be prepared for war. First the actors reminded the people of the fight against the Japanese, which had united the army and the people. The dancers moved together to form human squares; out of these rose various dancers, among them women—guerrillas, who looked about, fired shots, threw hand grenades, and then disappeared. Once a Mao quotation was sung. The last scene was a kind of Mao apotheosis, ending with a warlike living tableau.

During the discussion that ended my visit, I made a special effort to ferret out concrete examples of the general statements I had been hearing all day. I had been told, for instance, that the school's business was first, to "extend the revolutionary consciousness"; second, to develop understanding for the workers; and third, to spur people onward to ever greater achievement.

"Concretely, what does this mean?" I asked. "Can you clarify these things for me with specific examples?"

"Strengthening the revolutionary consciousness," I was told, "means that one must not rest on what has been achieved, but must constantly work anew for the revolution. In the beginning we had a man here who had joined the Party in 1934, and was thus a loyal follower of Chairman Mao. In 1949 he was awarded a high position in East Peking. In time he began putting on the airs of a highly placed gentleman; he separated himself from the masses and sat behind a desk giving orders that other people were supposed to carry out. Finally the revisionist poison entered his bloodstream. Of course he was criticized by the masses [during the Cultural Revolution]. He then realized that he would have to change, and came to us. Here he looked within himself. He came to understand that he was looking down on the people like a feudal prince or a capitalist, that in effect he had become an enemy of the people. A short while ago he returned to East Peking, cleansed of his mistakes.

"So far as understanding for the workers is concerned, we can give you the example of a woman doctor. She was working at a clinic in Peking. There all her patients were city people. She looked down her nose at the peasants. They were dirty, she said. She too was criticized by the masses and came to us. Life here was not easy for her, but she tried her best. When one of the peasant women was sick she moved in with her in order to give her better care. Here she did some of the dirtiest jobs herself, and so she got rid of her prejudices.

"Now for the third lesson to be learned here: out of love for Chairman Mao and the well-being of the Chinese people and our socialist fatherland, we must be ready to take on the heaviest burdens and do the most repellent jobs. What is the most repellent thing one can do? Cleaning the latrines. So, each of us has to do this job, not only here but also back home in the city. One of the men here was the deputy chairman of East Peking. There, of course, every child knew him. So it was a particular ordeal for him to go back to his own section of the city, where he had been one of the top leaders, and come in all dusty and sweaty after a long march, to empty the latrines there. He was afraid he would lose face entirely. But he overcame his revulsion and did it like the others; he emptied the latrines and shoved the stinking buckets onto his cart to bring them twenty kilometers back here, so that the contents could be spread on the school's fields. He had come to understand, you see, that emptying latrines is not a dirty job, but honorable work. In this way he helped frustrate the evil plans of Liu Shao-chi. It was Liu who had cultivated the feeling among the cadres that they were better than the masses, urging them to try to be as grand as the old-style city officials. You know the masses don't like snooty people. But when someone is brotherly towards them, and doesn't look down on them, and shows understanding for their work and can even bring himself to empty latrines, then they accept him even when he is a cadre, and they don't envy his car when he uses it, because it is faster to do urgent work in the service of Chairman Mao.

"That's the main thing about our school; here we have no officialdom, no rank; we are all students, workers in the heat of summer as in the cold of winter. This is good for all our cadres —not just the old ones, but also the young ones who have never known the difficult times of oppression and of the Japanese occupation. In these Seventh of May schools we put steel into their spirits, and when one day they are cadres or teachers or whatever, the masses will say of them, 'They're all right, they were in a Seventh of May school.'"

Certainly, they said, discipline was pre-eminent at the school, but it had nothing to do with militarism. At first the army had been involved, but that was long ago. And in fact I did not see a uniform during my entire stay at the school.

The revolutionary committee of the school was only founded very late, in October, 1969. "We came here from the most varied administrations and schools, so we first had to get to know one another through communal life and work before we could elect our leadership." The Party committee was formed in November, 1970. As in other places, the same people have leadership positions on both committees.

I talked at some length with one of the young people, a man

from the cultural administration of East Peking. I asked him his favorite quotation from the Little Red Book, which he carried in his outside jacket pocket.

"The first one in the first chapter," he said, and quoted it: "The force at the core leading our cause forward is the Chinese Communist Party. The theoretical basis guiding our thinking is Marxism-Leninism."

Had he read any of Marx and Lenin himself, I asked. He said yes, and so I asked him which of each author's works he particularly cherished. Once again the answer came promptly: *The Communist Manifesto,* which he knew had been published in 1848, and *State and Revolution.*

Where had he done his reading of these not entirely easy texts, I wanted to know.

"Lying on my cot."

"Is there no common study hall?"

"No."

Did he think everyone who came to the school knew what to expect there? "It may be that some don't," was the answer. "It happens to us time and again that new people arrive thinking they have come to learn about agricultural work. But that to us is secondary; we are not here to turn out professional peasants. Then again, some who have understood that the point of the school isn't training in agriculture but the thought of Mao Tse-tung, slip into the opposite mistake and try to withdraw into themselves to study. In the end they too come to realize that they're not here to learn something with their heads, but to change their entire being, their daily lives, and to follow the teachings of Chairman Mao. Then at last they are on the right track."

I asked about the collective study of Mao's works.

"Half an hour every morning and three evenings a week. The other evenings are free."

"And what happens during these study sessions?"

"We study Mao, we criticize the traitor Liu, and engage in self-criticism."

I got no answer to my question about how many Seventh of May students there were in all of China. Probably no one knew. From time to time, regional figures are given in the press: over one hundred thousand in Kwangtung province; in Honan, twenty thousand recruits from the provincial government alone.

Before I left, I asked what the students thought the future would be if a large percentage of them stayed on here for years, with a very slight turnover, so that only a very small number of the cadres and teachers of East Peking would be able to have this schooling.

"We don't know exactly; it's all new and in the experimental stage. We know we're still making many mistakes, but when we've ironed out most of the difficulties it may be that only a small staff will stay here permanently and the rest of the student body will come for shorter periods, perhaps for three months only."

"Are you thinking of founding a second Seventh of May school for East Peking in order to get more people through the school?"

The answer was a decided no.

"In any case, won't the schools be unnecessary one day, after everyone has changed and improved?"

Again, the answer came without hesitation: "The struggle between the two ways will continue indefinitely, so these schools are certain to exist for a long time."

8: The Yellow Clay Hill People's Commune

The people's commune is situated in the district of Fengtai, southwest of Peking. The hill of yellow clay from which it got its name no longer exists, since it was composed of good soil and had thus been carried off and made into wheat fields.

Several members of the revolutionary committee met me at the gate and led me through a series of courtyards. The last of these contained forty or fifty bicycles.

"A meeting?" I asked.

They nodded, and explained: "Discussion of spring planning, and self-criticism."

Let me add now that when we returned, after hours of inspection, the bicycles were still there.

First, as usual, tea was served. On one excursion I had been served nothing but hot water; tea still counts as a luxury but hot water is always available. China produces untold quantities of thermos bottles; today they are as much a part of everyday routine as the samovar once was in Russia. In every hotel a waiter sees to it that a thermos of boiling water is always on the table. I would buy tea for myself at a store in the hotel lobby; the best I saw cost fifteen yuan a pound (or about $6.00) but you could get some for as little as two yuan.

First my hosts gave me some basic information. The commune was founded in 1958, at the same time as hundreds of thousands of other people's communes, by bringing together a series of villages, now called brigades. Today the county of Fengtai, which is very heavily populated, includes five people's communes. The county is made up of about thirty-four thousand people on about 45,000 mu of land, and is divided into eleven brigades which in turn are divided into 106 teams. It has five "factories," a clinic, thirteen elementary and three middle schools. Also, each of the eleven brigades has at its disposal a small infirmary and a workshop for repairing machinery.

We visited only the two nearest brigades; even so, we had to drive a considerable distance. I was shown the following:

First, a chicken farm. The chickens were housed in low clay buildings, with glass windows about the height of a man that open to the south, but low and windowless to the north. Each building was about one hundred yards long and could contain about a thousand chickens. Two men and a group of girls were in charge.

Second, greenhouses. The buildings were similar, but they were heated. I was shown how cucumbers were grown. Along the window, warmed by the spring sun, was a green lattice from which cucumbers were hanging. Each one was weighted by a stone that hung from a string around its middle, "so that the cucumber grows nice and straight." I saw an old man who was in charge of the heating system, and two girls who took care of the cucumbers. The commune sold quantities of greenhouse vegetables to Peking, among them tomatoes.

Third, a store: a bright room, measuring about 36 by 90 feet, with a sales counter and shelves along the walls. There were many different kinds of merchandise: clothing, shoes, stationery, candy, canned goods, and fruit. I saw here the same shirt I had bought in Peking, at the same price.

These establishments belonged to the brigade; there are others that belonged to the commune. They included:

The hospital. Consisting of a group of houses, it was set off by itself, surrounded by fields. It was only a few years old. I visited the dispensary, the pharmacy (with both traditional Chinese and Western medications), the delivery room, the maternity section (complete with mother and baby), the treatment room (where one woman was having an arm treated with infrared light and another was getting hot packs), and the operating room. The hospital's expenses are borne by the commune out of its own earnings, and in addition each member of the commune pays a yearly fee of one yuan. I met some of the personnel: the head doctor, a woman with a refined, intellectual face; a couple of giggly nurses; a young pharmacist who immediately launched into a speech about his medicines, above all the herbs gathered by women in the commune. Finally there were two "barefoot doctors."

The barefoot doctors do not have bare feet; the phrase is part of the expressive new terminology used by the Chinese. What it means is simply that these are people who have had no academic training. With their help China is trying to assure herself of at least minimal medical care everywhere, even in the villages. The two I met were a woman of about thirty and a healthy-looking boy in his mid-twenties, both of whom had been trained at this hospital. Normally they would have been out with their brigade, where they took part in whatever work was in progress, becoming "doctors" only in cases of necessity.

I asked them what they could cope with. Broken bones? Only very simple cases, they said. Anything more complicated was taken to the hospital. Could they act as midwives? The young woman nodded; the boy looked doubtful.

My next visit was to a middle school, with 460 students and thirty teachers. A gym class—or, to be exact, a relay race—was in progress on the playground. There were experiments in this school too. Because some thought six grades were too many for a middle school in the country, three were being tried here. But no final decision had been reached. I saw three classes in progress. One was a math class where the students were busy with fractions. The teacher, a young woman, wrote fairly long and complicated equations on the blackboard, questioned the class, heard their answers, and went on writing, all at a very rapid pace. In a workshop, the noise was deafening as the students made shovels out of heavy tin, to be sold in the city; quantities of the finished product were piled in a corner.

Finally, I went to a class in acupuncture, the classical Chinese method of healing, which makes use of needles sunk deep into the nerve centers of the body. The teacher would ask where to put a needle for certain ailments, and the students would point to the proper spot on their own bodies. Then he called out two girl students, one to act as the patient, the other as the doctor. The "doctor" first disinfected her hands and the needle with alcohol; then, with a sure movement, she sank the needle into her patient's temple. The teacher examined, criticized, and demonstrated. The "doctor" pulled out the needle and applied alcohol to the puncture.

Of the "factories," I saw only one big workshop. It contained —if my count was correct—twenty-two lathes for turning out machine parts, some of them destined for use here and others to be sold. Farther on, I saw a mill where wheat and corn were being ground. The members of the commune had done all the carpentry for it themselves; the mill was turned by electricity, and was attended by personnel in white smocks.

Finally I saw a tractor station, which counted as one of the five factories. It was after working hours when I went in. A few workers with the Little Red Book in their hands greeted us. They showed us orderly rows of tractors and trucks, and also a jeep made in China.

The call for many small and middle-sized shops and industries within the framework of the people's communes is not new, but it has been stressed particularly during the last few years. The five "factories" of this commune had been founded toward the beginning of its existence. They employed seven hundred workers, all of them from the commune itself.

We drove across the fields threaded with irrigation canals, crossing canals that were as much as eighty-five miles long, and which the people of the commune had dug. In addition there were many irrigation ditches. The commune had also built four hundred electrically powered wells.

"We still have a great deal of sandy soil, and we've always had three enemies: drought, flood, and sandstorms. We've almost conquered drought and flood with our canals and ditches. Today 95 percent of our land is irrigated; in 1945 the figure was only 5 percent. We used to harvest about one hundred pounds of grain per mu; now we get three hundred and fifty. We've planted trees against the sandstorms [the long, straight, asphalt-paved streets of the commune were lined with trees] and other communes westward of us, where the storms come from, have done it too. So it won't be long now before we've conquered our third enemy."

Back in the reception room I asked a few more questions. The first was about the commune's finances.

"The commune receives 20 percent of the brigades' income. Out of this sum we pay taxes to the state—6 percent of the gross income of the commune—and we also pay for a series of investments, some of them at the brigade level. For example, the commune builds its schools, but the state pays for the teachers' salaries and for the electricity. And the state sometimes helps the commune with big investments."

"Why do you pay taxes?" I asked. "They told me in Tachai that the villages don't."

"Grain is tax free, but much of what we produce is vegetables and similar high-priced foodstuffs for Peking, so we have a relatively high income—which is taxable."

I had been looking forward with particular eagerness to my first visit to a people's commune. In 1957, when I was last in China, this particular form of agrarian organization had not yet been in existence. Then suddenly in 1958 the countryside was organized

75

entirely into people's communes, subdivided into brigades; and the whole world—not least of all the Soviet Union—was informed that the people's commune was the ideal form of socialist agricultural endeavor. After the heavy setbacks of the Great Leap Forward, less was heard about the people's communes; it seemed almost as though they had existed only on paper.

My visit to Yellow Clay Hill proved that the people's communes did exist, and that they had a function to perform between the levels of the brigade and the county. But there could be no doubt that the brigade was a far more dynamic entity. In the brigade everybody knows everybody else, and that's where life pulsates; people debate, quarrel, and make decisions. During my visit to Tachai I almost never heard the word commune, except when people told me how after the 1963 catastrophe they had declined the commune's help. The more vitality a brigade has, the more it works on its own initiative and maintains its autonomy: Tachai even has its own hospital. The brigades leave to the commune those things that are far beyond the scope of a brigade, and which can be more rationally accomplished by a larger organization. But even here the distinctions are fluid. There are brigades that even have a mill of their own, and Tachai, as we saw, had built its own noodle factory.

Essentially the people's commune consists of administration buildings and a few relatively large-scale enterprises. Whenever the cadres want to give a concrete picture of the commune's work, they are obliged to refer again and again to what is done in the brigades. It is quite natural for them to think that all the most important decisions lie within their domain; but to me it seems no accident that it is a brigade, not a people's commune, which is the model held up before the eyes of the entire nation: Tachai.

I asked my hosts at Yellow Clay Hill a few more questions, so as to verify some of the facts I had already gleaned. First I inquired about the incomes of the commune members.

"The workers in the commune factories get between 30 and 50 yuan a month. The director of the machine-parts shop earns 40 yuan, and a teacher and the doctor earn the same; agricultural workers get between 300 and 400 yuan a year."

76

"How do you decide on individual wages?"

"We discuss them." The factors that enter into these discussions have been covered elsewhere. But what is meant by "political consciousness" never was made clearer to me than in a story told to me here by a member of the revolutionary committee.

"There is a member of this commune, Comrade Feng, who takes care of pigs. It happened that one of the sows in her care, and a sheep she owns herself, were about to give birth the same night. She did not have an easy decision to make; but she remembered the teaching of Chairman Mao, and so she spent the night in the commune's sty, helping the pig—and when she got home in the morning her newborn lambs were dead through lack of care. She was very sad about this, but she was praised by her children because she had put the collective well-being ahead of her own."

9: Equality and the Silk Factory

Hangchow, which Marco Polo called a paradise on earth, even today remains the center of China's ancient silk industry. I was very eager to visit a silk factory there. The one I visited employs seventeen hundred workers, both men and women, and has 330 electrically driven looms that can handle up to fifteen different colors and about a thousand patterns and color combinations. It produces brocade and, since the Cultural Revolution, political designs as well—portraits of revolutionary figures from Marx to Stalin, and a whole series of woven silk pictures of Mao (among them one of Mao and Sihanouk together.)

After going through the factory I sat with my guides in the reception room, asking my questions while the faces of Marx, Engels, Lenin, and Stalin looked down on us from one wall and Mao reigned over the three others—all in pure silk.

My first question concerned bookkeeping. It was not exactly simple.

"What is the relation between your income and your expenses?"

"We don't calculate in those terms. The state places orders, sets planning goals, and provides our material; we deliver the product. We have no financial problems as they exist in the capitalist world."

"I can't really believe it's as easy as all that," I said, "or how could you know what you're doing, or plan ahead?"

"For us production is a matter of quantity, that is, statistics, and not bookkeeping. We've filled our quota the past years, and that's all there is to it."

But I still wasn't satisfied. "How can you deliver a product to the state without knowing its value? And how can the state supply you with raw material and machines as well as money for your salaries, without having somebody keep books? How much were you supposed to produce in 1970?"

"Four and a half million yards." I remembered in a general way the prices for silks and brocades I had seen in the stores, and ventured a guess: "Then the state must somehow credit you with about 9 million yuan."

My hosts looked at each other, laughed, and said that it might be something like that. My figure must have been more or less accurate, for during the rest of the conversation we used two yuan per yard as a point of departure.

"All right, the state sends you the necessary raw materials, provides electricity, water and so on, and gives you cash to pay your salaries. Is that about the way it goes?"

They nodded.

"Now let us assume that in 1970 your expenses were approximately equal to your income from sales to the state, and that in 1971, thanks to more highly developed automation or other labor-saving devices—in other words, thanks to your greater productivity—you produced 10 percent more. That would be about 5 million yards. So the state now owes you around 10 million yuan, instead of 9 million as before. Let us assume all this. Can you now dispose as you wish of this additional million yuan?"

To my hosts, the whole idea seemed very peculiar. They shook their heads energetically. No, of course not; theirs was no capitalistic enterprise, out to make a profit!

"But raising productivity is not a capitalistic principle! It's as

78

old as human endeavor. The better living conditions that have come about during the past thousand years have stemmed directly from the fact that mankind has raised its productivity by the most diverse methods."

"But that's exactly what we're doing, raising our productive capacity! And we're successful—we're producing 50 percent more than before the Cultural Revolution."

"This means that in 1965 you produced only 3 million yards, and earned only 6 million yuan from the state. Thus your income in 1970 should be 3 million yuan higher than in 1965."

I was immediately corrected. "Our productivity by the yard has risen by 50 percent since 1965, but the worth of our goods has risen only 17 percent. Before the Cultural Revolution we sold too dear and produced too much luxury material."

"Well," I said, "I'm not especially concerned with exact figures. I'm interested in underlying principles. Let me go ahead on my assumption that in 1970 you received 9 million yuan for 4.5 million yards. In 1965 you earned 17 percent less, as you've just explained to me [we were now all busily calculating on scraps of paper]; that is 7.7 million yuan; and this for 50 percent less material —that is, for 3 million yards. At that time the factory was earning two and a half yuan for a yard; now you're only earning two yuan. You have raised your yard production and lowered your price; thus you have raised your work productivity. What kind of benefits have you had from this?"

"We may be earning less per yard than in 1965, but the total earnings are better because our production has risen. This has allowed us to improve our machinery, expand the factory, and things of that sort."

"That's all for the good of the factory," I replied. "But how does it benefit the workers?"

Silence.

"Have their wages been raised?"

Decidedly negative headshakes.

"Has there been some indirect improvement, such as more or better houses to live in, or a bigger communal kitchen?"

"No. When we need new houses we place a request with the revolutionary committee of the city of Hangchow, and it decides whether or not we are to get them."

"And these decisions have nothing to do with your filling your production quota?"

"No, nothing at all. That's exactly the lesson we learned in the Cultural Revolution: that one does not work for oneself, but for the honor of Chairman Mao and our socialist state. And this change in our political consciousness indicates a victory of the thought of Chairman Mao over that traitor Liu Shao-chi."

"I keep hearing about the wickedness of this man," I said. "Just exactly what did he do?"

He tried to introduce capitalist ways, I was told.

"How, exactly, did this happen?"

"For example, he had his people in this factory, and they were the people who set the tone at that time. They started offering the workers additional sums for special achievements. Workers who produced more than others would receive extra money over and above the salaries paid to them in accordance with their wage category. The worker's material interest and egotism were supposed to be inflamed and this was intended to spur him on to greater achievement."

"Those additional sums that some workers earned—were they very high?"

"As high as 6 yuan."

"Per day?"

"No! Per month."

I was very surprised. "If the sums they earned were so small, why all the excitement?"

"They were errors committed against the principle of equality. Everyone sees the necessity for various pay categories; the strong workman belongs in a higher category than a weaker woman, especially if she has a family to take care of. Our highest salary here is 82 yuan, and the average is, of course, lower. If two people in the same pay category get different salaries, say one gets 60 yuan and the other gets 66, it seems unjust to us. This capitalist and revisionist method of payment disturbs the unity of the factory community.

"At the time there would be long discussions about why one had gotten 6 yuan a month more than another. Say a worker had achieved a seemingly higher productive capacity by cheating. He might even have done it so cleverly that the overseers never noticed, but his colleagues would know and be angry about it. Not only would the man have cheated, but he would have been rewarded for it. Instead of discussing better work methods, people argued about pay. The masses criticized this system of payment, but for a long time they could not get their way against those in power who were going the capitalist way. It took the storm of the Cultural Revolution to sweep these people away."

"And have things gotten better since 6 yuan a month are no longer being paid for special effort?"

"It's not a question of the 6 yuan; they're not really important. It's the meaning of the thing, it's that the followers of that traitor and scab Liu were encouraging egotism among the workers. Egotism is a bad thing; we declared war on it, and we have won."

"How are things better now?"

"We have achieved unity among the workers. We no longer sit around discussing salaries, we talk about how we can save overhead expenses, how we can do better, how we can deliver more to the state. Before, when someone found a better method of doing something, he kept it to himself in order to produce more than his colleagues, and thus earn more. Today, when someone discovers a better method of doing something, he immediately offers it to the collective, since there is nothing to be gained by keeping it to himself."

I asked for illustrations. One woman said: "A few years ago we imported some jet-type looms from Czechoslovakia. But we discovered that we could only produce very narrow fabrics on them. Nobody devoted any thought to how these could be improved, since it would be of no benefit to anyone personally, and at the time everybody was only interested in earning his bonus. But as soon as we had overcome this lapse into egotism, a group of us

81

took on the task of improving these looms, and now we can weave wide fabrics on them. At the moment we can do this only with one-color fabrics, but we expect to solve that problem too."

"If I understand you correctly, you've explained to me that first you conquered institutional egotism, and now you've conquered individual egotism too. You offer no benefits, no rewards, for high achievement. Do you really think things can work this way in the long run?"

"Yes. We simply assume that everyone is working according to his ability, and that within his own pay category he is doing his absolute best."

"Can you honestly say," I persisted, "that there is no one in this entire factory who gets more than the 82 yuan you mentioned, not even the cadres or the technical experts?"

My hosts looked around at each other. "Well," somebody said, "there are three who do. One of them actually gets 100 yuan, but he's the only one, and he has been here all his life. There's nothing above that. And this one exception is only a temporary thing."

"By the way," I asked, "what finally became of those followers of Liu you mentioned earlier?"

"Some of them changed their political orientation; they went through a period of self-criticism, and today they're still in the factory, some of them even holding their old jobs with the consent of the masses. The others are no longer here. One of the things the masses resented particularly was that Liu's people kept waiting for advice and aid from outside China, and relied on foreign methods and patents, instead of on the inexhaustible creativity of our own Chinese people."

"Now let us assume the following," I said. "You have a worker named Chang; he is strong, healthy and intelligent and has had many years of experience. He is a good worker, reliable, keeps his machines in perfect order, and has never produced defective goods; his family circumstances are orderly—in short, he's the best worker in the whole factory, but . . . but . . . he has one weakness: he has absolutely no interest in Chairman Mao and the Little Red Book. Then what?"

Everybody spoke at once. And the sense of what they said was that such a thing was impossible. Any worker who rejected the thought of Chairman Mao could not be a good worker. The two went hand in hand.

I said, "You appear to me like soldiers during a war. Every one of the same rank gets the same pay, whether or not he's brave or good at what he does. And a soldier isn't paid in cash for the number of the enemy he kills. Yet he gives his all, sometimes even his life. Do you think this is a fair comparison?"

They all nodded. The parallel seemed to please them enormously.

"All right," I said. "I'm talking about soldiers in wartime. Their country is in danger, their wives and children must be protected, and all of them know that one day all this will end. But you, here, want to perpetuate this state of mind forever. How do you suppose things will look in ten or twenty years?"

"We're absolutely persuaded that it will be just as it is today. As it has been since the Cultural Revolution."

"From the lessons of history," I said, "we have learned that small minorities can be ready to devote themselves for a lifetime, without egocentric concerns, to an idea or an ideal, and that for a short period whole peoples can be made to behave in this way. But do you truly believe that three-quarters of a billion people can live like this for an indefinite length of time?"

"Yes, we certainly believe it."

"Man's egotism is surely not his most laudable characteristic, but since the beginning of time it has been the motor of progress. For the first time in the history of mankind you are trying to eliminate this trait in the interests of an entire vast population. If you succeed in this, it will be a remarkable thing. I wish you all the luck in the world. But the five years that have passed since the beginning of the Cultural Revolution is far too short a time to reach a definitive conclusion. We really should discuss all this again in 1990."

"We're very sure we're right," my hosts repeated as we said goodbye.

I importuned the representatives of other factories I visited with similar queries. My persistent questions about pay systems encountered headshaking wonderment, and were dealt with as a standard symptom of my capitalist mentality. There are more important things in the world than pay and money, they kept telling me. To this I would answer that the relation between work and pay was a basic human problem with which Marx, Lenin, and Stalin had all grappled, so it should seem quite normal for me to be interested in these new Chinese systems.

The clearest and most concrete information I received about wages came from a small factory to the north of Peking. It had only 820 workers, so it was easy to grasp how things worked there. My two hosts were both workers, both named Liu, and both members of the revolutionary committee; the younger of the two was the committee secretary, the elder in charge of ideology and personnel. Here is the picture I got from them:

All in all, there are eight pay categories in this factory. (This seemed to be generally true of other factories.) The pay in the lowest category is 40 yuan; in the highest it is 100 yuan. A person's classification is based on three qualifications: experience, performance, and political consciousness.

Experience is judged essentially by a person's years of activity at the same job, although two workers at the same job for the same number of years may reach very different levels of performance, and this difference is examined. Just how political consciousness is measured I could never really discover, since I was not present at any meetings where the question was discussed in detail concerning each person.

I inquired into the pay category of every worker with whom I talked whenever we inspected a factory. One old master of his craft, who had been working at the same job since he was fifteen years old, was in the eighth and highest category. Two women whom he had trained were in the third and fourth categories respectively. The elder Liu was in the seventh, the younger only in the fourth, even though he was secretary of the revolutionary committee. The director of the factory (absent that day) was in the eighth. The amount of work produced is not reflected in the wage scale; thus there is no piece rate. Perhaps the old master of his craft produced less in quantity than the two women he had trained; yet because of his years of experience and the high quality of his work, he is in the highest category.

"If somebody has bad political consciousness," I asked, "does he get put down to a lower wage category?"

Both Lius spontaneously lifted their hands in gestures of denial. No, that never happened, they said.

"Then how does political consciousness enter into the wage scale?"

The younger Liu explained it this way: "Let us assume that you and Comrade Li [my interpreter] are both in category six. You have good political consciousness, Comrade Li's is bad. In this case, you will advance to category seven after a certain time, generally in about two years, while Comrade Li will remain in the sixth, because every two years there is a review of each worker's wage scale."

I asked questions about other details of organization. Again it was the younger Liu, a man of quick intelligence, who answered:

"The revolutionary committee of this factory was formed on November 23, 1967; it consists of thirteen people. The party committee of this factory was founded on the fifth of March, 1970, after the old one had been disbanded by the Cultural Revolution."

"What is the relation between the party committee and the revolutionary committee?"

"The party committee guides the revolutionary committee."

"Is there any overlap?"

"The leaders of the revolutionary committee are also members of the party committee."

"Is the director of the factory also a member of the revolutionary committee and the party committee?"

"Yes."

"Does the director, who is in the eighth category, receive the same pay as the old master of his craft who is also in the eighth category, or are there two different pay scales, one for workers and another for administrators?"

"The director of the factory who is in the eighth category gets exactly the same amount of money as the old master who is also in the eighth category."

"Do you believe that the parallel functions of the revolutionary committee and the party committee will continue, or do you think the two will merge?"

Again the younger Liu: "Things will stay this way for a long while yet because the two groups serve different functions; the party committee has a leadership function, the revolutionary committee is administrative."

Liu also told me that workers of both sexes can continue with full pay beyond the age at which they are pensioned, and after they are pensioned they receive 70 percent of that same pay for the rest of their lives.

Also in the course of this conversation—much too long to be reproduced here in full—I was of course told at some length about the excellence of the teaching of Chairman Mao, and the misdeeds of Liu Shao-chi, and how bitter, in this factory too, the battle between the "two ways of thought" had been. It was not, I was told, primarily a matter of achieving greater production, but a matter of a change in the spirit of man and, finally, of revolution in the whole world. For half an hour before going to work every morning, and for an hour after work every evening, all the people devote their time to study of the thought of Mao Tse-tung. For many workers, the elder Liu said, the study of Mao had become as much a part of life as morning prayer in a convent.

10: Tea and Rice

It was a landscape out of a Chinese painting: rice fields under heavy rain clouds; steep, bizarrely shaped hills; tiny huts; people wearing wide hats and rain capes made of woven reeds, balancing heavily laden bamboo poles across their shoulders.

About ten miles southwest of Hangchow, we turned into a valley and followed the course of a narrow river. At one place I saw a number of people working in the open, although it was pouring rain. They were constructing a dike by the side of the river, filling the ground to the height of the dike—about four hundred of them, both men and women—and they worked away undismayed, not heeding the disagreeable weather.

About half a mile farther on, where the valley grew narrower, was the village of Meichawa. Here, when I met the chairman of the revolutionary committee, I asked whether it was customary to work out of doors in such weather, reminding him of Mao's statement that one must ever be watchful of the health of the people. He said, "I have just come from the fields myself—please excuse me for being late—and I went there to tell the people they should stop work because of the heavy rain. They were reluctant to follow my orders. They said that in a few days it would be time to harvest the tea, and in the meantime they wanted to finish the work they had begun. I finally let them go on, but only on condition that they did not return to work outside this afternoon."

As we returned to the village, wearing raincoats and protected by umbrellas, we saw the four hundred people walking home in a long column with their baskets and hoes, wet from head to foot and covered with mud to the hips. As we were on our way to visit the school, we stood aside to let them pass. We returned to the road only after the column had gone on a bit farther, and suddenly I noticed that the water in the stream, which a short time ago had seemed so clear, was now a muddy brown. I soon discovered the reason: four hundred people were washing themselves and their clothes in that stream.

Here and there I saw women with small children in their arms, soaking wet, running through the rain; they had gone to fetch their children from the communal nursery and were taking them home for lunch.

We were visiting a brigade that belongs, with thirteen others, to a commune south of Hangchow. The chairman of the revolutionary committee is Mr. Tsu; the vice chairman is Mrs. Cheng. The brigade's main product is tea. Before 1949 about five hundred mu of tea were planted in Meichawa. Four-fifths of all this had belonged to one big landlord and a few peasants; the remaining 20 percent belonged to the villagers, who at that time numbered about 750. Since 1949 the area planted with tea has been increased to 1,035 mu thanks to the new terraces, and the population has about doubled, to a total of 1,340 people.

The production per mu has also risen, from 220 pounds in 1965 to 280 in 1970. And in the same period the income per family has gone up accordingly, from 900 to 964 yuan. The stages of collectivization are in keeping with the pattern elsewhere. In 1952 a "mutual aid team" was founded, followed in 1955 by a "cooperative of the higher type," and in 1958 by a people's commune, which Meichawa entered as a brigade. The brigade's income rose steeply, and today, without outside help, it can produce tea of the finest quality, ready for market. The villagers now have 240 electrically powered ovens for tea drying—which means that they can complete the entire process of curing in their own village.

What is new is that the brigade, which formerly only raised tea, now has 150 mu of rice paddies. This area has not been taken over from tea cultivation, but has been wrested from previously unreclaimed ground. The moving of rocks and soil that I had seen on my way here was a step toward the creation of new rice paddies.

I was told that the villagers had decided to clear another 150 mu for the same purpose. "At the beginning, with the first 150 mu, we had bad luck. In both 1968 and 1969, our new rice fields were washed away and destroyed. There were those of little faith who thought we should give up the whole idea of growing rice; as tea producers, they said, we knew nothing about it. But the masses remembered the saying of Chairman Mao: 'In agriculture, learn from Tachai!' So we learned from the example of Tachai's flood catastrophe in 1963, and after our own floods in 1968 and 1969, we simply reconstructed our rice fields, and built higher dikes against possible new floods. Since then everything has gone well. Last year we took to heart Chairman Mao's declaration of the twentieth of May, proclaiming our solidarity with the peoples of Indochina, and in honor of their battles we made a special effort to increase our rice production. As a result, we harvested about 200,000 pounds. That covers the greater part of our own needs."

I asked why the people of the brigade were so intent on raising their own rice. "Aren't you possibly carrying Mao's words about standing on your own feet a bit too far? Your valley produces a tea that is famous throughout all of China. [I had been told this again and again.] If you're going to take the trouble to reclaim land, why don't you plant it with tea? For generations your people have planted and harvested tea; there is nothing you don't know about it, and the climate here is ideal. Why not stay with the thing you know, and buy your rice from places where it is more easily grown?"

"If we did that, we would be putting a burden on the state for our own food."

"Not at all, since you would be delivering tea, which is more valuable to the state because it can be sold abroad for foreign currency. You would be the opposite of a burden to the state; you would be a great asset."

"You don't understand. We are following the words of Chairman Mao, in which he says that everyone must store away food reserves for use in case of war."

So that was it! I had no further arguments.

My next questions concerned finances.

"You have about a thousand mu under cultivation with tea, and you harvest about 300 pounds per mu. I have learned from you that every twenty years the tea plants must be cut back almost to ground level and then a few years must go by before you can harvest tea from these plants again. So it is likely that you are not harvesting three hundred times a thousand—that is, 300,000 pounds—each year, but somewhat less. Can you tell me the size of your 1970 harvest?"

The two chairmen knew the exact figure: 240,000 pounds.

"And what did the state pay you for them?"

"Three hundred and seventy thousand yuan." (The state pays between 2 and 20 yuan per pound, depending on the quality.)

"So your 1970 income was about 370,000 yuan. What were your expenses? In the first place, there are salaries. You have about 250 families, and you tell me each family earned about 1,000 yuan. So you needed about 250,000 yuan to cover your salary expenses. That leaves you about 120,000 yuan. What became of them?"

The answers now came more slowly. The two men talked for a few minutes, and then they came up with the results: 30,000 yuan had gone for taxes (which incidentally were paid directly to the state, not through the commune), 30,000 into investments of all sorts, 50,000 for such items as electricity and fertilizer, and the remaining 10,000 yuan were listed as miscellaneous.

"I was told in another commune, in the north, that agricultural workers pay no taxes. Why did your brigade have to pay taxes?"

"There's a simple answer to that: earnings from grain are not taxable, but other earnings are—such as tea."

"And how do you set your wage scale?"

It turned out that this brigade also worked according to the point system. As at Tachai, ten points per day was generally the maximum. Each point was worth fourteen fen (in Tachai the figure was 15 fen). There was an average of 290 working days in a year. Thus a ten-point wage-earner would have an income of approximately 410 yuan a year.

Next I began to ask about relations between the brigade and the commune. The commune gave support to projects beyond the means of the individual brigades, as we have seen before. The commune worked out the production plan for the entire commune as well as for individual brigades. These were discussed with the brigade in question, but the final decision lay with the commune.

In this brigade the revolutionary committee consisted of seventeen persons. In accordance with the "three in one" principle, some representatives of the military sit on it (in this instance, there were four members of the brigade's militia), some cadres (a total of eight), and some representatives of the masses (a total of five). I asked how one got to be a member of the revolutionary committee. Following a rather prolonged discussion, this is what I was told:

Candidates are suggested by members of the brigade and then discussed in an open meeting. Some candidacies vanish in the process, and so the list of names grows smaller. When it has dwindled to a manageable number, elections take place. Every working member of the brigade (there are no stated age limits) writes a maximum of seventeen names on a piece of paper, which is stuffed into a ballot box. The seventeen people with the most votes are elected.

"Is the person with the most votes automatically made chairman?"

"No. The seventeen members of the committee vote on their own chairman and vice chairmen. Our brigade has four of those."

"When was your revolutionary committee voted into office?"

"In August, 1968."

"Have there been re-elections since?"

"No. Since we were voted in for a term of only one year, at the end of that time we asked the masses whether they desired changes in the composition of the revolutionary committee. They didn't, so we remained in office. A year later it went the same way, and we shall probably go on in this fashion."

"Are these annual decisions arrived at by secret vote?"

"No."

When I asked about the number of members in the brigade's Party leadership, I got no direct answer. That depended on local conditions, I was told. I generally found that the people of the brigade were much more willing to talk about the revolutionary committee than about the Party; perhaps because the reconstruction of the Party had not yet been completed in the village. I was finally told that of course, Party leadership in the village had fewer members than the revolutionary committee.

Were all its members also members of the revolutionary committee?

"No; but a few are members of both so as to ensure unity of leadership." (Both the chairman of the revolutionary committee and his deputy belonged to the local Party leadership.)

"And how does one become a member of the revolutionary committee of the commune?"

"The brigade sends one or more representatives. Our brigade has one man on the revolutionary committee of the commune, who also sits on our own revolutionary committee. The masses decide who sits on the joint revolutionary committee."

"Is this also by secret vote?"

"No."

Our conversation was taking place in a big room that did not look as though it had been recently built. Even the carpentry of the chairs seemed to me old-fashioned.

"Did this house once belong to a rich peasant?"

"Yes. He made his money exploiting the poor peasants; so during our land reform it was taken away from him and returned to the people."

"What happened to him?"

"He is dead now."

"And the other rich peasants?"

"They are dead too."

"And their children?"

"Some of them are members of our brigade. We don't discriminate against them; they had no part in exploiting the people. But of course they must now live like the rest of us, without special privileges."

Tea, the lovely green tea that is the pride and the chief product of the brigade, was served once more. Then I took my leave.

11: "The Morning Sun"

In Shanghai, where I had lived for several years during the early 1940s, I was interested in what had changed in the old part of the city, as well as in the new developments surrounding it.

On my first day there we drove off to visit a new district called Tsaoyang ("The Morning Sun"), situated northwest of Shanghai. The oldest of the new districts, it was begun in 1951 and has been expanding steadily ever since. Today it consists of eight subdivisions, housing about 68,000 people who make up 14,700 households.

The inhabitants are mostly workers in a nearby textile factory. The houses are from two to five stories high. Thirteen day-care centers and kindergartens provide for 2,300 children; there are fourteen elementary schools for the first six years (with 15,000 students), and seven middle schools for the next three years (with 17,000 students). The district has a movie house which is also used as a theater, a House of Culture for festivities of all sorts, a bookstore, a hospital (each subdivision also has an infirmary), a department store (each subdivision has a general store, a rice shop, and a vegetable store), a bathhouse, a post office, and a bank.

I was able to see most of these places and gather my own impressions. The department store was not much different from those in the city, although the selection was slightly more limited. There were great heaps of apples, pears, and tangerines. In the rice shop you could buy three different grades, priced at 55, 60, or 65 fen a pound. As it is weighed out, the rice slides down a tin funnel into a sack the customer has brought along. Rice is rationed (as cotton is) and the rations are posted on a blackboard: children ten to fourteen years old receive 28 pounds a month, women receive 32. The highest ration (for grown men who do heavy work) is 55 pounds a month.

The hospital is alive with activity. While one patient is being treated, all the others watch. Here is someone being treated with acupuncture needles, there is someone else being given an injection, or having drops put into his eyes; and medication of every sort is being prescribed and dispensed.

The bank is very simply furnished. There are no counters; the employees sit behind a long table. It was here that I finally found out that the interest on a savings account is 3½ percent (in Tachai, you will recall, no one knew exactly). When I asked about the size of an average savings account, no one could give me a clear answer. There were, I was told, accounts with more than 1,000 yuan.

At the day-care center for the one-to-three-year-olds, the "older ones" sang and danced for me. Each performance had some political content—"In Peking there is a golden sun . . ." or "We have seen Chairman Mao," or "The light that shines from Chairman Mao has penetrated deep into our hearts"—and each was accompanied by the appropriate gestures. Here as anywhere else, the kindergarten children were particularly appealing. And after I had made my rounds, I was treated to a performance that began with a formal greeting by the diminutive announcer to "the uncle from West Germany." I saw scenes out of a new opera, and a dance

93

entitled "The Exploited People Fighting Against Imperialism," in which the dancers stood with little fists clenched and fierce looks on their faces.

In a song and dance routine called "The Penny," a little girl dances alone and finds a penny on the ground. A boy dances by. She asks, "Uncle, is this your penny?"

"No."

A girl dances by. "Auntie, is this your penny?"

"No."

A boy appears dressed as a policeman.

"Uncle policeman, I have found this penny. People all say it doesn't belong to them, so I am giving it to you for the state."

The policeman takes the penny and thanks the little girl.

It was a delightful spring day. The sun broke through the clouds from time to time and the trees had that pale-green shimmer of early spring. The people in the streets and shops looked at me curiously but in a friendly way. I said to my two companions from the revolutionary committee, "Might I see where someone lives?"

So they took me to a nearby house. We crossed a hall on the ground floor, and a door opened. A middle-aged woman greeted us from a spotlessly clean room and began immediately to prepare tea (I had the distinct impression that the "foreign guest" was not entirely unexpected.) Mrs. Kuo, is fifty-nine years old, she is plump and healthy-looking; her husband is 66, and they are both on pensions. Mr. Kuo had been a worker in a textile factory, and his wife had worked in a silk factory. The pensionable age is fifty for women, sixty for men. Pensions are set at 70 percent of the last salary. (For Mrs. Kuo, this is 42 yuan.) The couple has a son who had moved into another house in the same district, with his wife, the year before. The older couple pay 3.10 yuan a month for rent, and about one yuan a month goes for electricity. The two of them live in this one room and share a toilet and a kitchen with two other families. The toilet has running water, and in the kitchen there are three separate gas burners placed on three tables.

The room contains a wide bed, a table, three chairs, a commode, and four chests set one on top of another, containing clothing and household effects. The walls are covered with quotations and pictures of Chairman Mao.

What do they do with their free time?

Mrs. Kuo spends a lot of time helping out in the neighborhood, taking care of the sick and looking after young children while their mothers are at work.

Is this work assigned?

The answer is no.

How does she find out where she is needed?

"Oh, around here it's easy to find out what's going on."

Three times a week there are political sessions. The participants are members of the three families that make up this little community, and every now and then they choose one from among themselves to lead these studies.

When we were back in the street I asked, "Could I see one more apartment?"

We went into another house, where a woman was in the process of washing down the hall. She led us to her apartment, which consisted of two rooms—one for herself and her husband, the other for her children. Mrs. Tsou does not go out to work, and calls herself a housewife. Her husband is a worker (he was absent at the time of my visit); her eldest son had finished a higher technical school and is a technician working in a factory, her second child is in the army, her third is an apprentice, and the two youngest are still in school. Only the three younger children still live at home. It was not quite as clean here as it had been at Mrs. Kuo's —one realized here that there were children in the house. On a bookshelf I saw a statue of Mao, and on the walls there were pictures of Mao, as well as two framed diplomas. One of these stated that Mr. Tsou was considered an activist in his factory, the other that the second eldest son had served well in the army.

Back in the reception room, I asked for information about the activities of the revolutionary committee and the Party committee. First I was given an explanation of the administrative setup. The city of Shanghai covers 140 square kilometers and has six million inhabitants. In the environs of Shanghai, covering about 2,880 square miles, live another four million souls. The city of Shanghai is composed of ten boroughs, and each of these is made up of nine districts, of which "The Morning Sun," where I now found myself, is one. Since the district itself is subdivided into four quarters, there are four levels of administrative division. I was dealing here at the lowest level, with the district and its quarters. At each level, every division or subdivision has its own revolutionary committee.

There were a few questions I kept asking over and over—for example, "What is the structure of a revolutionary committee at the quarter level?"

Each block of dwellings in the quarter comprises a group. These groups gather in open meetings, at which candidates are proposed and discussed, the list shrinking in the process.

"At the end, when there is a manageable number, we vote. Not by ballot—we just raise our hands. At the quarter level, the members of the revolutionary committee are mostly housewives and pensioned people."

"And at the level of the district?"

"Here the 'three-in-one' principle works doubly. On the one hand, the army, the cadres, and the masses must be represented, and on the other hand the elder, middle, and younger generations must also be represented."

To my remark that this "three-in-one" had been decreed by the 1969 Party Congress only for Party cells, the response was that there had been a decision to follow the same principle in the composition of the revolutionary committee.

Incidentally, the two representatives of the army on the Tsaoyang revolutionary committee had not been elected, but had been dispatched from a unit stationed in Shanghai. The other eighteen members of the revolutionary committee were elected in this fashion: each of the block groups in the various quarters sent out an elector —which would mean that there were about five hundred of these for the entire district—and the electors then chose the eighteen members of the revolutionary committee by secret ballot. My two hosts at Tsaoyang are both members. The woman runs a day-care center, and the man, who is about thirty, is a cadre. Before becoming a member of the revolutionary committee, he had been a cadre in the borough of the city that was responsible for this district, and so people here knew him.

"Is the revolutionary committee subdivided?"

"Yes, we have ten departments."

"What are they?"

"Politics and propaganda, organization, supplies, collective enterprises (for example, common vegetable gardens or small workshops), youth, Intellectual Youth to the Countryside, education, culture, store supervision, and administration."

"Does every member of the revolutionary committee belong to one of these departments?"

"Not necessarily."

The woman with me was kept so busy with her day-care center that she took part only in plenary sessions or meetings of the revolutionary committee as "representative of the masses," whereas the young man represented the cadres. His full-time job was to head the organizational department of the revolutionary committee. In order to make sure that I wouldn't suppose he was imbued with officialdom, he hastened to tell me that he was frequently in conversation with the people "in order to learn from the masses."

Here, once again, I asked about the relation between the revolutionary committee and the Party committee. The revolutionary committee had been in existence since April, 1969, the Party committee since May, 1970. There were seven members of the Party committee, one of them the woman from the day-care center.

As for the relation between the two, the revolutionary committee was an organ of state power, and had in its ranks some who were not Party members; membership in the Party committee, on the other hand, was limited to those who were. According to its latest constitution, the Party's job is to issue directives, at the district level as well, whereas the revolutionary committee has the function of an executive office.

"What sort of executive offices existed before the revolutionary committees?" I asked.

"There used to be administrative bureaus."

"Do they still exist?"

"No, the revolutionary committee has replaced them."

97

The revolutionary committee and the Party committee meet in the same building, the 1969 Party Congress having decreed the necessity for "unified leadership." But this principle does not mean that a member of the Party committee must now sit on each of the ten departments of the revolutionary committee.

My final questions were concerned with the department of the revolutionary committee that deals with "Intellectual Youth to the Countryside."

Before the Cultural Revolution, I was told, young people had hesitated to go out into the villages. But since there had been an upswing in political consciousness, young people were swarming to the countryside; they knew it was the task of all to further the revolution and follow the words of Chairman Mao. Applications were reviewed by the department of the revolutionary committee in charge of such matters, and it made decisions about work assignments.

"Is the individual allowed to state preferences?"

"Yes."

"Are these respected?"

"Sometimes."

"Does he know in advance how long his assignment will last?"

"He doesn't ask. He has only one thought in mind, and that is to serve Chairman Mao and the state as well as possible. The state decides how long each person is to stay. Some stay forever."

12: The Schools Function Once More

As we drove up to the gate of the middle school, located in a side street near the center of Peking, a reception committee had already lined up: a man and a woman in civilian dress, a man in uniform (rank not discernible) and two youngsters wearing the red arm bands that identified them as members of the Red Guard formed in 1966. Just behind the gate, at the spot where in a traditional Chinese compound there would have been a wall to keep away evil spirits, was a big picture of Chairman Mao. To my left was the playground; straight ahead and to my right were the school buildings. One of them looked as though it had once been a church. They were all of gray brick, as so many Peking houses are.

We were led into a reception room and I was seated, as guests have always been in China, against the back wall with an interpreter to my right. The five representatives of the school sat down on the other side of the table. The man in civilian dress greeted me formally and explained that he was a member of the revolutionary committee (but for simplicity I shall refer to him as the school's director).

Then he introduced the others: the man in uniform, who belonged to the revolutionary committee in accordance with the "three in one" principle; the woman, who was a teacher of Chinese language and literature; and the two youngsters, who were thirteen and fourteen years old. In turn, each of the persons introduced stood up, made a quick bow, and sat down again; I did the same. I was told by the director, in answer to some of my questions, that this had originally been an English mission school and had been taken over by the Communists in 1949. Today it is a middle school, composed of six grades; the students are graduates of the district's elementary school, which also has six grades. There are 1,500 students in all. Twelve subjects are taught: politics, Chinese, mathematics, chemistry, physics, biology, agriculture, revolutionary culture, military education, geography, history, and English. At the time of my visit, the experiment of decreasing the number of school years, requested by Chairman Mao, was in progress. Some people were in favor of five years of middle school; others thought even four would be enough. Every year the students worked one month each in industry and on the land. The agricultural work was done in the environs of Peking; about the industrial month I was to learn more later on. We went into the courtyard just as a gymnastics class was beginning. A teacher with a microphone stood on a kind of podium and gave orders to fifteen hundred students: "Arms out! Bend!"—and so on. Between movements they recited Mao quotations in chorus. When the gymnastics class was over, the children closed ranks so as to form columns. I had already turned to go when I heard loud applause. Looking back, I found the entire group applauding, and was given to understand that this was for the "foreign guest." I applauded too, as I had learned to do in Russia and had come to realize was also the custom here.

Next we visited four of the school's workshops. In one, cables for automobiles were being made; in a second it was other automobile parts; a third was making parts for electronic switchboards by a photochemical process; and a fourth was putting together small transistors, some of them so tiny that the work had to be done using a microscope. Each of these shops was staffed by students from the second class; they would be working here for a month, and then their places would be taken by students from another class. Other students of the second class, I was told, were working that month in factories allied with the school.

In each shop I was greeted by a student who explained to me what was being done. Each one, as part of the explanation, declared that the workers were following the teachings of Chairman Mao, that it was not a matter simply of turning out various products but of changing the students' basic consciousness. Formerly the school had been concerned with academic learning, but now "politics are in command."

So far as I could tell, the work was being done correctly and carefully. Every single piece was later tested, sometimes with rather complicated devices. Some of the machinery looked quite old, some looked homemade—and this was pointed out to me with great pride, since it showed that Mao's directive to rely on one's own strength was being followed. The teachers were not technicians in their fields, as I had supposed at first, but ordinary teachers who had learned the appropriate techniques.

In my conversations with teachers and students, I discovered that although ancient and modern literature were covered, they concentrated on the period since the fourth of May, 1919, the date of the great youth demonstration before the Gate of Heavenly Peace, which was followed almost immediately by the formation of the Chinese Communist Party. One might almost have supposed that the only Chinese history that mattered had begun a mere half century ago. In literature courses the classics had their place, the teacher told me, but here too the emphasis was on the poems of Chairman Mao and the works of Lu Hsün.

There was no longer an entrance examination, as there had been before the Cultural Revolution. Anyone who had completed elementary school could enter the middle school. Once here, however, he had to take periodic tests and examinations.

After our tour of inspection we went back to the reception room, where the same cast of characters had soon reassembled, and I had a chance to ask further questions. The school's revolutionary committee had been founded very early, back in the spring of 1967, and as everywhere it consisted of the "three-in-one alliance" —namely, the army, the cadres, and the masses. Three men from the army had been assigned to the school; they remained soldiers but were responsible for the school's ideological posture; they were present at all conferences as well as—naturally—at Mao studies, and they organized campaigns and marches. The cadre category also had a part in administering the school, as director, and so on. And the masses were represented by both teachers and students: the teacher and the student at our table were both on the revolutionary committee.

We had long discussions about how marks were awarded. It was hard for me to arrive at a clear picture despite these long discussions. I shall simply pass along what I discovered. There are five marks; the highest is five, the lowest is one. Three criteria enter into the mark: political consciousness, scholarly excellence, and health. I did not pursue the health factor. Scholarly excellence can obviously be measured by certain objective criteria. But how, I asked, can political consciousness be measured?

One quickly realizes that the students know each other well; at all class meetings every student is discussed, and it is here that a final decision is made about marks. In an effort to get a clear idea of how things are done, I asked the two boys with us how they had fared at the end of the last school year. The thirteen-year-old, who was in the second grade, answered, "On the positive side, I have been active in political matters; but I had three points against me: I'm undisciplined, I talk too much, and I have a tendency to apply Chairman Mao's principles more to others than to myself."

The fourteen-year-old, who was in the third grade, said, "They told me I had studied the teachings of Chairman Mao very thoroughly but then had grown arrogant about knowing it all."

Were comments of this kind written into your report card? I asked. The answer was, Sometimes yes, sometimes no. And I could find out nothing more on this subject. . . .

Since I had been assured several times that factual knowledge was always combined with practical application and emphasis on the state of consciousness, I asked the director, who was also an instructor in mathematics, how that worked out. This was his answer: "To combine theory and practice in my field, for example, we go to our school's meteorological station. There we keep track of temperature, rainfall, and wind. Then we calculate monthly averages. This is a practical application of mathematics.

"Political consciousness in my field can be introduced in several ways. We can talk about positive and negative figures. For example, China has no foreign debts; thus everything we produce is on the positive side of the ledger, since it adds to the well-being of the people. On the other hand, the American imperialists and the Soviet revisionists both have enormous debts, incurred in financing their monstrous arms race. These are negative figures, and they show why both these states are in decline."

While all this was being translated, I had time to look around me. On one wall were pictures of two Germans and two Russians —Marx, Engels, Lenin, and Stalin, the latter in his uniform as marshal of the Red armies. On the opposite wall was an enormous portrait of Mao, and on the remaining two walls were color prints depicting scenes from his life. Through the window I could see a building that must once have been the school chapel, but was now a lecture hall. From time to time students, wearing heavy fur caps, would pass the window, behind them the clear, cold Peking sky.

The faces of my interlocutors were what might have been expected: both teachers were intellectuals. This was notably true of the director, who had been teaching at the school for sixteen years, and who looked the way anyone would expect a teacher to look. The man in uniform had the heavy face of a sergeant. The elder of the two boys appeared the more alert; he followed the conversation intently, and seemed to have a sense of humor. The younger one seemed a bit less quick. At the beginning, when I questioned him, he took a long time to answer. But once launched, he was remarkably articulate.

I turned to the soldier: "What happens to the graduates of this school?"

"In former times, every one of our graduates wanted to be a cadre or a teacher or some other kind of leader. Today they are assigned according to the country's needs, although of course their preferences are taken into account."

"Can you give me an idea of what happened to your last year's graduates? There must be about 250 of them, I suppose."

He answered without hesitation: "Eighty percent went into industry, 10 percent into agriculture, and 4 percent into the People's Liberation Army; the rest are scattered among various professions."

"Of the 10 percent who went out into the countryside, were any sent to remote places?"

Again there was no hesitation: "Of last year's class, there were none."

I asked whether these quotas were assigned to the school. The answer was yes. One thing I noticed, incidentally, was that all my questions were answered very promptly, without any questioning exchange of glances between those from the school. Only when I touched on the subject of further developments at the school, I was told that things were just getting started, people were experimenting, and all of them knew that the revolution in education was the most important one of all.

Later I spoke with the youngsters about what they would do when their schooling ended. They both said very nearly the same thing: that they were ready to undertake any work the state asked of them. The elder one said that if he could choose, he would like to join the army and defend his homeland against its enemies. The younger said he would like to work in a factory. He was, by the way, a member of the Communist Youth League, whereas the other boy was not; according to what I was told, only about 3 percent of the students were members. The percentage of student membership in the Red Guard seemed to be higher; I would put it at about 10 percent, judging from the number of red armbands I saw during the gym class.

At the end, the director of the school asked me whether I wished to say anything about my impressions. I replied that I had seen similar schools in the Soviet Union about forty years before. At that time I had seen the same close cooperation between schools and factories, and had seen them de-emphasize book learning in favor of practical experience and the development of political consciousness. But then, beginning around 1934, the system had begun to change, and Soviet schools had begun adhering more and more closely to the traditional school system. Now they stress scholastic discipline, and are among the toughest schools in the world.

The fourteen-year-old student spoke up.

"Stalin was a great Marxist-Leninist but he wasn't able to direct everything at the same time, and so the revisionists, who were already entrenched in Moscow at the time, betrayed the revolution and reintroduced book learning into the country. But in China, thanks to the teaching of Chairman Mao and his comrade-in-arms Lin Piao, politics rather than academic learning will always be in command. The hopes that the imperialists and revisionists place on the third generation of Chinese revolutionaries is misplaced. I'm still young, but my brief experience has taught me that if you rely on the teaching of Chairman Mao you will always be victorious."

He ended his little speech with a quotation from the time of the Great Leap Forward (1958): "When you come to China the next time you will be able to see for yourself; under the leadership of Chairman Mao, one day in China is worth twenty years."

On this crescendo note, my hosts and I parted at the gate.

My chance to visit an elementary school came in Nanking. . . . It was raining. The reception committee stood at the gate with umbrellas raised. The school yard was surrounded by one-story

104

buildings. As everywhere, there was a large reception room, with tea waiting, where we could talk before we set out. The fundamentals were explained by the principal, Mrs. Li, a woman in her middle years. Also present were another teacher and an old worker named Wang. The revolutionary committee here consisted of five persons, the three already mentioned and two other teachers I did not meet.

The school has six grades, with about 1,200 boys and girls who were divided into twenty-five classes (with about 50 to a class) and about 48 teachers. School starts every morning at 8:10, recesses at 11:30, starts again at 1:30, and ends at 3 o'clock. The children are all from the section of town surrounding the school. In the four lower grades the subjects are: politics, Chinese, mathematics, sports, and revolutionary arts (singing and painting). In grades five and six, two subjects are added: English and "general studies" (history, geography, and science). In accordance with the request of Chairman Mao that school time be shortened, an effort was being made to reorganize the subjects into a course lasting five rather than six years. A student's main business is education, Chairman Mao had said on May 7, 1966. There are ten months of school during the year (two months of vacation), yet in grades five and six all students have a month and a half of practical work in villages or factories; for grades three and four the time is one month, and for the two first grades it is two weeks. Besides this, there were the school workshops.

"Even this elementary school experienced the struggle between the two lines of thought," explained Mrs. Li. "That anti-revolutionary revisionist Liu overemphasized academic schooling; he tried to make the children into bookworms, he wanted to educate them to be officials and then look down on people who work with their hands. But during the Cultural Revolution the revolutionary line of Chairman Mao won out, above all when the propaganda troops appeared." (More about them in a moment.)

Then she gave two examples: a teacher who formerly had emphasized book learning alone, but who now understood that the main point in education was a change in consciousness, and a little eight-year-old girl who had twisted her ankle and had been taken home, but who returned in the evening, despite her swollen foot, because there was a rehearsal of the theater group to which she belonged.

The little girl had told her protesting mother that Chairman Mao had said one must be deterred by neither pain nor death, and had also reminded her of the story of the sailor who went on fighting Chiang Kai-shek's soldiers despite a severe head wound. With this prelude, we went out to visit the classrooms.

Every subject except arithmetic is filled with Mao's thought. In the second grade, where the children were learning to read, the four characters for "the continuous revolution" were written on the blackboard. The students in a politics class were reciting in chorus, "We must carry the revolution to the very end." The first word in the beginning English reader is "Mao," printed in Latin characters.

The school is a model of discipline. The children all sit with their arms folded and resting on their desks; open in front of each were the Little Red Book and another text. A child who wants to answer a teacher's question doesn't frantically wave an arm in the air, but lifts the right hand, keeping the elbow on the desk and the other hand lying flat. Their concentration on the teacher is so intense that even the appearance of a rare bird like me occupied them for only a few seconds. The little ones in the second grade were already in the process of learning the complexities of the Chinese abacus. Next we visited the shops, where even the smallest of the children were already working with bits of wood and metal. There were no toys, nothing but real machine parts—albeit simple ones, of course.

Children are always a joy to watch, whatever the color of their skin, and almost any class of schoolchildren gives me enormous pleasure. Thus I have always made a point of visiting schools, endless numbers of them, in nearly all parts of the globe. So I believe I have acquired an eye for the differences and the special character of a school. There are dull schools and alert schools; there are schools where the children are simply crammed with facts, and others where the goal is to develop character. There are classes who stay with the teacher every step of the way, and others who simply sit waiting for the bell to ring. My impression of the ten

106

or twelve classes I visited in that Nanking elementary school was unmistakable: the children there were *learning* every instant they were in school. I seemed to be surrounded by eager faces asking, "What's the next question? I want to answer! Faster, faster!" A child who was called up to the blackboard sped to it from his desk, wrote what was called for, and then skipped back.

I did not get the impression that the preoccupation with quotations from Chairman Mao was at the expense of scholastic work. The children learn Mao quotations, but they also learn—everything. It may make a difference in the childish psyche whether one learns to spell from words like "cow" or "mother," or from words like "Mao" and "revolution"; but so far as learning to read is concerned, it probably makes very little difference. I also got the impression that, as contrasted with the universities, the Chinese schools are no longer in a phase of radical experimentation. Those in charge seem to have a clear idea of their aims, and to approach them with determination.

We returned to a reception room that had been transformed during our absence. Along one wall there was now a small orchestra composed of Chinese instruments—all played by children in soldiers' uniforms. Part of the room was now the "stage," and a door served for exits and entrances. Before each of the eight or nine numbers, a child would jump onto the stage and announce the next number. The "uncle from West Germany" was greeted during the first announcement. Then a sort of miniature whirlwind in dance and song broke out. Tiny soldiers marched or ran across the stage, sang or danced, accompanied by an orchestra and a little chorus. There were solo dances and songs by small performers, both girls and boys, all of them just elementary school children. A tiny eight-year-old girl (presumably the one with the twisted ankle) played a Chinese instrument which she dragged onto the stage by herself, together with the table she needed. The whole thing, done at breakneck speed and without any intermission, lasted about twenty-five minutes—and was done with enormous verve and spirit, as well as obvious pleasure.

I saw no original skits; instead, there were childish adaptations of modern Peking operas and ballets. Two of the solo performers, for example, mimicked the heroes of *The Red Lantern* and *Tiger Mountain* down to the rolling eyes and facial contortions of the adult actors. One number was, of course, the song and ballet "The East Is Red," with all the children wearing huge paper flowers. I would really have liked to spend the rest of my time at this school hugging all the soloists, but I needed every minute that remained for a conversation with Wang, the workers' representative.

So following the last tableau, after I had applauded the performers and they had applauded me, I watched them file out and turned to Mr. Wang.

It had been during the summer of 1968 that the first propaganda corps marched into and took over a university—Tsinghua University in Peking. During the weeks and months that followed, the same thing went on in most of the universities and then it spread to the schools. Mr. Wang was the first person I had met who belonged to such a group.

"How long have there been these propaganda groups in the elementary schools?"

"Since the end of 1968."

"How many members are there here?"

"Four."

"All of them out of the same factory?"

"Yes, we're all from a car repair workshop."

"How long will you stay here?"

"For a year. Then we return to our workshop and others will come and take our place."

"Are you now employed partly in the school and partly in the workshop?"

"No, our work is entirely in the school."

"And who does your work at the factory while you're gone."

"Our comrades. We can afford it; our productivity has risen greatly since the Cultural Revolution."

"Who pays your salary?"

"The workshop continues to pay my salary, since we are its employees during the time we work at the school."

"What is your job in the school?"

"To see to it that the teachings of Chairman Mao are followed."

"And how do you do this?"

"Since there are only four of us and there are twelve hundred children, we have to concern ourselves mainly with the teachers and not the students. Mostly we study the ideas of Chairman Mao with them. This is how we follow his instruction that the working classes must maintain leadership in all areas."

"Are you a member of the Party?"

"Yes."

"For how long?"

"Over ten years."

I had one last question for Mrs. Li: "How many of your children failed last year and had to repeat a class?"

"Six out of the twelve hundred," she replied. "At the time of the traitor Liu Shao-chi there were many more, since under his influence the school concentrated on the particularly gifted children and neglected the rest. Now we give everyone a fair chance."

13: Shanghai's Factory University

My time in China was flying by, but every day I crossed off an item or two from my list of requests. One of the most important items on it, however, was brought up again in city after city: I wanted to visit one of the new universities. I never did cross that item off my list. This came as no great surprise. For years the Chinese press has reported more about the revolution in the universities than about their achievements. Their experiments with a new form seem thus far not to have jelled. Anticipating this, I had listed a substitute request: to visit the "university" of Machine Tools Factory #1. The nearer we came to Shanghai, the more curious I grew about whether or not this request would be granted. Then, one day, there it was: "Tomorrow morning we shall visit Machine Tools Factory #1."

The location is in an ugly industrial region, at some distance northeast of the city. The area encompassed by the factory is so large that this time we were met not at the gate but in front of an administration building. Here we found the usual reception room and the emissaries from the revolutionary committee, one woman and four men.

I said to them at once, "Three years ago I was sitting at my desk in Germany when I read the investigation report on university reform dated July 21, 1968. It was then that I began to be interested in your work. A few days later Chairman Mao declared in a directive that . . ."

At this point my hosts broke in on the interpreter to recite in chorus the directive declaring their factory to be a model for university reform, and thus making them famous overnight throughout China: ". . . it is essential to shorten training time, revolutionize education, and put proletarian politics in command . . ."

(The entire text of the directive is given in the document section)

"So," I continued, "you can see that this aspect of your work is what interests me most."

My hosts declared they understood me perfectly—though I had the impression that they would much rather have spent the whole time taking me through various shops. For them, the business of their factory was to produce machine tools, and the experiment with new teaching methods was merely a sideline. Before 1949 all this had been a small workshop that produced only the most primitive implements, such as hoes (one lay on the table as an exhibit). This was, of course, because the imperialists would not allow any kind of real industrialization, since they wanted to keep China as a market for their own products. Now there were 6,000 employees, working in three shifts and turning out machines of great sophistication.

In answer to my request, my hosts now turned to the matter of university reform. They had long been dissatisfied with the experts the old university had sent them. When they said "old" university, they didn't mean the university of the time before the Communist takeover, but prior to the Cultural Revolution—that is, before 1966.

What was so bad about it, I asked.

"The old university," my hosts replied, "made narrow specialists who, once they had finished their education, thought only of themselves, their careers, their income, or their reputation."

I asked them to give me an example.

"We had an electrical engineer," I was told, "who came to us before the Cultural Revolution. He started designing all sorts of machines. One was intended to promote the growth of hair on bald heads by a particular treatment of the skin. Another was supposed to kill rats with light beams. The workers criticized him. 'Why do you want to construct such stupid stuff? We're a factory for first-rate grinding machinery.' And he would reply, 'No one has ever seen such a device for making hair grow, and nobody has ever made such a rat trap. If I'm successful, I'll be known throughout the world and I'll make a lot of money with my patents.' The workers were outraged."

"What happened to your ratcatcher?" I asked.

"Today he's a worker in our factory, learning to integrate theory and practice."

"What we need," said my hosts, "is the exact opposite of the electrical engineer we've just described. We need technicians and engineers who have risen from the ranks of the workers [from now on, for simplicity, I shall refer to them as worker-technicians], and who work not for themselves but according to Chairman Mao's instructions, and serve the people. Of course it has not been easy to carry through the right way against the wrong way of that traitor and scab Liu Shao-chi, and it was necessary to throw off certain ancient Chinese habits, such as an overwhelming respect for 'the learned.' But through the Cultural Revolution the right way has triumphed, and we began to train our technicians in the factories with a combination of practical experience and study. . . .

"Today we have two kinds of training for worker-technicians. We can either send workers who have the right political consciousness and suitable practical experience to a school or university outside the factory, and then have them come back and work here, or else we can give specially qualified workers the opportunity to attend and graduate from our own university, which we opened next to the factory in the fall of 1968, and then become a technician or possibly even an engineer."

111

"How many people have you trained in this way since your university was started?"

"Two hundred thirty technicians and ten engineers, almost half of the total number working here."

I asked to be shown the factory university.

"With pleasure; but you won't see anything there now because we're just at the end of a course and at the moment the students are completing their work in the factory itself."

We had to drive for some time before we came to the "university." It consisted of a number of barracks-like buildings that had obviously once served other purposes but now housed school desks, blackboards, and so on. By the way, I saw no heating at all, and in a Shanghai winter the temperature can hover around freezing for weeks at a time. The director, hurriedly summoned from his office, turned out to have come to the factory as an apprentice at the age of fourteen, had been sent from here to an outside school at eighteen, and had returned to the factory as a worker-technician.

In answer to my question about what subjects the university taught, he listed politics, military skills, agriculture, mathematics, mechanics, electrical engineering, hydraulics, the construction and production of grinding machinery, and English. Teachers were "workers, revolutionary technicians, and engineers." In the morning there were lectures, and in the afternoons the students read and did their assignments. At the end of the year there were papers and examinations.

"Where do the students do their afternoon's work?" I asked.

"Here." Wang, the director, pointed to the classroom.

"Would it be possible for me to see some students doing the work that ended the year?"

"Why not?"

We drove back to the factory. In one of the designing rooms we came upon a student working among his colleagues. He was visibly unprepared for my visit, and kept looking in perplexity at his companions, answering my questions only after they calmed and encouraged him.

He was born in 1941, had entered the factory in 1958 as an apprentice, and become a worker in 1961. In the autumn of 1968 he had been accepted at the newly opened factory university. For his first three months he studied nothing but theory. Then came six months of practical work combined with study, followed by a year of concentrated study with occasional work in the factory. For a few months now he had been working in the design department on his final paper—it might be called a thesis—whose subject of course lay within the realm of what the factory produced. When he had finished it, his studies would be complete. Along with fifty-one other students who had entered the university in the autumn of 1968, he belonged to the first group of students to graduate.

In another designing room, we met six other students. I began questioning a young woman, who had come to the factory in 1956 after finishing school and had also been taken into the factory university immediately after it opened. When I asked what she was studying, she named as her third subject not agriculture, as the director had done, but simply "manual work."

What did she plan to do after she finished her studies?

"My class-brothers have shown me their trust in sending me to the university; in order to repay this trust I will follow the Mao line all my life and carry out every task the state sets for me."

I asked whether I could meet one or two of the professors. I was introduced to a young man in his early thirties. He had graduated in 1964 from Tsinghua University in Peking (for many decades one of the leading institutes of technology in China) and immediately after graduating he became for two years what we would call an assistant professor, also at Tsinghua. Then, during the Cultural Revolution, he had spent two years working in a village. "After that I was assigned to this factory. I was warmly welcomed by the workers, since I came to them from manual labor in a village rather than from a university. A short time after that they made me a professor in their factory university."

I said, "You knew the old Tsinghua University. You know that the Cultural Revolution has changed everything there, and you now know the university here at this factory. What do you think Tsinghua will be like a few years from now? Do you think it will be like the factory university here?"

"The circumstances are so very different. Tsinghua has always

113

been a university; this place was and still is a factory. And there are also vast differences in the studies themselves: Tsinghua maintains many disciplines that reach in all directions. Here basically we have a single technological direction: grinding machinery. But Chairman Mao has said that all universities are to follow the example set here, so I assume that in essentials the Tsinghua University of tomorrow will resemble this place. I've read that Tsinghua is getting another factory, where they'll build trucks, and that production workshops have even been put into schools. Of course, there will still be one important difference: Tsinghua is directed by the state; the factory university is directed by the factory."

I talked to the head of the design department. He had been an ordinary worker, then had taken courses and become involved in "three-in-one" activity, and was now a professor at the factory university.

I had now met with the "three-in-one" concept several times, and wanted to know more about it. In China today there are several three-in-one arrangements, and it is not altogether easy to define them. This one meant that in design teams it was not technicians or engineers alone who advised and decided, but workers and cadres as well. Workers, administrators, and "revolutionary cadres"—that is, those cadres who have been purified by the Cultural Revolution—make up the three-in-one teams for machine design and similar work. It was explained to me that this was an excellent method for making technicians out of workers and at the same time making use of their experience in design.

Another man, I was told, had begun as a sweeper; then he became a skilled workman and after that a technician, finally rising to the grade of engineer; now he is the chief engineer of the factory. "We no longer have the title of chief engineer," it was explained, "but that's really what his job is." Another worker-technician had become vice chairman of the revolutionary committee of the factory, as well as a member of the revolutionary committee for the city of Shanghai.

"Things are not easy for us in China. The Soviet revisionists tore up all our contracts for technical assistance, and the imperialists are out to do us harm. So our old workers, with their decades of

114

experience, are a great help, especially when they also have some technical training. Of course, we often have to experiment for a long time before we succeed. A group of our worker-technicians did more than 3,000 experiments over a period of three years so as to perfect a complicated grinding machine that was urgently needed. Again and again they studied the thought of Chairman Mao, especially his essay 'On Practice,' and read his maxim that 'failure is the mother of success,' as well as his saying that one must go from practice to knowledge and then back to practice.[1] So their failures never discouraged them, since they were not working for gain or fame but "for the honor of Chairman Mao and our Chinese fatherland."

At the end of every visit I made, someone would always say, "Despite our best efforts to follow the teachings of Chairman Mao, we are still inadequate in many ways and we must seek to improve many things." (This too is typical of the new situation, my friends among the diplomats in Peking tell me; it didn't happen a few months ago.) After that there would generally be a few examples. On this occasion a man from the revolutionary committee added, "For example, our production is uneven."

"What does that mean?"

"It means that at the beginning of the month we work too slowly and then at the end of the month we work too hastily and make mistakes."

"Why is that?" I asked, though I could imagine what the answer would be.

"Because we have quotas that we have to fill every month."

"Who sets these quotas?"

"The masses discuss a program, and then they make a production projection for the next year. The factory revolutionary committee reviews these suggestions and then sends them to the corresponding section of the Shanghai revolutionary committee. From there it comes back to us as our final plan."

After this visit I was no longer surprised that my request to visit a university had not been granted. There will have to be many more experiments before Machine Tools Factory #1 is really the

[1] Little Red Book, Chapter XXII.

model to follow, and before that model can be built into a university system that can answer the requirements of a modern industrial power.

14: The Little Red Book and the Song of the Helmsman

Over the long hours I spent in traveling with my two Chinese companions, we developed a game of our own. I would be reading, say, the *Peking Review*, and whenever I came on an important quotation for which I wanted to know the source I would inquire: "Mr. Li and Mr. Tao, when and on what occasion did Chairman Mao say, 'Fewer troops, but better ones and less cumbersome organization'?"

Very often they both knew, or at least one or the other of them did, but when it turned out that neither of them knew, an eager search would begin. They both, of course, always carried the Little Red Book with them in an outside jacket pocket. But not every quotation could be found there. Mr. Li had the advantage that wherever we went, he carried in his luggage the *Selected Works* of Chairman Mao in Chinese—a volume of over 1,400 pages—and also in English—four volumes. As soon as he had found the place in the Chinese edition, he would show it to me in the English. Both gentlemen seemed to enjoy this game. And they failed me only once during the entire trip.

As we were driving from Sian to Yenan, the place of the sacred sites, we passed a village where the statue of Mao seemed particularly imposing, even from a distance. This was Lochuan, where Mao had held an important conference of the Politbureau during the war against the Japanese. The three of us began talking about the conference and what Mao had said there, and of course Mr. Li immediately hauled out his Mao volumes and with speedy assurance tracked down the reference in the Chinese edition. . . .

The complete quotation read: "On what basis should our policy

116

rest? It should rest on our own strength, and that means regeneration through one's own efforts."

I cannot begin to count the number of times in the course of my trip that this was quoted to me!

Mr. Li and Mr. Tao are particularly well-educated men. But whenever I had a chance I would quiz others I met on their knowledge of Mao—such as the local people who were our companions from time to time. At one point our conversation turned to Mao's thinking about matter and consciousness: that matter can change into consciousness and consciousness into matter. . . . We were soon immersed in dialectical discussion. When I mentioned at one point that I had attended the same high school as Hegel, the German philosopher who was the father of modern dialectics, it turned out that Hegel was known not only to my two faithful companions, but also to the local guide. They all knew that Karl Marx had developed his dialectical materialism out of the teachings of Hegel on contradiction.

"Since Marx always associated dialectics with the class struggle," I said, "some of his disciples later declared that after the proletarian revolution and the disappearance of the bourgeosie—that is, with the disappearance of the two main classes—contradictions would also disappear, and with them the basic element of dialectics."

"But you see," said our guide, "Marx only imagined the victory of the proletariat, so he cannot have foreseen that contradictions would outlive the moment of the proletarian victory. The Russians, though, should have known, only they didn't understand it. That's why it's so important for Chairman Mao to have established that contradictions live on, and made this thesis a cornerstone of his thought. Look at his article, 'On Contradictions,' written in 1957."

I wanted to see how thorough his knowledge of this article was. It was particularly familiar to me since I had happened to be in China in 1957 when it first appeared, and everyone was discussing it at the time.

"There is a difference," I began, "between the two kinds of contradictions . . ."

Mr. Li promptly finished for me: "Some are antagonistic and others are non-antagonistic."

117

"On the one hand there are contradictions between the people and their enemies, and on the other hand there are contradictions among the people," the local man said, and went on to elaborate: "The Russians believe, in their superficial and un-Marxist way, that there can be no further antagonistic contradictions in a socialist system. But thanks to Chairman Mao we know that they continue, which is why the revolution must go on even during the socialist epoch. I really cannot grasp why the Russians don't understand this . . ."

". . . and seem to believe that they have a state made up of the *whole* population, and a party made up of *all* the people," the local man continued. (This was from the current program of the Communist Party of the Soviet Union.) "These contradictions will always exist," he concluded, "since where there are no contradictions there is no movement and no life."

I asked a man once which quotation from Mao was the most important to him personally. He replied, "We reach for the thoughts of Chairman Mao whenever a problem arises, and the particular quotation naturally varies according to the problem. I myself am particularly fond of the story of the foolish old man."

Mao had used this story in his final speech at the Seventh Party Congress on June 11, 1945, to underline the will for tough endurance.

The so-called foolish old man, with his two sons, was trying to level two high mountains that stood before his house. When a so-called wise old man came by and ridiculed this enterprise he answered, unabashed, that after him his grandsons and his great-grandsons would continue with the task, and in this way the two mountains would finally be leveled. Mao then added, "God was moved by this, and he sent two angels, who carried away the mountains on their backs." [1]

At this point I said, "But Chairman Mao doesn't believe in God, so how can he tell a story like that?"

"Chairman Mao ended his story saying that we too have two mountains before our door: one is external—imperialism, and the other is internal—feudalism. But if we work hard enough we too

[1] Little Red Book, Chapter XXI.

will move the heart of God. But God in this case is the Chinese people, with whose help the two mountains will be leveled."

(The story is one of the most typical of Mao's parables for today's China, and has been included among the documents in Part IV.)

As we made the rounds during our visits, I would often ask when the workers or students did their Mao studies. I was usually told, in the morning before work and in the evening after work. At my hotel the waiters on my floor would gather in the television room at about six in the evening to do their Mao studies. One of them would lead (not always the same one), while all the rest sat around him, each with a Little Red Book open on his knees. I would hear them recite a quotation in chorus, and discussion and teaching would follow. The proceedings were often quite noisy and cheerful.

In the beautiful city of Hangchow I often saw groups of students who had come to visit the famous sites, sitting in groups on a lawn, their packs piled into a neat pyramid, their Little Red Books open in their hands, reading or reciting.

I shall never forget the scene I witnessed every morning in Shanghai. The Chinese live sensibly, and go to bed early. So they also get up early. At no later than 7 A.M. the loudspeakers begin to drone "The East Is Red." A moment later you hear the first rhythmic whistles and shouts from the street. I would look out of my window on the fifth floor of the Peace Hotel into the narrow street below and see the beginning of morning exercises. The employees of the Bank of China, which was across the street, would stream out through its door—from the director (so I was told) down to the last messenger boy. Two men with lists and pencils stood checking off those present. A man in uniform, presumably a member of the revolutionary committee, called out the orders, and once a day the entire company would march up and down the street at a fast trot. There would be a pause, during which everybody would pull out his Little Red Book and meditate on the quotation announced by the man in uniform through a power megaphone.

No sooner had the bank employees disappeared into their offices than another group would appear and do exactly the same thing; it would be about nine-thirty before the street quieted down.

There seem to be Chinese marching somewhere every minute. At any time of the day there are surely millions marching to something or other; it may be a military exercise, or it may be that they're marching into the countryside to help the peasants in the fields, or they may be simply marching for the sake of marching. Always there is a red flag. Often the first man in the column carries a picture of Mao. If the marchers are out for any length of time, each one has a padded sleeping bag, sheathed with plastic to ward off rain and snow, carefully rolled according to regulations and tied with cords that also serve as pack straps. Many will have a little red pad about the size of a postcard, inscribed with a Mao quotation, tied to their packs so that the person behind will have it directly in his line of vision.

The marching rhythm is set by a kind of whistle (usually in a strange syncopated rhythm: *one*-two, *one*-two-three). Sometimes encouraging shouts from the line of marchers are answered by Mao quotations shouted in rhythm; sometimes there is a song.

There are three songs that I must have heard a thousand times —in the street, over the loudspeaker on trains, on television (as background music, whatever may be going on), as intermission pieces in films and operas, and during school performances. Two of these are tied for first place.

One of them, "The East Is Red," has grown very popular during the last few years, mainly because of an enormous production by the same name that was performed by an army ensemble in 1964. It is set to the melody of a folksong from the north of Shensi Province (the locale of Mao's Yenan), and it is said to have been written by a peasant of the region during the civil war. I could get no more precise information; it has become a folksong, with author and origin already forgotten. I am dubious that anyone would have written the words to "The East Is Red" at a time when the guerrillas were being pressed by the Japanese and by Chiang Kai-shek's troops, who happened to be coming from the east. (The complete text of song, as well as the other that is most popular, is included among the documents.)

120

Two lines from the "Song of the Helmsman" are known to everyone:

For a voyage at sea you need a helmsman . . .
To make a revolution you need the ideas of Mao Tse-tung.

Both the melody and the words were composed by a not particularly distinguished composer named Wang Shuang-yin. The song became famous in 1967, when Lin Piao applied it to Mao, whereupon it was on everyone's lips. It is set to a catchy march tune, whereas "The East Is Red" has a more stately beat.

The "Internationale," the song of the Paris Commune of 1871, is often heard. Certainly I heard it as many times during my weeks in China as I did in the years from 1934 to 1936 when I lived in the Soviet Union, where it was supplanted by the Stalinist national anthem.

On many occasions you hear the call, *"Mao chuhsi wansui—* Long live Chairman Mao" (literally "Mao, the chairman, 10,000 years") repeated with a strongly accented beat. Spoken in chorus, it sounds like "Maochi wansui, Maochi wansui." While it is recited, the pace is speeded up, growing faster and faster. The Little Red Books are usually waved at the same time—at the end of a performance, for example, when the actors come forward once again to take their bows.

China watchers in the West and in Hong Kong believe they have seen a slight diminution in the importance of the Little Red Book since 1970; they point out that a little book by Lin Piao and a new red book by Mao (though its contents are not new) have appeared in the same format. I saw quantities of these in bookstores during my trip, and of course I bought some copies for myself and my Institute; but whereas quite literally all who can read and write (and surely some who are too old to learn) carry the Little Red Book on their persons at all times, I scarcely found anyone who had the work of Lin Piao at hand. Nor can I confirm that the old, already classic Red Book is being replaced by the new volume, whose title is *Five Articles by Chairman Mao.* This contains the "Three Constantly Read Articles," the "Report about False Views in the Party," and "Against Liberalism," written in

1929 and 1937. Nor has the Little Red Book been superseded by *Four Philosophical Articles*, containing "On Practice," the two articles on contradictions mentioned earlier, and a passage entitled "Where Do Correct Ideas Come From?"

Whenever people in China mention the Little Red Book, they still mean the book of quotations, the "Mao Bible" as it is often called outside China. . . . There are stacks of these in every hotel. In every classroom a copy lies on each child's desk, whatever the subject that is being studied. Whether you arrive at a factory, a brigade, or a school, whether or not anyone has known you were coming, it is immediately pulled out and waved in front of the chest with short, quick motions. It is read, meditated on, and memorized. As a theologian knows his New Testament, or as Shakespeareans know their *Hamlet*, so millions of people in China today know their Little Red Book. . . .

The effects—one is tempted to say, the miracles—ascribed to the Little Red Book are innumerable. Outside China people joke about them. Inside China those effects are taken for granted. They run all the way from the practical details of agriculture (see the document on tomatoes) to the most refined strata of knowledge.

For example, Chen Chung-wei, a forty-two-year-old doctor in Shanghai's Hospital #6, has become famous throughout the world for his success, in 1963, in grafting limbs severed by work accidents back onto the body. All the while, as he told me about his work, he held the Little Red Book in his hand—as did the assistant beside him—and many times he broke off his description to quote from it. (His patients of course, greeted me from their hospital beds by waving their Little Red Books.)

A professor of physics at the University of Kirin told in similar language of how he had improved his scientific qualifications by studying the works of Mao. His account (see "Redeemed by Mao," in Part IV) is the more extraordinary since it deals with an experience that is probably much like that of many other intellectuals since the beginning of the Cultural Revolution.

Even the world high-jump champion, Ni Chi-chin, whom I met at a banquet in the Great Hall of the People, insisted that he owed his 2.29-meter leap entirely to the Little Red Book.

It was quite obvious that everyone made an effort to give a "philosophical" base to whatever he did or tried to do, and to show at all times that he held the correct philosophical point of view. You find this in reports such as the one by a worker in a Tientsin textile factory, entitled "The Usefulness of My Study of Philosophy." [2] The author declares that Liu Shao-chi and his agents did not want the workers to achieve better production results through their study of philosophy; he became aware of this during the three months he spent at a Party school, before the Cultural Revolution, where he was "bombarded with seventeenth- and eighteenth-century philosophies."

He writes: "We had to read thick books by people like Hegel and Feuerbach and puzzle over every sort of technical language . . . I was in despair, lost my appetite, and slept badly. I had never in my life been the least bit nervous; now I was close to a nervous breakdown. I grew dizzy. The more I studied, the emptier I felt, and the more confused I became. I had less and less energy." Then he discovered the works of Chairman Mao, and everything was changed.

15: Maoism's Sacred Sites

During our ten-hour drive from Sian north to Yenan, the deeper we went into the mountains of Shensi, the more I felt like a pilgrim to a holy place. I felt this especially during the second half of the trip, after we reached the area held by Mao and the Red Army from 1935 to 1937, following the Long March, from which he had directed the war against the Japanese and the army of Chiang Kai-shek. I could also feel a rising excitement in my traveling companions. We consulted the Little Red Book and Mao's *Selected Works* more and more frequently to refresh our memories about the speeches and articles dating to that time.

Looking up as we descended into a narrow valley, all of a sudden I could see on a hill, at a distance of several miles, the nine-

[2] *China Reconstructs,* January, 1971, pp. 29–31.

story pagoda that had become a monument of that historic period. Like the Arc de Triomphe in Paris, this pagoda symbolizes the battles and the victories of an entire people. Soon the valley opened onto the level plain along the Yen River, and Mao's city lay before us.

Our quarters in Yenan were especially luxurious. I was assigned two comfortable rooms, rather than the usual modest pilgrim's quarters; in my bathroom there was hot water day and night, and each morning and evening a great gust of warm air swept through my rooms—for at an altitude of close to three thousand feet, the nights were bitterly cold. The food was excellent.

Before each visit I would be asked whether I would rather see something other than what had been scheduled, yet I have the impression that my visit scarcely diverged from a well-tried program. Over the years, countless Chinese have made the pilgrimage to Yenan, many of them on foot and from great distances. They are shown four places where Mao lived between 1935 and 1947; one place that had been Chou En-lai's home and one that was Lin Piao's; two exhibitions and three Party buildings (two of these were the meeting halls of the Central Committee, and one was a Party office building, including a lecture room.) The visitor who isn't afraid of climbing stairs (I wasn't) is taken to the previously mentioned pagoda, which has an excellent view over the city and valley of the Yen.

Mao first lived in the city. Then he moved to a "cave" house in the near-by Yang-chia Valley, into which the Yen River flows. He lived there for five years, from 1938 to 1943. The pleasantest of his houses was the Date Garden, in a village with the same name about three miles outside the city. From 1945 to the end of 1947, he lived in a house nearer the city, next to the headquarters of his army.

Mao always occupied three rooms. The one in the middle would be the living and working room; from it a door led to the bedroom. The room where he received visitors had a separate entrance. The furniture he used, which has been carefully preserved, is very simple. The double bed is made of boards covered by a thin mattress. There are deck chairs. Each of the dwellings contains a desk, on which copies of the works written there are exhibited. Each one of the four houses had its own guide, who greeted us at the door with a Little Red Book in his hand.

In the spring sunshine all these houses looked quite cheerful, but in bad weather and during the cold of winter they must seem rather forbidding. Throughout China, millions of people live in genuine caves dug into the mountain sides. The famous caves inhabited by Chairman Mao and other high Party officials have only their backs cut into the mountain; their façades project and are made of brick. They are built on a kind of terrace. The houses of Chou En-lai and Lin Piao are like Mao's, only a little smaller. These days, the houses that once belonged to Liu Shao-chi, Ho Lung, and other victims of the Cultural Revolution are, of course, not shown to visitors.

The Seventh Party Congress was held in 1945, in the main hall of the Party compound in the Yang-chia Valley. In the lecture room of the Party's office building behind it, Mao gave in May, 1942, the talks about literature and art that are of such importance even today. The conference room in the Date Garden had been the scene of the meetings of the Party's Central Committee. A few hundred yards away is the stone dais from which Mao gave on September 8, 1944, the lecture called "Serve the People," one of the "Three Constantly Read Articles."

The two exhibitions are made up of photographs and documents from the historic Yenan days. Mao himself appears in many of the pictures. Others show soldiers marching or at work. Also on exhibition are clothing, homemade weapons, primitive tools, and even spinning wheels used at that time. Among those of other party leaders, I saw about ten pictures of Lin Piao, three of Chou En-lai, one of Mao's wife (in which she looks young and cheerful), and one of Kang Sheng, who was then head of security. There are several pictures of Mao that I had not seen before: some of these show him relaxed and even smiling; in one, he is playing ping-pong. The second exhibition, now in the place that once housed the military academy, was opened in 1966 and is devoted mainly to Lin Piao. Twice I met peasants who still remembered the days here with Mao. One is now sixty-seven years old; he had been the headman at the Date Garden village. He told me that **Mao** said to him one day, "You are the headman here, so I must obey you." The old man laughed cheerfully as he told me this. The other peasant had had fields close to the army headquarters during those years, and had thus been near the fourth of Mao's houses. He is to be seen in a well-known picture that shows Mao talking with the peasants, and he reported that Mao often did this.

Of course, there are now stories connected with every single place in Yenan. As you go through a room in which Mao gave one of his talks on literature to a group of artists, you are told: "The peasants were glad about the visit of writers and artists and gave them a present of hard-boiled eggs. The artists ate the eggs and threw the shells on the ground. Then Chairman Mao said, 'If you want to find artists, just follow a trail of eggshells.' So the artists thought about this and from then on they had more consideration for the work of the peasants."

And as you visit Mao's house in the Date Garden you are told the following story: "Chairman Mao wrote his great works by the light of this oil lamp. And as he sat here, thinking about what he would write next, he would turn the wick all the way down to save oil." In passing, it should be said that the theme of studies conducted under the most frugal circumstances is an old favorite in Chinese literature.

Everything that happened in Yenan has become part of the legend. The pagoda that was built during the Sung era (A.D. 960–1280) has lost its old religious associations and is now a monument to the City of the Resistance. The lovely Taoist monastery on the mountain peak across the valley is now famous only because it contained a Communist radio station, and the graceful contours of Peacock Mountain are famous because Mao's first house was situated at its foot. Given the strong historical feelings of the Chinese, I would guess that the city of Yenan will remain a place of pilgrimage for a good while. After all, I had seen Chufu, the city of Confucius, in all its glory in 1957, two millenniums and a half after his death. The term "sacred sites," which I have used here several times, was applied by me not by the Chinese. An album of postcards which I bought in Yenan carries the heading "Yenan—Sacred Site of the Revolution."

Later, in Canton, I visited another sacred site. Here the left-wing city government of the year 1925 had taken over a sixteenth-century temple of Confucius and made it into a school for revolutionary peasant leaders. This was during the time of close cooperation between the Kuomintang and the Communist Party. Since Mao was one of the relatively few Communists who had a village background and knew how to talk to peasants, he was made director of this school. It lasted only six months, however, and was disbanded after the break between the Kuomintang and the Communist Party.

While he worked in this school Mao concerned himself most intensely with the peasants' problems; it was here that he wrote his first important work about classes in China. And it was here that he conceived the idea of giving the peasants a leading role in the scheme of things—as opposed to Marx, whose main concern was with the industrial proletariat. Thus it can be said without exaggeration that this is the place where Maoism actually had its beginning—a peasant-based (and later a guerrilla-based) Communism. Later Mao elaborated on the ideas conceived here. Today the grounds of this school, located in the middle of the city, have become a cult museum. In the front garden is a huge marble statue of a teaching Mao. The rooms are filled with mementos. There is a particular reverence for the room where Mao lived and worked, which contains a cot, a desk, and two carrying baskets he used to transport his few books and personal effects. On the wall a painting, added later, shows him meditating at his desk. One room is filled with photographs of Mao's relatives who lost their lives in conjunction with the revolution; one of his sons died in the Korean War. The long, low building next door, where the students once slept, have been made into exhibition rooms containing quotations and photographs. Among these is one of the young Chou En-lai, taken at the time when he was an instructor at the school.

Classes were held in one of the two main temples (the other

was used as a communal eating hall). It is filled with rows of simple tables and chairs, and along one long wall is a podium with a table on it. A picture on the wall shows the young Mao as a teacher on this same podium, surrounded by intently listening students.

There is already what may be called a Mao iconography, in which the sacred sites occupy an important place. Many pictures have been made of them, sometimes individually, sometimes to form a composite. The most popular of these would seem to be China's "Bethlehem"—Mao's birthplace at Shaoshan. In addition, there are about three dozen portraits of Mao, including both paintings and photographs. Finally, there are pictures of Mao in action, nearly all of them paintings—some done from photographs, others from the artist's imagination. I saw many copies of two of these. One shows Mao on the beach of Peitaiho, a seaside resort not far from Peking, walking toward the viewer with his coat flapping and the sea behind him. The other painting, by far the most popular of all at present, shows his triumphal march—there can hardly be another word for it—in the summer of 1968.

At that time it was reported that the painting had been done earlier, by a painters' collective, but had been suppressed by malicious people who were enemies of Mao. In this battle between good and evil the work of art had finally won out, it is said, because "the masses of workers, peasants, and soldiers encouraged and supported the painter, their pioneer on the art front."

The picture shows the young Mao in 1921, the year the Chinese Communist Party was founded, on his way to Anyuan, where he was to organize a strike. His left hand is clenched into a fist, and under his right arm he carries a worn umbrella. He is walking (to use the words of the *Peking Review* of July 23, 1968) "as is his habit, without fear of effort, working hard for the revolution." Prints of this painting were carried by plane into the provinces, and they were said to have been greeted everywhere with enormous enthusiasm.

Those pictures of Mao that have been painted from imagination are almost always in the same style—a kind of heroic naturalism that reminds you of Soviet painting during the time of Stalin. There is almost no relation between these paintings and the ancient art of China.

Never in the history of mankind, I believe, have so many portraits of one person been painted, drawn, printed, embroidered, hewn in rock, and poured in concrete and plaster within that person's own lifetime. In the old silk factory in Hangchow I saw machine upon machine, in serried ranks, embroidering portraits of Chairman Mao in silk, which would be sold in tens of thousands of shops and hung on millions of walls.

Portraits of Mao go with his people wherever they go, all through the day. I even saw one painted on the front of a locomotive! And how many times I saw that portrait attached to a pole, standing next to a fluttering red flag, overlooking the bowed figures of peasants at work! It was as though his image had been designed not only to strengthen the workers in their labors, but also to ward off drought and flood.

The Mao badges that almost everyone wears pinned to his clothes, just over his heart, seem to have the character of a talisman. And the Mao portraits in people's houses amount to a kind of icon corner, or so it seemed to me. Family pictures very clearly take second place.

In the streets there are Mao portraits everywhere. In old Russia when the faith was at its height, icons were never so ubiquitous. There is hardly a courtyard whose entrance wall does not carry the face of the leader, hardly an official building without its gigantic picture, often framed in electric bulbs. When your train pulls into a station, the first thing you see is not the name of the place but a portrait and quotation of the leader. Television news broadcasts begin and end with a portrait of Mao surrounded by beams of light to all sides, like a shining sun. While it is being shown you hear the "Song of the Helmsman," the song of Mao.

Mao is everywhere.

16: The Fatherland and the Yangtze Bridge

In Peking a wise foreigner said to me, "On your journeys, don't just try to see what you want to see, see what the Chinese themselves want to show you." One of these latter was the bridge over the Yangtze River near Nanking. For someone from the West, a bridge is a bridge. But since the Chinese wanted so much to show it to me, I devoted half a day to it. And I don't regret that I did.

First, a few technical details. At this place the Yangtze is 1,574 feet wide and 45 feet deep. The bridge rests on nine pillars set 160 feet apart; it is 60 feet high and 19.5 feet across; and it has two levels—the lower one carrying two railway tracks, the upper one for street traffic. The first train crossed the bridge on October 1, 1968, the anniversary of the founding of the state, and it was opened to general traffic on January 1, 1969. Within a twenty-four-hour period it is crossed on an average by 140 trains.

For an understanding of China today, it is essential to realize that Chinese technology is capable of building such a bridge. But there is another aspect that I find much more interesting: politically, the bridge is China's Aswan dam, but with one important difference: "We did it all by ourselves!" So its primary importance is not the technological achievement; rather, it is a symbol of national strength. I came upon very few picture postcards during my journeys in China, but when I did I always found a picture of the bridge taken from various angles.

The bridge has become the predominant structure in Nanking. On both sides the approaches are several miles long, and may be seen from a distance. You can see them from afar looking like elevated highways. On the city side, a People's Park has been laid out at the foot of the supporting towers, and the bridge may be reached from it either by elevator or from the street.

After more than two years, a kind of folk festival was still in progress. People were arriving here from everywhere, on buses or on foot, to admire the technological marvel. Even we approached it not as a secular monument but as a temple or a palace might

130

once have been approached. The supporting towers contain exhibition halls, to which many provinces and cities have sent wall hangings, pictures, or statues, among which the visitors move about as though they were in a cathedral.

An elevator took us up to the height of the railroad tracks, halting as a train went by with a thunderous roar. The elevator then took us up to a platform high on the tower, where there is a spectacular view of the river, the city, and the bridge itself. Finally we arrived at a lecture hall, also in the tower, which contains a model of the bridge, along with many drawings and photographs explaining its construction.

Listening carefully, I began to grasp what I was being told. If you look beyond the technical data, which is heaped on you in overwhelming detail, what you find is the depiction of a titanic struggle between the forces of righteousness and the powers of darkness, in which the Good, as manifested in the bridge, is triumphant. The story goes like this: There were once certain imperialist nations who had no interest in building such a bridge because they were not interested in the economic development of a semicolonial nation such as China, but wished to keep it undeveloped as a market for their products. Thus it was in their interest to sabotage such a bridge. American engineers came and declared that a bridge over the Yangtze could not be built just here because the bottom was unsuitable and the current too strong.

Then came the Russian revisionists, and their behavior was reprehensible. True, they did help build the first Yangtze bridge near Wuhan; but that, as I had been able to see for myself, was in no way as beautiful a structure as this one. Then, in the summer of 1960, the Russians tore up all the contracts, including those made in 1959 for the delivery of steel girders to be used in the Nanking bridge. At that time the Chinese had not been able to make the supports themselves, but the Russians simply left everything unfinished, gathered up their belongings, and departed. Never again would the Chinese depend on foreigners! But in that very same year they decided to build the Yangtze bridge by themselves—which brought dire prophetic warnings from Moscow about their foredoomed failure.

Then there had been a third enemy to overcome—that traitor and malefactor Liu Shao-chi. With his fawning attitude towards foreign countries and his mistrust of the Chinese people, he had insisted that the Chinese were incapable of completing such a structure themselves, and that one would have to turn to outside experts.

"But," said our guide at the bridge, "neither the hatred of the American imperialists nor the meanness of the Soviet revisionists, nor the machinations of that Chinese Khrushchev, Liu, could deter us! Ten thousand Chinese workers rallied under the banner of our great leader, Chairman Mao, "to guard our independence, keep the initiative in our own hands, and rely on our own effort." And so they went to work. They surpassed every quota and broke all records. The four mighty towers at the ends of the bridge were erected in twenty-eight days, instead of the projected nine months! And you must remember that we had to start from scratch, since the Russians had taken away with them every last blueprint."

After that we walked across the bridge. The cars in which we arrived had been sent ahead, and were waiting for us at the other end. Trains roared underneath us and loudspeakers droned overhead. But around us there was hardly a car to be seen—only pedestrians and people pulling handcarts. China is still in the era of the train and the bicycle, not of the car. But psychologically that is unimportant; what is important here is the meaning for the Chinese of having achieved this technological advance by their own strength.

I was aware of the same note of patriotism at the industrial exhibition hall in Shanghai. In 1957 it had been shown to me, since it had been built by the Russians, as an expression of Soviet-Chinese friendship. In the meantime the statue of Stalin has been replaced by a gigantic marble figure of Mao, and every Soviet emblem has been carefully removed. Even so, the wedding-cake style that is typical of Stalinist architecture remains unmistakable.

The exhibition hall is divided into many sections, showing everything from a huge truck with a loading capacity of thirty-two tons to children's toys and artifacts. The exhibits are handsome and graphic: the machines and tools don't just stand there, you see them at work. A girl holding a Little Red Book stands beside every big machine, ready to demonstrate how it works and how it embodies the thought of Mao Tse-tung.

Implicit in the words of each of these girls is the same underlying theme as at the bridge in Nanking: we have done this on our own!

At almost every machine the girl would say, "We once had to import this machine, and in order to raise the foreign currency we had to export our rice. Now we manufacture it ourselves, and thus bring honor to Chairman Mao and our socialist homeland."

A frequently quoted sentence from Mao goes this way: "We must have what others [in the West] have, *and* we must have what those others do not have." Again and again you are told, "Every single part of this machine was made in China. . . ."

You meet patriotism as a driving force everywhere in today's China. Among the emotions released by the Cultural Revolution, some are strongly nationalistic. They are manifested negatively in an aggressiveness towards the outside world, and positively in a vast effort to build up the nation. In Peking I visited a workshop where transistor parts were being made. In 1958, at the time of the Great Leap Forward, it had been a modest neighborhood establishment that produced rather primitive weighing scales. Spurred on by patriotic exhortations, its employees—mostly housewives who also had homes and families to look after—wanted to do more for their country.

"We studied the words of Chairman Mao," one of the women told me, "and found our inspiration in Chapter III of the Little Red Book, where it says that China is poor, but that poverty gives rise to the desire for change, the desire for action, and the desire for revolution."

"So," she went on, "we wondered how we could be useful to Chairman Mao and our Chinese fatherland. One day we read that our country needed transistors in order to be independent of foreigners. We chose four people from among us, one of them a woman, and sent them away to be trained. It was not easy for them; the woman worker didn't even know what was up and what was down in a technical drawing. But they learned to make the intellectual effort. All this time, our workshop went on producing scales; but then we began to change over, and in 1967 the first transistors left our shop. By then it was growing by leaps and bounds, and now we can produce even very complex things."

The shop was in what had once been a private house, now somewhat expanded. There were 350 workers in all. I could not judge the quality of what I saw them making, but I was able to see that they were doing complicated things with hundreds of little wires, tubes, and soldering points. I was introduced to the woman who in 1966 hadn't known what was up and what was down—she laughed with chagrin when this was mentioned—and saw her handle, along with three other worker-technicians, what appeared to me an excruciatingly complicated apparatus.

I was repeatedly told that all this had been made possible only through intensive study of the thought of Chairman Mao.

"When do you conduct these studies?" I asked.

"We have an eight-hour day. The first half hour of it is devoted to Mao studies. In addition, we meet three evenings a week for about an hour and a half."

I asked whether there were meetings outside the working day which everyone had to attend.

"No. We have a chorus and a ping-pong room, but of course those are optional. Also, some of the people who are interested occasionally go to the theater or the movies together. But that's up to them."

In Nanking I visited another small factory. We drove many miles into the southern part of the city; at first we went along wide, tree-lined streets, and then through tiny alleyways in the old part of town. Standing in front of a gate I saw a group of people carrying Little Red Books—the reception committee.

In 1958, responding to Mao's call for small-scale industrialization at the time of the Great Leap Forward, a group of young people had started a workshop here. With only the most primitive facilities, they had begun making glass test tubes and other laboratory equipment. The enterprise had soon grown to its present size, with about a dozen workers.

"Though we didn't realize it at the time, we were up against two formidable obstacles. One was that traitor and enemy of the people,

Liu Shao-chi, and his accomplices, who promoted only the university graduates, played on their personal ambitions and promised them an easy life instead of respecting the workers and allowing them to develop their skills. Our other enemies were the Soviet revisionists, who showed themselves for what they were when they called back all their advisers in 1960. This strengthened the determination of the Chinese people not to depend on others any longer. What really angered us was that the Moscow revisionists broke all their contracts, and refused to deliver even the materials they had promised. Among other things, these included mercury rectifier tubes.

"The young people on our staff were determined to come to the aid of Chairman Mao and our Chinese fatherland; so we decided to try producing the tubes ourselves. We managed to obtain some from the U.S.S.R., but it was difficult to copy them since we had no experts in this field. We showed them to one laboratory after another, but they couldn't find out what kind of gas had been used to fill the tubes; and of course the Russians gave us no help at all.

Naturally there were people among us who thought we should continue to produce the old test tubes, and who didn't want us to experiment with new things. But the majority kept on trying, and finally we found the right gas. That was in 1963.

A year later, the Czechoslovakian revisionists also broke their contracts. This meant we were without several other important instruments, which Prague up until then had supplied to our Chinese boiler industry. We were outraged, and more determined than ever to make up for this loss. There was one part, for instance, in which a fine metal thread—a third of the thickness of a hair—had to be inserted through a long, thin spiral tube. The Czechs wouldn't tell us how they did it. For weeks we racked our brains; and of course we studied the Little Red Book. There we found the wise saying of Mao that the old should be made to serve the new—and one day one of us suddenly remembered an old story. The story tells of a king who didn't know how to hang a very tiny, intricate, much-loved ornament on the wall because it had nothing that could be attached. Nobody could think what to do until an old man came up with the idea of tying a thread to the leg of an ant and letting the ant crawl through the narrow opening. The ant went on and on,

135

and every time it got tired the old man would blow smoke into the opening, which made the ant scramble on again. Finally it emerged —along with the thread—on the other side of the ornament. We immediately tried this solution, also using an ant, but the glass tube was too slippery for the ant to make any progress. All the same, we now had an important clue to the way the thing could be done. We had only to find something that could be made to move through the tube like an ant, pulling the thread along with it. And we found it!"

Proudly, they showed me their secret—which, unfortunately, I have promised not to give away. It's astoundingly simple. They were obviously gleeful at having done it—and at being able to tell the story. It was like putting together a jigsaw puzzle—all for the fatherland.

On my tour through the factory, I saw extremely crowded work-shops where the workers, most of them women, were making tiny precision instruments. The machines they used were very simple, and about 80 percent of them were homemade. I was told that except for one university graduate who had just joined them, none of the workers had had more than nine years of schooling. They attributed their success to the constant application of Mao's teach-ings, and to their own inventiveness.

"For one product we once conducted a thousand different experi-ments; when we finally succeeded, we called it 'Product 1001.' To-day we make about a hundred different products, which the state once had to buy from the revisionists. The revisionists had us in a stranglehold; they wanted to keep us dependent on them. Our little factory is proud to have contributed to our liberation from this shameful dependence. Many of our customers tell us that our products are better than the ones we used to buy abroad."

Here, too—and I saw the same thing over and over again in other places—was the insistence on the patriotic nature of each individual achievement.

17: Mao's Wife, Too, Is Everywhere

The theater is in the southern part of the city, not far from the old Temple of Heaven, and is known as the Tientsiao, or Bridge of Heaven, for the quarter in which it is found. The building is large and brightly lit, but quite plain on the outside. By the time we arrived, a large crowd had already gathered. Uniformed guards kept the road open for the few who were arriving by car. Repeatedly, I found I was reminded of Russia—first of all by the open square in front of the theater, then as we pushed our way through the crowds around the entrance to the foyer, where the first thing you see is a gigantic portrait of the Leader, in white on red. It was not present-day Moscow that came to my mind, but rather those first performances I had attended in the Soviet Union just after the revolution, between 1929 and 1931. Now as then, here in the Peking of 1971, I was surrounded by the proletariat, the masses. The place smelled of cheap tobacco, and as in Moscow, the people looked as though they had come straight from the factory or the road crew. The only difference here was that most people wore the usual dark, quilted jackets and coats. To cover their heads they wore caps of every imaginable kind, often made of fur, often—as I had also observed in Russia during that earlier time—with the earflaps dangling. Here, too, men and women were scarcely distinguishable; the girls showed not the slightest attempt at elegance and, of course, not a trace of makeup. All around me were the people of a nation in the early stages of industrialization (as had been true of the Soviet Union in those days now long gone), and among them many peasant faces.

Our seats were in the upper tier, giving us a fine view of the whole theater. Below us, a surging mass of people on rows of simple folding chairs, with here and there a flash of color: soldiers in green, sailors in blue-gray. No insignia, naturally no salutes to officers—these were really the Masses, the people Mao talks about. I found only one thing missing: the distinctive smell of Russian leather boots. In Russia, on the other hand, there had been none of the gauze face masks so many Chinese wear nowadays—a legacy

137

from the Japanese soldiers, who wore them during the occupation to ward off infection. Many of the Chinese wear masks covering their faces so completely that there is only a narrow slit to see through.

At exactly eight o'clock the lights went out. A woman in army uniform stepped smartly into the spotlight before the curtain and recited a quotation from Mao. She ended by calling out, "Long live Chairman Mao!" three times, while the whole audience joined in. Then the curtain went up.

I was in a high state of expectancy, since the ballet we were about to see was *The Red Detachment of Women*, one of eight plays that are the only ones performed on the Chinese stage today, and which were all—as every theatergoer knows—produced under the direction of Mao's wife, Chiang Ching.

Once again I found myself back in the early days of the Soviet Union, of a totally political theater glorifying deeds of legendary heroism in a civil war. This ballet is set in south China, or more precisely on the large island of Hainan, at some time in the thirties. A short prologue shows a dim underground prison, where a young girl, Ching-hua, has been imprisoned by her master, the landowner, for some misdeed; but she manages to escape.

The first act shows a forest at night. The landowner's bodyguards, carrying large paper lanterns, are looking for the runaway girl. They find her. The landowner (wearing a European-style straw hat) arrives on the scene and has the girl whipped. She is left for dead. Two Red guerrillas find her and bring her back to life. (How many Russian guerrillas had I seen playing almost identical roles!) They then tell her where their camp is hidden.

In contrast to the gloomy darkness of the prologue and the first act, the second act is bathed in dazzling light. We are in the partisan camp. A newly formed Women's Detachment is just being trained. Now comes a set piece: a dance in toe shoes, with leveled rifles. Ching-hua arrives, and expresses in a solo dance what she has suffered as a servant in the landowner's house. The other women ceremoniously present her with a gun and accept her as a member of the Women's Detachment. They then decide to liberate the peasants and servant girls who are enslaved by the tyrant.

The setting of the third act shows the house of the landowner.

138

Once again the stage is in semidarkness. It is the tyrant's birthday, and in the garden before his house a party is in progress. Mountains of gifts are brought in; visitors arrive; dancing girls are driven in, with whips at their backs, to perform for the guests. Then everyone disappears inside the house, where festivities continue. The guerrillas arrive on the scene. They stab the guards and hide in the bushes. The guests leave without noticing anything amiss; the landowner stays behind. Overcome by hatred, Ching-hua shoots him, but manages only to wound his arm. He escapes. The plan to do away with the menace has failed.

Ching-hua is a failure as a guerrilla. But in the fourth act, which once again is set in the guerrilla camp (and once again the stage is flooded with sunshine), with the guidance of the Detachment Commissar, she comes to grips with her failure. At that precise moment, a messenger rushes in: the landowner has called out the troops, and they are on their way.

The guerrillas retreat into the mountains. In the fifth act, there is a bitter fight. The Commissar orders his troops to retreat and save themselves; he stays, with just two comrades. In a heroic battle to halt the enemy in a mountain pass, both his companions die and he himself is wounded and captured.

In the sixth act, we are once again at the landowner's house. He is trying to persuade the Commissar to surrender by threatening him with a horrible death. The Commissar remains steadfast; he is then burned at the stake, standing proudly erect among the flames while a mixed chorus in the orchestra sings the "Internationale."

Meanwhile, however, the guerrillas have won their battle with the troops. They storm the landowner's house and kill his lackeys; the tyrant himself is shot by Ching-hua. Then they suddenly come upon the Commissar's cap; they see the smoking embers and realize what has happened. The members of the Women's Detachment kneel before the place of sacrifice, and all the other guerrillas follow their example. Again the chorus sings the "Internationale," and one after another the groups of dancers retreat downstage. The People now swarm onto the stage, closing ranks to form a massive phalanx, underneath a large red banner they all march to the front of the stage. The curtain goes down to thunderous applause.

The curtain goes up again, and now the performers too join in the applause. Against the backdrop appears the head of Mao, wearing a military cap, encircled by a bright red halo. Everybody calls out three times, "Long live Mao Tse-tung!" and then the final curtain falls.

What reminded me so strongly of Russia in the 1920s was not only the proletarian audience; it was the absolute black-and-white of the plot, the pathos of the gestures, and the unabashed glorification of violence. In Moscow at the time, the avant-garde theater of Meyernold and Alexander Tairov was already in decline, and heroic naturalism was the order of the day. The new theory was that art should have no subtleties; rather it should exert a strong persuasive influence on people's thinking. The same was true here.

If you happen to like naturalistic theater sets, you could find none prettier than these. The forest in the first act was really a forest, and the storm that drove away the girl's tormentors was a tempest to end all tempests. The sets for the partisan camp—sunlit mountains, trees and streams under a clear blue sky dotted with a few snowy clouds—were so enchanting that the audience burst into applause each time the curtain parted to reveal them. The setting for the fifth act showed a grandiose mountain landscape at dusk, with an absolutely spectacular thunderstorm at the end of the battle as our wonded hero collapses, with bolts of lightning striking all around him.

Traditional Chinese theater had nothing at all in the way of naturalistic sets, ballet, or Western musical instruments. That is all new. Now, the first thing you see after the curtain goes up is a toe dance by the heroine. In the camp scenes, however, the influence of traditional Chinese theater still lingers. Sword fights—or more precisely, sword dances—were a particularly popular element in classical Chinese drama, and it appears that Chinese audiences are delighted by them even now. The battles in *The Red Detachment of Women* are all fought—notwithstanding the partisan rifles!—with swords and halberds, which were standard equipment on the traditional stage. There is also a particular kind of kick in the scenes of hand-to-hand fighting that I seem to remember from old times.

The orchestra, which formerly sat on the stage, is now placed in a pit. So far as I could tell, there was not a single traditional Chinese instrument in it, except for a certain drum, used traditionally to represent the sounds of battle or in scenes of strong emotion. The music itself has lost much of the strangeness that Chinese music has traditionally had to a Western ear. Listening with my eyes closed, I could have sworn that I was hearing something from a film of the 1930s, or from the *Grand Canyon Suite*. But the Chinese seemed to like it very much. The theme songs, especially those sung by the guerrillas, are obviously very popular; during the performance I heard several people around me singing along with the chorus, and later, as we left the theater and went out in the street, people were still humming.

Another well-known play is *Taking Tiger Mountain by Strategy* —which, as you might guess, has a political theme.

A detachment of the People's Liberation Army receives orders to destroy one of the last strongholds of Chiang Kai-shek's troops— simply called "bandits" throughout the opera. This stronghold lies in the mountainous northwest region of China; the "bandits" are led by a much-decorated General known as The Vulture. His headquarters, a gloomy cave on Tiger Mountain, are next to impregnable; they can be reached only by a single path, which is heavily guarded. The Vulture's soldiers have treated the mountain people with such cruelty (they are shown killing women and children and leading men away in chains) that the Red Army can count on their support; but the mission can succeed only if they can somehow smuggle one of their own people into the fortress.

Young Yang Tse-yung is chosen for this dangerous mission. Disguised and carrying the papers of a Kuomintang prisoner, he gets inside the enemy camp. He lets his comrades know when they should attack: during a feast that will turn into an all-night drinking spree for the bandits. At one point the Vulture becomes suspicious, but just as he has unmasked Yang as a Red spy, the People's Liberation Army overruns the camp and destroys the enemy.

The play is called a Peking opera, because it is sung, as were the classical Peking operas. But it also contains some elements of ballet and acrobatics, which are generally more pleasing for the foreigner than the strange-sounding Chinese arias.

Some scenes stay in my mind with particular vividness. There is the lonely ride our hero takes through the snowy woods to the stronghold of the Vulture. Yang wears a thick fur hat, a tigerskin jacket, black trousers, light brown high boots, and a heavy, dark leather coat trimmed with white lambskin that catches the light dramatically each time he moves. He rides, but there is no horse: in traditional Peking opera style, the ride is simply suggested by his carrying a whip. So Yang "gallops" through the woods, over obstacles, across ravines, till suddenly the horse rears wildly, and we hear the angry roar of a tiger. The hero jumps off the horse and kills the (invisible) tiger with two shots from his pistol. Alerted by the shots, the Vulture's soldiers appear on the scene; they admire Yang's heroic feat, and simply assume that he is one of their own.

The greatest piece of acrobatic pantomime came during the ninth scene, when the soldiers of the Red Army race through a snow storm on "skis" (which again are no more than suggested to the imagination of the audience), on their way to Tiger Mountain. Over their uniforms they wear wide, white capes that fly out behind them as they rush on; their fur caps, adorned with the red star, are swathed in white scarves to complete the camouflage. They race over the snow, with short rapid steps or long, high leaps; they swarm from the rocks to the left of the stage, taking off like ski-jumpers, sailing headlong through the air in incredible elevations, disappearing in a green-and-white cascade of moving bodies, only to reappear immediately, three rows deep, facing the audience with their capes spread like wings, but with each of the rows in a different phase of movement: the first crouching low, the second just above and behind them with arms and legs spread wide, the third standing upright, the entire group advances together, three rows deep, towards the front of the stage.

A scene that, though not quite so impressive in color and pattern, had great dramatic power, was the battle at the end, in the cave of the Vulture. Duels and battles alternated with the speed of light, with the warriors leaping through the air in every direction, jumping all the way up to where the Vulture himself stood watching the battle. Swords, halberds, daggers, pistols, even bayonets went sailing through the air with a flash and were caught again. The movements were almost too quick for the eye to follow—until the end, when the victors froze into their motionless final tableau. When the curtain went up again, they were all waving their Little Red Books, and the audience joined in a rousing chorus of

> Sailing the seas depends on the helmsman;
> Making revolution depends on Mao Tse-tung's thought. . . .

I did not have many opportunities to listen to music. But one evening in Shanghai I did attend a concert. On the way to the concert hall I noticed what could have been easily a thousand bicycles, parked neatly and close together on both sides of the street. In the building itself we found a tremendous crowd, resembling the turnout for a major football game in the West. I was told that the theater held ten thousand people, and every seat was filled. Here we were among what could truly be called the masses (the tickets cost only between 15 and 40 fen), and it is quite likely that never in history has a piano concert drawn such audiences as seem to be the rule in China today—not even in Europe, the cradle of piano music, and not even, I think, in the U.S.S.R.

The performing arts in China are entirely confined to a few new operas, ballets, and concertos. Wherever I attended an amateur performance (even in the nursery schools!), the scenes either were taken from the prescribed new works, or were paraphrases that adhered closely in style and subject matter, including the abruptly frozen tableau at the end.

A kind of political variety show, given by the Performing Arts Ensemble of Kwantung, was playing in an open-air theater which seats 3,000 people. The performance was completely sold out, and was already under way when a park official showed us to special seats that had been hastily set up in the center aisle.

We had come in during what might be called a political ballet. The scene was a textile factory.

A male chorus entered and began singing a paean to a people's commune of their province, which had learned the lessons of Tachai and was now producing bumper crops.

The next scene was a ballet. Two girls, Red Guards of about fifteen or sixteen, are taught by army soldiers how to fight with halberds. The next scene takes place by the sea. A horrid reptile crawls out of the water: it is a frogman—a Taiwan spy, naturally. He tries to disappear in the crowd, but the girls find him out. He thinks he has an absolutely foolproof way of bribing them; he offers them his (American) wristwatch. Contemptuously, they throw it on the ground. The two girls attack the pistol-packing fiend all by themselves; soon a group of soldiers come to their aid, and the villain is defeated and taken prisoner.

We stayed to hear an even larger male chorus sing a rousing version of "We Shall Liberate Taiwan!," and then we left. . . .

Needless to say, the "new" music dominates all radio broadcasts. I didn't keep a tally, but it seemed to me that every Chinese radio station broadcasts at least one a day of the eight "exemplary plays." Throughout the entire trip, whenever I asked the name of the music coming from the loudspeaker or the car radio, I was invariably told it was one the operas. It never failed. As I walked across the mile-long Yangtze Bridge near Nanking, loudspeakers on the bridge were tuned to a radio station that was just then playing the concert version of *Huang Ho*—and since the piece is by no means lacking in fortissimi, the music of the "Yellow River" roared out over the wide expanses of its great rival the Yangtze. Strangely enough, no one seems to become bored with this unvaried diet. On the train I was the only person who ever turned off the radio; everywhere else, the loudspeakers were going full blast. On trips by car, I had to ask the driver to turn the radio down so that I could hear my companions; as soon as one opera was finished, the driver would turn his dial until he had found a station that was playing the next one.

But the new style has an influence that goes far beyond the jam-packed theaters, the concert halls, open-air auditoriums, and radio stations. In ancient Greece all art forms were nourished by the world of Homer's epics, and in the Middle Ages by the world of the scriptures. In China, the new theater stamps its indelible mark on all

144

of China's cultural life; at every turn, the visitor meets with it in some new guise.

Most of the postage stamps now in use (I saw fourteen different designs), as well as nearly every picture postcard I saw, and every kind of calendar, show scenes from these operas and ballets. They are on the covers of magazines. They are framed and hung in hotels, in railroad cars, in buses, in shops, in private homes. They are the standard gift for all occasions, either as prints or in embroidered wall hangings, sculptured in wood and even sometimes in jade. They are hung as giant posters along the streets. At the Industrial Fair in Shanghai I was shown a steel saw that turned out not machine parts but neat little silhouettes of the heroine from one of the operas.

In the last few years I have often come across essays and magazine articles about the new Chinese theater. I had read that the 1,300 Peking operas that were still listed in a 1963 catalogue had been replaced by only eight new works. But until I witnessed it at first hand, I had had no idea what such a monopoly meant.

The classic operas with historical and legendary heroes, which have always been a favorite form of entertainment for every Chinese down to the poorest rickshaw coolie, have now been completely set aside, and with them the rich history they represented. Whatever one's artistic judgment of the new dramas may be, they are certainly brilliant pieces of propaganda theater. They are also, in their combination of instrumental and vocal music, dance, pantomime, and acrobatics, a new and comprehensive type of performing art.

Although the impact of the new Peking opera is tremendous, it is not easy to get information about the role of Chiang Ching, Mao's wife. People would look at me almost blankly when I mentioned her name; but they were immediately full of interest when I told them that a book about her had been published in Hong Kong, or that a German journalist is writing her biography.

Theatergoers mostly knew that Chiang Ching had something or other to do with the performance, but when I asked for anything more precise they gave me only vague answers—probably not because they were reluctant to talk, but simply because they didn't know much about her. Eventually some Chinese acquaintances brought me material which explained the extent of Chiang Ching's influence on the new theater.

There is evidence that Chiang Ching—a former actress who met Mao Tse-tung in Yenan in 1940—always favored a stronger political coloring of theater and films, and that after the establishment of the Chinese People's Republic she had taken some steps in that direction. As early as in 1954, when she was a member of a film committee in the Ministry of Culture, she denounced a movie about the Boxer Rebellion, but without immediate success.[1]

After 1963, with her husband's political comeback, she began really promoting her ideas. Essentially these were the ideas that were to become all-important in the years that followed: those of the Cultural Revolution.

For many years Chiang Ching met violent opposition from the cultural establishment. The first sign of a breakthrough came in July, 1964, at the Opera Festival in Peking. For the first time, several contemporary revolutionary works, among them *Tiger Mountain,* received wide publicity. Mao supported her efforts by attending several performances and offering some well-publicized comments. The theater, he said, concerned itself only with the past, or with a number of foreign classics; the Ministry of Culture might as well be renamed "the Ministry of Emperors, Kings, Generals, Chancellors, Scholars, and lovely ladies," or "the Department of Dead Foreigners." [2]

In connection with the festival, a seminar was held for "Workers in the Theater." Chiang Ching made a speech at this seminar. Opposition to her ideas was still so strong at that time that her speech was not published until three years later: today it is one of the important documents of the developments that led to the Cultural Revolution.[3] Chiang Ching drew a sad picture of the situation as it existed in 1964. "Our Operas," she said, "are full

[1] *Peking Review,* 1967, #15, p. 5ff.
[2] Quoted in Lin Piao's speech at the National Congress in 1969.
[3] See *Peking Review,* 1967, #21.

of emperors, princes, and such. . . . Our repertory theater, too, is completely dominated by classical and foreign themes." Workers, peasants, and soldiers ought to supply the themes and subject matter for the theater. New works should be written, old ones drastically revised; villains ought to be more villainous, heroes more heroic. . . .

I wanted to find out exactly what Chiang Ching had done on a practical basis, to make sure that her instructions were carried out —as indeed they were.

People I asked about this couldn't give me much of an answer. One of them finally turned up a brochure entitled *On the Revolution of the Peking Opera,* published in 1968; it gives some current information about people connected with the theater. We are told that in 1961 Chiang Ching started a theatrical survey. Among some two hundred plays on contemporary revolutionary subjects she found a few she considered useful. But in her opinion even these were too tame and colorless; she wanted certain strong, well-calculated effects. She "reorganized the troupe, changed the cast, and made her voice heard on the committee that was rewriting the libretto." One play was rewritten. She told a Shanghai ensemble to go to a village in Kiangsu province and live there among the peasants for a while, to hear at first hand the details of the civil war battle with which their opera was concerned.

Her contribution to *The Red Lantern* was described as follows:

The counter-revolutionary revisionists wanted to put on a play called *The Dragon Flirting with the Phoenix,* which dealt with the depraved lusts of a feudal lord. . . . Comrade Chiang Ching came to our theater in 1963, and told us we should concentrate on creating literary and artistic works that supported the revolution. She personally took charge of our efforts to create *The Red Lantern,* and struggled courageously to liberate the stage from the clutches of the bourgeoisie. . . . Thanks to her constant instruction and advice, we slowly began to understand the true meaning of our main character, the proletarian hero Li Yu-ho. . . . She worked tirelessly to help us portray the truly heroic character of Li Yu-ho. . . . She argued vigorously with the counter-revolutionary revisionists about the scene entitled "Battle in the Face of Death," the climax of the opera. . . . We cut out the details of the torture of Li Yu-ho and his mother, because we refused to cater to naturalism and sensationalism. . . . At long last she overcame all obstacles and setbacks; she made the figure of Li Yu-ho, a proletarian of truly heroic stature, tower over the stage of our socialist fatherland and enter into the hearts of millions. . . . Many changes in the music, the text, and the choreography were suggested by Comrade Chiang Ching herself. . . . We will always remember those intensive, creative rehearsals of *The Red Lantern;* our friendly and charming Comrade Chiang Ching was so often among us, always listening patiently to our ideas and giving us sensible advice. . . . The energy she gave to *The Red Lantern* is incalculable!

She received new public recognition for her work in 1966, when at the invitation of Defense Minister Lin Piao she acted as chairman of the Forum on the Work in Literature and Art in the Armed Forces.

When the mass demonstrations of the Cultural Revolution began, the political breakthrough in the arts was no longer in doubt. Chiang Ching had meanwhile become one of the five members of the group in charge of the Cultural Revolution. A mass meeting held in the Great Hall of the People on November 28, 1966, was dedicated entirely to literature and the arts. At this meeting, which Chou En-lai also attended, her appointment as Adviser to the Armed Forces for Cultural Affairs was announced; her speech was received with "thunderous applause." [4]

On such festive occasions of course, all tributes and glory go finally to her companion in life and in battle, Chairman Mao. Yet there seems to be no doubt that Chiang Ching played a leading role in the development of political theater, or that she is mainly responsible for the disappearance of the traditional theatrical forms.

We also know something about her influence on China's musical life. It was she who introduced the piano to the Chinese concert hall, where it has had its phenomenal success. The Philharmonic Orchestra of Peking, which had been "in the hands of pro-capitalist elements" and was "dangerously like orchestras in the U.S. and the Soviet Union," was completely changed after a visit from Chiang Ching in 1964, during which she apparently "lighted the flame of the revolution in the field of symphonic music."

The revisionists apparently did succeed in delaying for two and a half years Chiang Ching's efforts to launch the grand piano as the instrument of revolutionary art in China. It wasn't until May,

[4] *China Reconstructs,* March, 1967.

1967, after the Cultural Revolution began, that the piano was used openly. And even then "the counter-revolutionaries did not take their defeat lying down." They said, "Anyone who plays the piano is a traitor," and demanded that "all pianos be smashed." They wanted, "to shake the comrades' determination to revolutionize piano playing. The musicians, however, stood firm—and "with the support of Comrade Chiang Ching" this "new form of proletarian art" began its triumphant conquest of China.[5]

I asked my acquaintances why the piano had been introduced in China. They weren't at all sure; perhaps the piano represented an effort to replace traditional Chinese musical instruments as well as traditional Chinese theatrical forms, since the old instruments might, by their very sound, recall something of an old and now discarded world.

With the return to order after the Cultural Revolution, Chiang Ching's public appearances have become rare. One recent occasion was the Party Congress of 1969, where she was sixth in the vote count (this includes Mao himself).

When we consider the unbelievably wide impact of the new theater—the thousands of stage productions and movies; the hundreds of thousands of amateur performances in schools, in factories, and in villages; when we consider that the "eight exemplary works" are now the only ones in existence, and that the next generation will know no other heritage—when we consider all this, it would seem that never before in history has a single woman had so incalculable an influence on the cultural lives of hundreds of millions of people.

If Mao has shaped the spirit of the new China, then surely Chiang Ching has shaped its style—and her influence will be felt for a long time to come.

[5] *Peking Review,* 1967, #15, p. 5ff.

18: The Yellow Emperor

I had gathered that on our drive from Sian to Yenan I might have a chance to see two places of special interest. The first one, the cave in which the "King of Medicine" had lived, was about three hours from Sian. According to the guide, we would be able to see it from the road. In China this scholar—whose main work dates from the year 652, and includes more than five thousand prescriptions and formulae—is considered one of the greatest physicians of all time. Thus I was hoping to pay him my respects, at least from a distance. But this was not to be; the cave is now hidden by the dust and smoke of a cement factory. Since my companion wanted to reach our destination before dark, I did not insist on a detour. So I put my hopes on the second landmark.

For many travelers along this route, the small provincial town of Huangling, or "Yellow Grave," is a desirable place to spend the night. In the local hotel, which is mainly intended for "foreign visitors," we were the only guests. . . .

During dinner, I kept asking about my second sightseeing project. At first I was told that it would be too far out of our way; but when I persisted, it was decided that the next morning we would get up at six instead of seven. After breakfast we were on our way to the Grave of Huang-ti, the Yellow Emperor. According to legend, Huang-ti was the first of the five original emperors, who introduced the basic elements of civilization to the Chinese people in about 3000 B.C.: the wheel, the forging of metal, and the making of pottery.

It was because I wanted to trace the course of five thousand years of Chinese history in a day—from the Yellow to the Red Emperor of China—that I had been so adamant about the excursion.

No two authorities seem to agree on the exact location of the grave of the Yellow Emperor—whether it is in this temple or in a large burial mound farther up the mountain. At my request we continued along the very steep and winding road that leads through the woods to the mountain top. In front of an intricately stratified burial mound, we found a pavilion with a tall stone tablet bearing the year 1957. Carved on it, in the handwriting of Kuo Mo-jo, were the words, "The Grave of Huang-ti."

My hurry was so great that I stumbled and fell at the very threshold. My companions, as true Chinese, didn't miss an opportunity for a joke. Since, they said, I seemed so determined to pay my respects to the Yellow Emperor, he had allowed me to make a kowtow before his grave! We then decided that if his spirit could still play such pranks here after thousands of years, this spot must indeed be Huang-ti's final resting place.

My companions' reluctance to make this trip had not been simply because they disliked getting up at six in the morning. Their feeling was, Why bother with these old stories when it is clear that the true achievements of civilization have nothing to do with some ancient emperor, if indeed he ever existed at all. Since civilization stems from the masses, according to their point of view, history ought to begin with Mao Tse-tung.

I met with this scornful—and oddly insecure—attitude towards the past over and over again. The only two kinds of places I was not allowed to visit, despite repeated requests, were the universities and most museums. Of the latter I was allowed to see only one, the Museum of History at Sian. It is housed in a former Confucian temple, and was apparently already used as a museum by the year 1090, when many ancient stone tablets, known as the Grove of Steles, were installed here. The chief attraction is a collection of over a hundred black stone tablets, more than six feet tall, covered on either side with the 560,000 characters of the twelve classic scriptures. They date from the time of the Tang dynasty, which ruled China from A.D. 618 to 906.

One stone in the museum at Sian tells the story of the monk Hsuan-tsang, who in the seventh century went on a twelve-year journey to India and brought back some important new Buddhist texts. This treasure, well known in the West, is a bilingual stele telling of the arrival in China of the Nestorian (i.e., Christian) missionary Olopan, and of the building of the first Christian chapel in the year 636. When the Jesuits started a new Christian mission in China in the seventeenth century, they had this ancient stone to point to as a precedent.

Since I am not a student of ancient scriptures, however, my interest was captured chiefly by the exhibits of early Chinese sculpture—horses, leopards, a rhinoceros, tigers, and more horses. Most exquisite of all, and famous throughout the world, are the horses from the tomb of the Tang Emperor Tai-tsung. They are almost life size, and very lovely; some of them are portrayed at a full gallop.

Beautiful as it all was, I was still interested primarily in the museum's more contemporary significance. I was shown around by two museum employees, one an elderly, scholarly-looking man who said very little, the other a clear-eyed, energetic woman of about thirty. It was she who constantly related everything we looked at to contemporary politics. As we were stood before the horses of Tai-tsung, for instance, she began a bitter denunciation of the American imperialists. There had once been six horses, she said, and the Americans had tried to steal them all. To make transportation easier, they had sawed the reliefs into several pieces, as could still be seen. Luckily though, the thieves had been caught in the act by "the masses," they had still managed to steal two of them, which were now in the infamous possession of the United States. I have traced the two missing horses to the University Museum at Philadelphia. According to the curator, the provincial government of Shensi, through a certain C. T. Loo, sold them to an American, Eldridge Johnson, to obtain money for the building of schools, and in 1920 Johnson had presented them to the University of Pennsylvania.

As we stood before the stele of the monk Hsuan-tsang she talked about religion, which as "opium for the people" had been needed by the rulers for the oppression of the masses. Showing us another stone, on which there was a portrait of Confucius, she spoke of Confucius' "reactionary character."

But whatever we might think of him now, I said, didn't she agree that at least for his own time—two and a half millenniums before—Confucius had been rather progressive?

This she fervently denied. Confucius, she said, had been an advocate of slavery, and therefore a pawn of the ruling classes. How could it be, then, I persisted, that Confucius had an influence even in our own century, when the age of slavery was long forgotten and had been succeeded by two thousand years of feudalism and even early forms of capitalism?

She hesitated for a moment. Then she said, "Because Confucius was in favor of private property, and private property still needs an advocate, even after slavery has been abolished."

"All right," I replied. "But if Confucianism only served to justify private property, and Buddhism only to keep the people ignorant, why do you have this beautiful museum with its thousands of inscriptions, which are about either Confucianism or Buddhism?"

Now she launched into a long lecture, which can be summed up as follows:

"These museum pieces are kept and displayed first of all as 'negative examples.' [She said this several times, always using the same phrase.] In the second place, the painstaking work on these stones was done by the common people—by the masses—and now we display them to show how great their skill and precision were. In the third place, they serve to strengthen the patriotism of the Chinese people, and to give them pride in the great heritage of their country." This third reason was given only after considerable hesitation. When I finally asked where or when Mao had ever indicated his own attitude towards the history of China, the reply was vague.

There is still another ancient monument, which in its way fits the Red Emperor's teachings better than either the Grove of Steles or the grave of the Yellow Emperor. It lies outside the gates of Sian, among newly built factories and housing developments; there, covered by several huge pavilions, is the excavation site of a 5000-year-old settlement dating to the Stone Age.

Its discovery was an accident. Workmen came upon the settlement in 1953, while they were digging foundations for a factory. The factory was built elsewhere, and during the next few years about a fifth of the settlement was carefully excavated. Since 1958 the museum has been open to the public. Wooden platforms have been set up all around the old foundations of the village, which once stood on the banks of a small stream. About forty of the ancient buildings are now clearly visible.

The archaeological finds are exhibited in a neighboring pavilion:

stone axes, fishhooks made of bone, and some stone vessels. Colorful drawings and scale models help visitors to imagine what the settlement and the interior of the houses looked like. People explained to me that here, already five thousand years ago, "the masses" had lived and worked peacefully together, without tyrannical emperors or treacherous monks. It was quite clear from the size of the storage cellars dug deep into the ground, I was told, that they must have contained food for more than one family; thus the settlement must have been a kind of commune, where the families—though they were still separate units—lived very close together. One fairly large house, the only rectangular building in a group of otherwise circular ones, was thought to have been a meeting place, where community affairs were democratically discussed. (No one suggested it might also have been a place of worship. When I asked whether any idols or statues had been found, once again I couldn't get a direct answer.) The eyes of the museum director shone with enthusiasm as he spoke of those intrepid ancestral Communists (though this wasn't what he called them).

But there was still another historical monument I wanted to see before leaving Sian. This was in Lintung, about thirty-five miles east of the provincial capital, at the foot of Black Horse Mountain. Lintung has been famous for centuries for its hot springs. But I was interested in a historical event that took place here on December 21, 1936, and which has gone down in history as the Sian Incident, or "double-twelve" (the twelfth day of the twelfth month). At that time Chiang Kai-shek had come to Sian and set up his headquarters near Lintung's hot springs in order to negotiate with Chang Hsüe-liang, the son of Marshal Chang Tso-lin, the long-term ruler of Manchuria.

During the Japanese offensive in 1931, the "young marshal" and his troops had been forced back from Manchuria, and several of these units were then stationed in and around Sian. Generalissimo Chiang Kai-shek demanded that Chang's troops join his own in the fight against the Communists, who, after the Long March, had dug in near Yenan, just a few hundred miles farther north. But Chang Hsüe-liang in turn tried to persuade the Generalissimo to concentrate first on the fight against Japan, and to form an alliance with the

Communists. When Chiang Kai-shek refused, the "young marshal" decided to spring a surprise on the General.

Shortly after midnight on December 12, 1936, the "young marshal" ordered his troops to surround the area of the hot springs. Chiang was awakened by an exchange of fire between them and his own guards. He tried to escape, but was captured and held prisoner until he signed an agreement with Chou En-lai, who had been hurriedly summoned from Yenan to represent the Communists.

Mao, in his communiqué of December 28, 1936, sought to justify the Communists' part in the alliance. As Mao explained it, Chiang had begun to change his mind about the Communists, and this was proved by his having agreed to fight the Japanese instead, and his having ordered his troops to withdraw from Shensi (i.e., from the vicinity of Yenan). The alliance, Mao said, also struck a blow against the Japanese imperialists, who had much to gain from a long civil war in China, and against the traitors within Chiang's own camp, who had counted on Chiang's anti-Communist stand in Sian to further their own pro-Japanese ends. By "traitors" Mao meant first of all Wang Ching-wei, who in fact did leave Chiang two years later to form a counter-régime in Nanking, which had by then been occupied by the Japanese; Chiang, meanwhile, had moved to Chungking, and remained there for the rest of the Sino-Japanese War.

Lintung has become what amounts to an anti-shrine for the Communists. I was shown Chiang Kai-shek's bedroom in one of the pavilions, with the bullet holes still in the windows; the window from which he had jumped, "in his underwear"; the corner "where they found his false teeth"; the place where he had hurt his foot while scrambling over a wall; the trail he had taken on the steep slopes of Black Horse Mountain. Now a long flight of stone steps leads along Chiang's escape route, ending in a narrow crack between two rocks where the Generalissimo finally got stuck and where, around eight o'clock in the morning, he was hunted down and captured.

There is a building on this spot, a ludicrous one for two reasons: its style is imitation Greek temple, and it was erected—in 1946— by a friend of Chiang's. Perhaps the temple was intended to

155

counteract the unpleasant associations that went with the place; and this could also be the reason for the euphemistic name, "Pavilion of Honesty," which Chiang's friend chose to give to the temple. The Communists chipped away this inscription, and have replaced it with a new one, reading "Pavilion of the Capture of Chiang."

It would appear that under this régime, historic monuments have a better chance for survival, if they are in public parks. The seven-story Pagoda of the Great Wild Goose in Sian is a good example. It was built of the yellow clay that is everywhere in Shensi and in large parts of China a dazzling contrast to the clear blue skies of spring.

Massive yet marvelously proportioned, the pagoda stands in a well-kept park, which attracts many visitors, and especially many children. At the time of my visit, several groups were having picnics around the teahouse. There was continued traffic on the wooden steps inside the pagoda, as groups of Chinese tourists clattered up and down the stairs. When the "foreigner" appeared, they all stopped and stared; even though the pagoda is the great tourist attraction of Sian, they obviously found me a more engrossing sight.

In Peking, the Temple of Heaven and the Summer Palaces are also in public parks. Despite beautiful weather, the large park surrounding the Temple of Heaven was not at all crowded; as I walked about the grounds, I kept meeting the same faces. I was enchanted once again by the tranquil beauty of the place, but I did notice some changes.

To begin with, a great number of Mao portraits and quotations have appeared since 1957. As soon as you set foot in the park, you are faced with a gigantic billboard with Mao's picture on it. As you come nearer, you see that there are other pictures, representing various important stages in his life—the house where he was born, the Long March, and so on—in short, all the shrines of the New China. And walking southward from the largest temple towards the middle one—in my opinion the most nearly perfect of all—I saw yet another huge portrait of Mao. This one was solidly attached to large stone blocks. It appeared to me that the temples were being used simply as a background for his face.

Chinese buildings are not like Greek temples or Romanesque churches, which endure for centuries. Very often they are built of wood (in the case of the Temple of Heaven, without using a single nail!) or of glazed tiles, which are also not eternal.

On my first four visits to China, between 1929 and 1943, the Temples of Heaven were rather run down. Obviously nobody was spending much money on them, though the last dynasty had fallen only in 1911, and until then they had been protected. But in 1957 they were in beautiful condition; the new China, just come to power, obviously wanted to emphasize its great historical heritage.

But this time I found the temples in about the same shabby state as on my first visit. The bright colors had faded, many of the window frames were broken, and entire sections were missing from the glazed-tile wall around the south temple.

People who lived in Peking during the Cultural Revolution told me that for a time the Red Guards used the temple grounds as their bivouac; since they were violently opposed to everything "old," they had done a good deal of damage to the buildings. Afterwards there had obviously been some effort at restoration —but as far as I could see, not much effort had been expended.

How quickly anything that is neglected can fall into oblivion! In the Temples of Heaven, certain built-in architectural tricks were once known to every Pekingese, and on visits to the Temples they liked to play with them and show them off to visitors. Of these the best known was an acoustical trick at the middle Temple, which stands in the exact center of a large circular courtyard surrounded by a high wall. If you speak in a whisper with your face close to the wall, a person standing by the wall on the opposite side can hear every word; the sound travels all the way around the wall. As I entered the courtyard this time, there was a great deal of shouting going on. In the middle of the courtyard stood a group of Chinese tourists, looking bewildered and disappointed as they tried making all sorts of noises. They vaguely remembered that there had been some kind of acoustical effect, but they had no idea

157

how it worked. When I showed them how, they were absolutely surprised and enchanted, and they did it over and over.

On the next day we went to the Summer Palace, a few miles northwest of the capital. This turned out to be in much better condition, and despite the bitter cold the gardens were crowded. People always seem to have liked this park better than the severe trinity of the Temples of Heaven.

Personally, I have never liked the Summer Palace. All those long, useless galleries with their postcard-sized pictures, all those imitation pavilions and temples! And above all, there is that awful marble steamboat in the middle of the lake, an absurd memorial to the foolishness of the "Old Buddha," as the reactionary and all-powerful widow of the emperor who ruled around the turn of the century was called. With the money wasted on this marble folly, the Chinese navy could have been modernized. It was the lack of a navy that made possible Japan's easy victory in the war of 1894–95, paving the way for the collapse of the old China.

This time, however, I had a special reason for wishing to revisit the Summer Palace. Early in the fall of 1966, a few weeks after the beginning of the Cultural Revolution, I had been in Hong Kong. I had tried to find out as much as I could about the situation in China, and among the people I questioned was a young journalist who had just returned from a visit. This rare eyewitness gave me, along with several other listeners, some very dramatic reports. One of these was about how the Red Guards had badly vandalized the Summer Palace, especially the galleries.

In the spring of 1971 I found no trace of vandalism. On the other hand, the pictures didn't look as though they had been restored. I wondered whether restorations could really be so perfect as to be invisible, or whether my young informant had invented the whole story? This shows once again, at any rate, the necessity for extreme skepticism when it comes to hearsay.

The condition of the Ming graves is yet another indication of the official attitude towards the past. The Ming emperors, whose dynasty was the last dynasty but one to reign over China, are buried on a wide plain in the mountains about fifty miles north of Peking. They have long been tourist attractions. While I was still a student, I had been on several hiking trips to the site. From the very beginning of the Cultural Revolution the graves were declared off limits, and I was among the very first to be allowed to visit them afterward.

I was especially interested in the tomb of the Emperor Wan Li. (d. 1620), excavated as recently as 1956. Built of enormous stone blocks, it is composed of many vaults and chambers deep underground inside a burial hill; the coffins of the emperor and his two wives stand in the remotest of these chambers. The graves are brightly lit with electric lights, and have been open to Chinese tourists since mid-1970, though the entire grave site is closed during the winter season.

I was met there first by a small group of soldiers, who unlocked the entrance gate for me, and then by the museum director. Here again, the mausoleum has become primarily an object lesson for the present, rather than a tribute to the past.

The "underground palace"—as the tomb is called—and two new exhibition halls were both full of objects, not only from the graves themselves but from "feudal times, when the masses were oppressed and enslaved while the lords lived in luxury." There were, for instance, documents showing how the poor were forced to sell their children; there was a painting of a typical feudal estate in the time of the Ming dynasty; and in one of the museum buildings, a huge mural covering an entire wall depicted the oppression of the workers during the building of the mausoleum itself.

When I saw the rows of glass display cases full of jeweled crowns, golden bowls, and quantities of gold ingots, I supposed them to be imitations, and I wondered where the originals were kept. But my guides insisted that these were the real thing. No other country in the world would dare to leave such treasures—probably worth millions of dollars—lying about day and night in flimsy pavilions, protected only by the most ordinary windows and doors! But then, what would anyone do with jeweled crowns and golden bowls in today's China?

I made one more nostalgic excursion into the past: to the former Legation Quarter in Peking. Here, during the second half of the nineteenth century, the West (including Japan) had built a little world that kept entirely to itself, staying completely aloof and recognizing no Chinese law or authority. A walled district with its own troops and its own army barracks, it stood no more than a stone's throw from the Gate of Heavenly Peace. It was this district that in 1900 was held by a handful of foreigners against the fanatical Boxer rebels, who were secretly supported by the Chinese government. Even after the fall of the monarchy, when all the embassies moved to Nanking, something of the West still lingered at the heart of Peking. When I visited there for the first time in the late twenties 1,500 foreign soldiers were still stationed there. When later, at the time of Pearl Harbor, Japanese troops cordoned off the Legation quarter and jailed the Americans and the British, China had no say at all about what happened. . . .

I had expected the rulers of the New China to have torn down the foreign quarter altogether, since it could only remind them of their humiliation by the Western barbarians. But it is still there, though a few things are changed.

My Chinese guide was not at all pleased by this excursion. He didn't know his way around that part of town, and had almost no interest in it; worst of all, he wasn't quite sure how to react to this embarrassing relic of his country's semicolonial past. He was visibly relieved when our walk was over. To me, however, those two hours were a vivid revelation of how incredibly the world has changed in the past seventy years. What a tremendous contrast there is between the humiliation China suffered during the Boxer rebellion of 1901, and today's ping-pong diplomacy, eagerly accepted by what may be the most powerful nation on earth.

19: Hero Worship

In China there has been since time immemorial one day every spring when "the graves are swept" and the dead are remembered. Although the new China has little use for ancestor worship, it has adapted this particular custom for its own purposes, in the same way that the Christian church once absorbed pagan festivals into its calendar. During the weeks before and after the period set for sweeping the graves, the new China honors the martyrs who sacrificed their lives for Chairman Mao, for the working and peasant classes, and for the fatherland itself. As it happened, I made visits to several cities during these weeks of hero worship, and everywhere I went I had the same experience. Here are two scenes:

It was our last day in Hangchow. The city and its lovely environs were at their most dismal: the countryside was shrouded by a gray veil of driving rain, and the temperature stood at just a few degrees above freezing. When we set out on our morning drive into the country, it was obvious that the weather wasn't going to improve. But this was the day on which the schoolchildren of Hangchow were to pay homage to their war heroes, and nothing could alter that.

As we drove through the outskirts of the town we passed endless processions of children. The leaders of each convoy carried red flags and paper garlands, and often they had pictures of Chairman Mao. Of the schoolchildren who marched behind, a few wore raincoats or carried umbrellas, but the vast majority were in their ordinary clothes and practically nobody wore a hat. Yet I saw no unhappy faces. The children looked as if it were the most natural thing in the world to be marching for miles through an icy downpour to commemorate war heroes. Many of the groups were singing; others were chanting Mao quotations.

A week later I was in Canton. Once again, there were long columns of young people carrying red flags and paper flowers, moving towards a large park near the center of the city. This time I joined them. From a vast square, already jammed with young people, they followed a broad avenue leading through an area newly planted with trees to a grassy hill enclosed by a marble wall. This hill, according to the official figures, contains the bones of five thousand people, all of whom were killed when Chiang Kai-shek wiped out the Canton commune in 1927. The monument was built to mark the thirtieth anniversary of that massacre. Here, too, the graves were being swept, trees planted, and roads repaired.

The impact of all the different forms of hero worship on the Chinese youth of today must, I think be taken very seriously.

Surely it is no accident that most of the current stories being dinned into the ears of the young are about youthful soldiers.

At one hotel where I stayed, the guests were offered booklets containing nothing but stories of this kind.[1]

Here is a sample, from a story entitled "The Heroic Diving Squadron": During the construction of the Yangtze bridge near Nanking, divers from the Chinese navy were called in. "No one had worked at such a depth before. . . . In his brand-new Chinese diving suit, he plunged into the water, silently reciting 'serve the people' as he dived deeper and deeper. At 40–50 meters [about 150 feet] he felt cold all over. The comrades above read to him Chairman Mao's teaching: 'Be resolute, fear no sacrifice and surmount every difficulty to win victory.' This instantly filled him with warmth. He dived straight to the bottom, worked tenaciously for several hours and successfully completed the job."

Another story in the same booklet told about Wang, a young aviator, who was in the hospital after a serious cancer operation; a kidney had been removed, but the cancer had already spread to his lungs.

"On the early morning of March 3, 1969, Wang Teh-ming heard over the radio the news of Soviet revisionist social-imperialism's armed invasion of China's Chenpao Island area and the grave incident of bloodshed it created. Incensed at the wanton intrusion, Wang Teh-ming, who had been elected Party branch secretary of the wards, immediately called a meeting of his ward to denounce the towering crimes of the new tsars [i.e., the Soviet leaders].

"Waving his fist, he said: 'Comrades, the new tsars bully us to such an intolerable extent, what should we do?' All replied: 'Chairman Mao teaches us: We will not attack unless we are attacked; if we are attacked, we will certainly counter-attack. . . .' The angry shouts of the slogans of 'Down with Soviet revisionist social imperialism!' and 'Down with the new tsars!' resounded throughout the wards and the whole hospital."

Other brochures, available for only a few fen, bore such titles as *A Worthy Son of the People,* or *A Brave Fighter for Chairman Mao.* These heroes all have the two characteristics so highly prized

[1] *Fear Neither Hardship nor Death in Serving the People* (Peking, 1970).

by Mao: they are "poor and blank," they are like clean sheets of paper, on which the "newest and most beautiful words" (meaning Maoism) can be written without conflicting with earlier "inscriptions."

Mao's words, "Learn from the People's Liberation Army!" were spoken at the same period that he set up Tachai as an example to the entire nation. The old guerrilla leader, who still regards the Long March with his troops in 1935 as the high point of his life, has always had a special feeling for soldiers and for military life. It is not the laborer, not the peasant, the intellectual or the manager, but the soldier who finds it quite natural to fight to the limits of his strength for ideals that are more important to him than his life.

So it is hardly any wonder that Mao should have turned once more to the army when he was disappointed by the materialism of the people generally, and especially of the bureaucracy, after the Great Leap Forward. Once more the army became the shining example; since 1963, the majority of folk heroes have been soldiers.

One thing these heroes compare themselves to is oxen. The idea goes back to a remark made by Mao at Yenan in 1942, during his second speech there about art and literature: all revolutionaries, he said, must serve the proletariat and the masses like "willing oxen." [2]

The "ox" of Tachai is Chao Hsiao-ho, whose life story I saw portrayed in the village by a series of drawings. Before the revolution, Chao worked as a shepherd boy for the Tachai landowner. One day, the story goes, he was sold, along with his sheep, to another landowner. After the Communist victory he returned to Tachai. At first he had not wanted to join the commune; but finally, thanks to patient guidance by Chen, the Party secretary, and intensive study of Mao's writings, he found the right path and became a hard-working stableboy for the brigade. One day a horse he took care of suddenly shied and bolted, and would have plunged into a ravine if Chao had not thrown himself in its path. In so doing, Chao broke his leg. Because of an error in treatment, when the

[2] *Selected Works,* Volume III.

broken leg healed it was shorter than the other. Chao told his comrades to break the leg again, refusing any anesthetic (he steeled himself for the ordeal with Mao quotations). The leg was reset, this time without mishap. Afterwards he served the brigade faithfully for many years, until his death in another accident.

In China the young are continually offered such examples of unwavering zeal, and a strong influence on their thinking and behavior is only natural. Those of us who are not "willing oxen" but skeptical foreigners find such things overdramatized and even in bad taste.[3] But the China of 1971 is worlds away from Europe and America. In 1943, when we were all at war, and inspired by a nationalist fervor of our own, we might not have thought these stories either so strange or so flagrantly simple.

20: With Prince Sihanouk

I had last seen Prince Sihanouk in his own country in the fall of 1968. There, at the lovely little university town of Kompong Cham, he had been mobbed and cheered by the population, especially the young people. Now I was meeting him again thousands of miles from his own sunny land, in the still wintry capital of China. Yet he appeared not to have changed: still lively, witty, and charming, he also had the same intense concern over the crises in and around Southeast Asia.

The gate to Sihanouk's residence in the former French Embassy is flanked by a pair of Chinese lions, and the first thing you see inside is an enormous red plaque on the "wall against evil spirits," bearing the words "Serve the People" in Mao's handwriting, magnified in the usual fashion. Behind the wall are the spacious gardens of the compound, with buildings to the right and left, and the colors of Cambodia flying from the main building at the far end. On the first floor are offices and a large reception hall; upstairs are the Prince's living quarters, which include a formal dining room. The government Sihanouk formed shortly after his

[3] See "He swam for Mao," Document 7, in Part IV.

arrival in Peking, led by Premier Pen Nouth, has offices of its own in another section of the city. Pen Nouth, with his wife, lives in one of the annexes just a few yards away.

On March 18, 1970, when the first reports came of General Lon Nol's coup in Cambodia, Sihanouk happened to be in Moscow. Theoretically, he might have returned to Paris (where he had just been), or he could have stayed in Moscow instead of flying on to Peking, as he had been scheduled to do on his way back to Phnom Penh. But to retreat quietly to some safe spot like the French Riviera would have been entirely out of character. He spoke of the Moscow government with bitterness.

"When I heard the news of the coup, I asked Premier Kosygin not to recognize the illegal military government of Lon Nol, but to support the government I would be forming in the next few days. But even today, more than a year later, the Soviet Embassy is still in Phnom Penh."

The Prince told me, nevertheless, that he had not given up his efforts to influence Moscow; he based his hopes on a Soviet declaration of May 24, 1970, in which Lon Nol was warned against siding with Washington and Saigon. The Soviet government, according to this declaration, was following the developments in Cambodia very closely, and their future attitude would depend on whether Phnom Penh "chose the way of peace and neutrality, or joined the forces of aggression and turned into a military base against its neighbors."

The Prince showed me a copy of a letter he had written to Kosygin on January 15, 1971. In it he said that Lon Nol had done exactly what the Kremlin had warned him not to do in its declaration of May 24, 1970. He was accordingly asking the Soviet government to recognize his own government in Peking as the only legitimate Cambodian government, or at least to send immediate help to the Cambodian Resistance forces. . . .

Sihanouk's request was never answered. "I can understand," he told me, "that the Russians have some interests in Phnom Penh —a large hospital, a factory, a university. So I suggested that they might leave a medical, economic, and scientific mission in Phnom Penh, but that they should close down their embassy. Still there was no reaction. The Cambodian resistance fighters received help from China, from North Korea, from North Vietnam, from Laos —but not a penny from the Soviet Union."

Sihanouk's move to Peking was the only logical one, and in keeping with one of his deepest convictions. In all talks I have had with him over the past fourteen years he never varied on one point: America, he insisted, will one day pull out of Asia; the Soviet Union is far away; but China will be in Asia forever. After Cambodia gained its independence at the Geneva conference of 1954, Sihanouk considered it his most important political mission to remain on friendly terms with Peking. He often went to Peking on state visits; he defended its foreign policy, he sent one of his sons there, he refused all American economic aid, and finally he broke off diplomatic relations with the United States.

Sihanouk believes that if the United States withdraws from Vietnam—as he thinks it will do—a pro-American government cannot stay long in Cambodia. By now, he says, the present government would surely have been overthrown by the guerrillas and the Viet Cong, had it not been for the South Vietnamese army, which is of course supported in turn by massive American air power.

The fiercely patriotic Sihanouk sees no advantage in having Cambodia become part of a new Greater Vietnam, to include all the territory of former French Indochina—i.e., Vietnam, Laos, and Cambodia. He wants his country to remain a sovereign state. And the more strongly he is supported in Peking, the better are his chances of having Cambodia's neighbors respect that sovereignty.

With this conviction always in mind, Sihanouk has met with representatives of the government of Hanoi, with the National Liberation Front of South Vietnam, and with the Laotian guerrilla leader Souphanouvong. He has made agreements with all of them guaranteeing mutual respect for territorial integrity and sovereignty. He showed me, for example, a document signed February 8, 1971, by himself and Ton Duc Thang, the president of the Democratic Republic of Vietnam. It says in part: "The Democratic Republic of Vietnam confirms that it will continue to recognize and respect the territorial integrity of Cambodia within its present borders,

166

and guarantees Cambodia the right to settle its internal affairs without outside intervention."

Peking has given Prince Sihanouk a high degree of prominence. Many issues of the *Peking Review* have given him generous space. His frequent radio speeches to Cambodia are broadcast from Peking, and parts of them are carried verbatim in the Chinese press. Every official visit Sihanouk makes to the Chinese provinces receives extensive coverage.

In Sian, in Nanking, in Shanghai—everywhere, people showed me photographs of large crowds that came out to greet the Prince, waving Chinese and Cambodian flags. In many shop windows I saw photographs of Sihanouk and Mao together; he was given the place of honor next to Mao at the big parade before the Gate of Heavenly Peace on May 20th, 1970. Two declarations were read to the one million participants at the event, Mao's speech was read by Defense Minister Lin Piao, and Sihanouk's was given by Sihanouk himself. Whenever I came to a place he had visited, I had only to say I was a friend of his, and every door was immediately opened. It is, of course, not surprising that at a banquet given in his honor he should be seated to the right of Premier Chou En-lai. It *is* surprising, however, that though he is not a Communist he was invited to attend a dinner given by the Central Committee of the Communist Party in honor of Vietnamese Communist leaders, just before they left on their way to Moscow.

It is not always easy to live in exile and to be completely dependent on one's hosts. But I could see no signs of strain in Sihanouk. Not once during our talks did he seem tired or discouraged. His sense of humor, his ability to laugh at himself, is of course a great asset.

On the day after the banquet for the Indochinese Communist leaders, he said to me: "The whole world rushes to Moscow to attend the Party Congress—except Cambodia and China." His laugh was totally without bitterness; he seemed genuinely amused by the comical linking of giant China with tiny Cambodia.

And finally I believe he is sustained by a determination (which to my mind is genuine) to withdraw from political life once the war is over. Then, but only then, he wants to go and live quietly in France. I had never taken this very seriously, but I am now convinced that he really means it—or at any rate for the moment.

He feels—and he has said so quite openly on television—that Cambodia after the civil war should be led by those who have fought that war in the jungle, who have not been far away in Peking. They are the true patriots, he says, even if some of them are Communists.

At this moment, however, he sees his role in Peking as crucial. He coordinates the various campaigns to aid his Cambodian guerrillas; he addresses his countrymen almost every week over Radio Peking; and he maintains Cambodia's friendly relations with Mao and Chou En-lai. I have often observed him and Chou together; they obviously like each other; probably they might even be called personal friends. Chou En-lai, of course, does not simply follow his feelings but considers the interests of the state; yet political considerations and friendship are not necessarily in contradiction.

Nor does Sihanouk rely on feelings alone. "I have every important guarantee for the future independence, freedom, and neutrality of my country down in black and white," he said, patting his jacket pocket. He spoke to me especially of the Chinese declaration of October 10, 1970, just a few hours after Lon Nol had proclaimed Cambodia a republic. In this declaration, the Chinese government states that a nation is not judged by whether it calls itself a kingdom or a republic, but by the political road it takes. Because Sihanouk had never faltered in his policy of independence, peace, and neutrality, the statement went on, he had won the support and affection of the Cambodia masses. The Chinese government once again firmly stated that there was only one legitimate Cambodian government, and that it was the royal government headed by Prince Sihanouk. The Chinese declaration also expressed complete faith in a total victory in the fight against the United States, and in the "establishment of the independence of the kingdom of Cambodia."

Sihanouk is convinced that Peking cannot go back on such a declaration, with its clear emphasis on the independence and the sovereignty of his country. Also, since his move to Peking he has taken every opportunity to expound his views on the future of

Cambodia over the radio and in the press; this would make it even harder for Peking to change its mind. And no doubt it must also suit China's political purposes that in the post-American phase, Vietnam, Laos, and Cambodia should exist as separate independent nations.

I, too, hope that one day there will be a free and independent Cambodia, and as a personal friend I wish the Prince well; I have nothing but sympathy and admiration for the courageous, steadfast, even cheerful way which he faces a time that must be bitter for him.

I was most impressed by his attitude during my interview with him for German television. I had warned him beforehand that I would ask him some hard questions, being convinced that he could deal with them. I asked him, among other things, "How can you, a descendant of kings and of the founders of Angkor Wat, a devout Buddhist and a Cambodian patriot, collaborate with the Communists without becoming a mere puppet? Do you really believe that in the future it will be possible for Cambodians and Vietnamese, who have hated each other for so long, to work together? Why do you stay in Peking instead of joining your guerrillas in the jungle?"

Sihanouk answered all these questions without evasion, and explained his position as I have set it forth above. He seemed to me deeply and genuinely convinced that this meant the best for his country.

PART II: COMMENTARY

The first section of this book was devoted to the impressions I absorbed with my own eyes and ears during my recent visit to China. The section that follows deals with the thoughts and reflections evoked by those experiences. Such subjects as I could not discuss in China, or about which I could learn nothing worth telling—such as foreign policy or, what will happen after Mao—are not touched on here.

21: 1957 and 1971: A Comparison

My two most recent visits to China are separated by an interval of fourteen years. At a cursory glance, they appear to have one thing in common: the quality of order and quiescence. The year 1957 was the lull before the storm, which broke out a year later when China embarked on the Great Leap Forward, thus leaving the well-trodden path—and the camp—of the People's Democracies. When I returned in 1971, she had weathered the even greater turbulence of the Cultural Revolution.

One enormous change greets you, of course, the instant you cross the border: Mao is everywhere. There was nothing fourteen years ago to prepare one for such a development, however improbable this may seem now that the Little Red Book and the millions of Mao portraits are so omnipresent. At that earlier time, Mao's name appeared relatively seldom, even in connection with the Great Leap Forward, which may be recognized today as a forerunner of the Cultural Revolution. Many China observers, myself among them, believe they can recognize the work of Liu Shao-chi in the Great Leap Forward; it was he who in May, 1958, made this phrase a catchword.

In the years that followed, Mao seemed to have faded into the background; months would go by without any news of him. Years later, he was to say of that period between the Great Leap Forward and the Cultural Revolution, "At that time most people disagreed with me. Sometimes I was all alone. They said that my views were out of date." Again to use his words, at the time "it appeared quite probable that revisionism [that is, the political line of his enemies in China and Moscow] would triumph, and that we would lose." China just then was at a point of extreme instability—only nine years after its founding in the midst of all sorts of revolutionary upheavals, and was ruled by a monopoly of onetime revolutionaries who had become party hacks.

Compared with the quivering tension you feel everywhere today, China in 1957 was almost boring. Of course there were campaigns at the time—against the intellectuals (after the Hundred Flowers

173

had withered), against rats and flies (and today's traveler will still be grateful for those campaigns), along with the Hsiafang, the "sending down" of cadres for physical labor on the land. What was missing then was a dynamic ideology, an irresistible momentum, and a recognized leader of the masses.

On July 16, 1966, when Mao emerged from the Yangtze River —or more precisely, on July 25, when the press announced that he had swum nine miles downriver in sixty-five minutes, thus proving to the world that his health was excellent—he took his place as the leader of his nation. (As a signal for a historic turning point, the swimming of the Yangtze was in its own way no less original than the linking of politics with sport in the spring of 1971 by inviting the Americans in to play ping-pong.) It was then that the Little Red Book, which had hardly been known to the masses, became spiritual nourishment for everyman.

The economic and social changes—increased production, a wider choice of consumer goods (though not an increase in salaries), the equalizing of status differences—have been discussed elsewhere. The nation's intellectual life, which in 1957, during the days of the Hundred Flowers, was so impressively varied, has shrunk to an unprecedentedly narrow conformity. Patriotism and national consciousness have increased strongly, as the outside world has been more and more effectively cut off. The Soviet Union, fourteen years ago China's most powerful friend, has become its Enemy Number One.

But of all the changes since 1957, the most important is the way the population has been infused with *one* spirit, the spirit of Mao-Tse-tung. In villages, factories, and schools, the Chinese by hundreds of millions are marching in step—or so, at any rate, it appears to an outsider. As for what is really happening inside, I cannot be sure, since I cannot see into other men's hearts.

22: Peking and Moscow —No Longer Comparable

The last time I flew over Poland en route to the Soviet Union, from thirty thousand feet up you could tell with absolute certainty where the border was: suddenly the neat, narrow little fields belonging to individual Polish peasants gave way to the vast stretches of the kolkhoz. In March 1971, the picture at the border between the British Crown Colony of Hong Kong and the People's Republic of China was quite another matter: along both sides were the small, carefully built terraces typical of the region, and at first glance it is impossible to tell whether they are worked individually or collectively.

I believe that the most important border in the world today is in Asia, running along the Amur and the Ussuri. This was not so when I visited China in 1957. Whatever I saw at that time— factories or village collectives, schools or universities, party committees or national minorities—everywhere, the Soviet model was more or less closely followed: the country could have been named Soviet China. But since my visit in 1957 China has changed so much that the differences between it and the Soviet Union are now greater than they are between Russia and the West.

I visited both the Soviet Union and China in 1970–71 within a span of eight months, and in what I noted, six basic points of contrast leap to the eye.

1. The Soviet Union is now to a great degree an industrial civilization. Productivity and automation, efficiency, competition, profits, and a controlled market are the concepts that operate in the country's economic life today. In practical terms, Stalin's words, "The cadres decide everything," today means that the technicians decide everything: the experts, the specialists, the university graduates, the highly skilled and privileged technicians are the decision-makers —with the exception, of course, that the Party always has the last word.

China, on the other hand, remains to an overwhelming degree an agrarian society where technology is still at a very low level of development. As I traveled throughout the countryside, I saw hundreds of thousands of peasants but only a few hundred agricultural machines. I saw tens of thousands of handcarts, but only a few trucks. I even saw plows pulled by people. And never, anywhere, have I heard or read so many derogatory remarks about experts—technicians or engineers—as in today's China. One would almost suppose they must be a gang of saboteurs and ignoramuses. The word has gone out that only the masses are creative; specialists are mocked and held up to ridicule. Military and economic experts would seem to be the only exceptions to the rule; apparently they were mentioned in the twelfth of the Sixteen Points that were made public on August 8, 1966, and which placed technicians and scientists under special protection during the Cultural Revolution.

2. In the process of industrialization, the Soviet Union has become more and more of an achievement society. Work more and you'll have more; work still more—study, earn diplomas—and you'll have that much more still: your own apartment, a car, a dacha in the country.

But China is an egalitarian society. Not that the Chinese work less hard—the production level of manual labor per person must be far above that in the Soviet Union—but individual achievement is not gauged by a fluctuating pay system. More work is not stimulated by higher earnings. To measure achievement for purposes of monetary reward is an insult to a man of true "consciousness," much as a tip is unworthy of a free man. It is taken for granted that everyone will do his best, and thus the system of supervision and control that absorbs so great a proportion of Soviet society does not exist. It took my Western mind a good while to fully understand their pay system. It has very little in common with the Soviet system, which is much like that of the West.

3. The U.S.S.R. is on its way to being a consumer society. Billions of roubles and of work hours are invested today in things that make life more pleasant but are not "essential": the construction of private houses and country dachas, fashionable clothing, novels, cosmetics, records—even some Western music.

The new China, on the other hand, is striving with all its might toward being a production society. Even by Soviet standards, salaries barely amount to a kind of pocket money. And whenever I asked, "Why do you work from early morning till late at night?" the answer, as the reader knows, was invariably, "To win honor for Chairman Mao and our socialist fatherland."

4. In the Soviet Union, state and society are hierarchical in structure. There are clear status differences and social levels, the Party being incontestably at the top. From top to bottom the population is organized bureaucratically into countless layers. Lenin—to say nothing of Stalin—did not think much of the masses; they were there to be controlled by the Apparat.

In China, the Cultural Revolution broke up the kind of social encrustation that had begun since the triumph of the revolution, and the effect has been that both government and society have acquired a high degree of spontaneity. On the one hand there is Mao, the charismatic leader, and on the other there are "the masses." Everyone in between is in the midst of flux.

5. It would seem that with every passing day these two countries diverge still further with regard to the ideology they once had in common. In the now pragmatic Soviet Union, that ideology is eulogized at Party congresses, in editorials, and in political reviews, but in the daily life and talk of the people it plays almost no role. *Das Kapital* and the works of Lenin are kept on the bookshelf, as the Bible is in the West. As for the leaders, Kosygin and Brezhnev—are they still concerned with ideology? The Brezhnev doctrine, at any rate, is understood and practiced as a formula for power.

How different all this is in Mao's China! Every discussion is ideological, and Mao is quoted in at least every third sentence. During my entire stay, I found hardly a person without his Little Red Book in hand, or at any rate within reach.

6. Finally, the Soviet Union today is gradually becoming an open society. Soviet specialists (carefully selected, of course) take part in all sorts of conferences abroad, and every year thousands of foreigners attend conferences inside Russia. Every year, hundreds of thousands of tourists visit the country. Foreign books appear in editions of millions of copies, and millions of Russians listen to the foreign radio and dance to Western music.

But China today—despite ping-pong politics and the new rash

of journalists' visas— is still a closed society, and will be so for some time. I traveled three thousand miles through the country without ever meeting a non-Chinese except in the major cities, and without ever seeing a foreign newspaper except for one Albanian Communist Party newsletter. It is a country where a world event such as man's first landing on the moon is passed over in silence. These facts clearly speak for themselves.

I saw many things in the China of 1971 to remind me of the Russia I had known forty years ago. And how could it be otherwise? Then, when I was taken to the first automobile factory on the Volga, and to see the new dam on the Dnieper, these were shown to me with the same pride and triumph as is displayed today at the Yangtze bridge near Nanking. As I have said, the Chinese theater of today reminds me of the Moscow theater of that early time, when I saw W. W. Ivanov's *Armored Train #14–69* or W. W. Vichnevskij's *Optimistic Tragedy*.

It was during the 1930s that the Soviet Union underwent a great change, with the deproletarianization of the upper strata, who became a "new class," with the growth in size and importance of the military and of the diploma-bearing technocrats, and with the bureaucratization of the government. These were the years that saw the dwindling élan of the first Five Year Plan, which was then transposed to an economic basis. There was a resurgence of that élan during the Second World War, transposing it to the arena of patriotism; but little trace of it remains today!

For one who travels through China nowadays with his thoughts steadily directed to the Russian experience—to that country as it was forty years ago and as it is today—one question becomes obsessive: Will China follow much the same course in the forty years to come? And will the China of the year 2011 resemble the Soviet Union of 1971? Though no one knows the answer, it will be an important one for all of us. But anyone who has had that experience, who has seen and felt the degree to which the Chinese people have been gripped and changed by Maoism—more strongly than the Russians ever were by Marxism-Leninism—will, I think, refrain from hasty predictions.

23: The Unmastered Past

The attitude of the Soviet Union towards its own past went through two distinct and opposite phases. During the first, the whole of Russian history before the revolution and the triumph of the new doctrine was depicted as even darker than the picture painted of the Middle Ages by the Age of Enlightenment. Russia was "the prison of the people"; the tsars were tyrants and bloodthirsty criminals. History, for Russia and for the world, began with Lenin, perhaps prefaced by some mention of those who had paved the way for him—the peasant rebels and revolutionary intellectuals.

But then, at the beginning of the 1930s, Stalin steered a 180-degree change of course. One after another, historical figures suddenly appeared in new dress: even Ivan the Terrible now became Ivan the Exalted. From the princes of Kiev all the way to the Grand Dukes of Moscow and the Tsar—including the conquerors of Siberia and Central Asia—stretched the glorious span of Russian history, reaching its pinnacle of achievement with Lenin and Stalin. The most striking manifestation of this attitude is to be found in the restoration, during the Second World War, of the old guard regiments and the naming of military decorations after the tsarist marshals of the eighteenth and nineteenth centuries. Basically, since that time nothing has changed. Russian school-children generally know more about nineteenth-century Russian literature than about what is being written today. There may still be arguments about Stalin's place in history, but there are none about Peter the Great.

In this area, as in so many others, China has taken a diametrically opposite course. Naturally, both literature and history were accommodated to the goals of the revolution from the very beginning. But the great sites of the Chinese past were at first left undisturbed; in 1957 the Temple of Confucius at Chufu, his birthplace, and the Temple of Heaven at Peking were carefully looked after. On the stage throughout all of China, the classic figures of history and legend were regularly portrayed, and Kuo Mo-jo, Mao's favorite historian, was commissioned to honor the grave of the Yellow Emperor, the legendary Lord Ancestor of China, with a new inscription. In 1962, learned conferences about Confucius were still being held—the final one in November, 1962, ending with a visit to the temple at the grave of the sage.

It was not until the Cultural Revolution, beginning in 1963 with the battles of Chiang Ching, Mao's wife, against the traditional theater, that the storm broke over the Chinese past, and struck the "four old things"—old thoughts, culture, habits, and customs—a deadly blow. Now enemies were to be found not only among the intellectuals, but even inside their own camp—inside the Party's Central Committee, in fact. One of the articles marking the onset of the Cultural Revolution, by the well-known writer Yao Wen-yuan, and dated May 10, 1966, had this to say of the enemies that lurked in history: "Under a mantle of 'the search for valuable knowledge of ancient and modern times' they launched a mass attack against socialism. They cunningly idealized the feudal system and gave honor to the dead . . . they used . . . history . . . as a smoke screen, under cover of which they anesthetized the revolutionary vigilance of the people." [1]

Since that time, the past has been systematically withdrawn from the sight of the people. The old operas have been replaced by new ones for which Chiang Ching is responsible. Well-loved classics, such as *The Dream of the Red Chamber,* are no longer published; the bookstores are filled with nothing but technical books, the works of Mao, and a few Communist brochures. *The Rent Collection,* that accusation against feudalism that concerns itself more with the present than with the past, is proclaimed as the highest achievement of Chinese art. In the schools and universities the study of history and literature is essentially limited to the period since the triumph of Communism in China. Almost all the museums have been closed. Archaeological excavations on the site of the Ming graves have been interrupted, even though the first of these was highly successful.

It is possible to think of Chinese history without the mythical Yellow Emperor, whose tomb I had such trouble visiting; but it is not possible to think of Chinese history without Confucius, who has left such an indelible stamp on the last two thousand years. If coping

[1] Mehnert, *Mao's Second Revolution* (1966).

with him is too difficult or possibly even too dangerous, then you must bury him or limit yourself to phrases such as "the ideology of a slave." But can this be successful in the long run?

As in Russia during the 1920s, those early heroes of the class war, the rebellious peasants, do not come under the historical taboo. So in the Underground Palace, the mausoleum of the Ming Emperor Wan Li, there hang colossal paintings depicting the peasant rebellion of that time. But even where these events are concerned, some strange lack of assurance is quite evident; thus the Taiping rebellion of the last century is praised, but my request to visit the Taiping Museum in Nanking, the one-time Taiping capital, was not granted. Likewise, my request to see the houses of the writer Lu Hsün (1881–1936)—which have been made into museums—was not granted, even though he has been praised and quoted by Mao as a forerunner of Communism.

But there is one domain in which the ancestral achievements are respectfully extolled. This is in the natural sciences, especially medicine. For if you would travel under the banner of such mottoes as: "We must rely on our own strength," and "We must use the old in the service of the new," you cannot keep an entirely negative attitude toward history.

But with this exception, today's leadership does not wish people to be occupied with history, or at least not publicly. Possibly the reluctance to deal even with the forerunners of Communism (such as the Taiping rebellion) stems from a fear of turning up ideas or events that might confuse the Communist believers of today.

Mao's aversion to unmonitored history, and perhaps to history itself, was surely increased by an awareness that his enemies were using historical fact to wage a very contemporary fight against him. There was the case of a prominent person, deposed by Mao, appearing on stage in the costume of a minister of a former time. Critical allusions were made during the sixties, for example, to the rapid end of the Chin Dynasty, which increased production but was oblivious to justice and compassion, and to the fall of the Sui Dynasty, with its extravagant official construction and unjustifiable demands on the people's working capacity.

An example dating from May, 1971, is the bitter attack on a

film about the Taiping rebellion that had been shown shortly before the Cultural Revolution. Was its hero, Li Hsiu-chen, one of the Taiping leaders, truly a hero—as the film showed him to be—or a scoundrel, as the story goes today? Li had been willing to join forces with the emperor's troops against the European invaders (see the parallel with the collaboration of many Communist leaders with Chiang Kai-shek against the Japanese); furthermore, Li had made a confession of his own guilt while he was a prisoner of the Emperor's troops, in order to be set free (as the Communists of the 1930s also did in order to escape Chiang's jails); and finally, Li criticized his own commanders, who led the Taiping rebellion.

Mao himself must surely be aware of the contradiction between the antagonism toward history that he demands of his followers and his own often reiterated attitude toward Chinese history. As the reader will recall, the museum officials in Sian could not quote for me any anti-Confucian words spoken by Chairman Mao—for the reason that there are none. In the speeches and articles that are contained in the *Selected Works* he quotes the sage often and openly as a classic, without adding any pejorative remarks. He encourages Communists to study their historic legacy: "Our nation looks back over several thousand years of history . . . has created a treasury of great worth . . . is the end product of Chinese history . . . we must not cut the thread of historical continuity. We must gather up our history from Confucius to Sun Yat-sen and discover the worth of this valuable inheritance. This will help us to lead the great movement towards the future." Mao's criticism is not directed against Confucius in his own time, but against those who would make him a leader of the present.

In his literary speeches at Yenan in 1942, Mao said, "We must incorporate the best of our literary and artistic heritage . . . whether the work of our artists and writers is refined or crude; whether it is discriminating or coarse, whether it is on a higher or a lower level, will depend on this . . . so we cannot afford to neglect the work of the ancients and of foreign writers and artists, even when they come from the feudal or bourgeois classes; we must accept their legacy and use their example in our work."

These ideas may still be pertinent today for Mao himself. But will he permit them in others?

Fifteen years after those Yenan speeches he wrote a letter to the editors of the periodical that published his poems, saying that he had not allowed these to be published before for fear of "promoting wrong tendencies and influencing young people in the wrong way . . . or possibly narrowing their thinking." [2]

Even in his poem "The Snow" (1936), whose final words call for "a look at today," Mao sets aside the past, but only after a salute to the great emperors of the past—including Tai-tsung, whose horses we were shown in Sian.

Yet what Jove may do . . .

Mao would prefer to see the mind of the Chinese people as a blank page, untouched by history, so as to leave his own imprint on it without fear of other influences. Through the fever of the Cultural Revolution, the people were supposed to expel all the poisons of their past history and of foreign influence and to become immune against them both.

When all this has been achieved, will the strict isolationism be loosened? Are the ping-pong politics of early 1971 to be understood as the beginning of this relaxation? We must wait to find out. It will not be a rapid process. Mao remembers the Russian example that he hates. What he damns in it as "revisionism" was caused by lifting the taboos on Russian history and literature, as well as by a greater opening to the outside world.

I have no doubt whatever that the Chinese will some day rediscover their history. It stretches backward, in unbroken continuity, through thousands of years, to the origins of mankind. There is no other nation on earth of whom this is true.

[2] *Nineteen Poems* (Peking, 1968).

24: Mao's Ideas
—Have They Taken Root?

In China no one talks—or at any rate not with a foreigner—
about what will come *after* Mao. But the "foreign guest," faced
with a portrait of Mao at all times of the day and night, cannot
but wonder about the fate of Maoism when Mao is gone.

The Little Red Book and the *Selected Works* will have canonical
authority for a long time, perhaps for a very long time. In the end,
not every one of Mao's pronouncements will carry the same weight.
But it may be said of some of Mao's ideas that they have entered
the Chinese bloodstream.

First of all, there is the theme of self-help, the will to rise by dint
of one's "own strength," as the incessantly quoted phrase has it. The
new patriotism of the Chinese has made this theme a fundamental
one, for group effort as well as for the life and thought of the individual.

Tachai is this idea made manifest. Among the reasons for Mao's
elevation of this village as a model for the nation, the most important of them must be Tachai's famous "three refusals" after the
1963 catastrophe, when it refused help both from the State and
from neighboring villages so as to resurrect the village with its "own
strength." Today you will find Tachais all over China. Look from
the window of any car or train, and you will see it confirmed:
nothing but hard work, most of it manual. In due course there will
be more trucks and tractors and bulldozers, but that will not be
until some time hence, and in the meantime the "spirit of Tachai"
will continue to prevail throughout the land because its effectiveness
can be easily seen and measured.

The second central idea that has taken root is an unbounded
belief in the strength of the masses—a strength that can move
mountains and perform "miracles" that human logic declares to be
impossible, as in Mao's story of the Wise Old Man.

Here, once again, the foreign visitor sees endless demonstrations
of the idea in action. You drive past almost endless processions

of human beings, each one pushing a cart—empty carts going in one direction, full ones going in the other; carts by the thousands, two thousand of them at a single building site. On any day there must be over a hundred million handcarts and carrying baskets being pushed and carried back and forth an uncountable number of times. If there are a hundred million carts, and each one of them transports, let us say, roughly a half a cubic yard of soil, stones, or manure an average of twenty trips a day, the sum total would come to at least a billion cubic yards a day—literally mountains being moved throughout China every day the sun rises.

With millions of hands in action and at work, it is still the spirit and the will that set them in motion. In the language of ideology, this means: consciousness can be transformed into matter. This third thesis, once again, in these very terms, has been absorbed into the wisdom of the people. Whenever I stood before some great achievement wrought with very modest means, someone would explain to me in the most natural fashion: Here you see our will to achieve made manifest; here our consciousness has been transformed into matter.

What is harder to discern is the degree to which Mao's most personal (and peculiarly stubborn) interpretation of Marxist ideology has been assimilated: his teachings on contradiction and on the "continuing revolution"—the very themes that brought him into his earliest and most serious conflict with Moscow. But whatever may be the attitude of the new leading classes—and they are the first to be concerned—the "masses" seem to have accepted them. To be sure, I saw people in positions of authority in the villages and the cities who had been cadres before the Cultural Revolution (for example, Chen, the chairman of the Tachai brigade, who has been the head of the village since the 1950s). But the men and women who were my local guides impressed me as being activists rather than apparatchiks or bureaucrats—people who owed their position not to Party patronage but to personal initiative. But they still cannot regard their positions as a reward for good service, since any of them may be replaced at any time by someone else who is still more active. One of Mao's most often quoted maxims says the leaders must not live off the "capital" of their old achievements but must continually strive for further progress.[1] There is little place in his philosophy for "old comrades in arms."

All things considered, the impressions I bring back from my trip have minimized rather than increased my skepticism about the durability of Maoism. Whether the ideas will outlive their founder as distinctly and for as long a time as Confucianism is doubtful. Maoism lacks the strong base of the two hierarchical institutions that carried Confucianism from generation to generation over two and a half millenniums: the extended family or clan, and the whole of officialdom. During all those years, the rise to official position was tied to examinations based on a thoroughgoing familiarity with Confucian ideas and texts. Since Mao has drawn his own lines of battle against any sort of hierarchy, he will have a harder time.

25: Revolution Without End

At the time the Chinese Communist Party founded the new state, its triumph was as complete as any ever wrung out of a revolution.

That was more than two decades ago. Yet in today's China I heard no political term mentioned so frequently or so passionately as the word "revolution." The people are constantly being encouraged to "make revolution": as one needs a helmsman for a boat at sea, so one needs Chairman Mao for the revolution. ("Needs," not "needed"!) The cadres and the people are "revolutionary cadres" and "revolutionary masses." Every single village boss is called the "chairman of the revolutionary committee," and what happened in 1966, seventeen years after total victory, was the Cultural *Revolution*.

How can this be explained? The question touches on the essence of the problem named Mao Tse-tung. And here too, as you grope for an answer, it is useful to remember China's powerful neighbor.

The Soviet Union underwent one great upheaval, the October

[1] *People's Daily*, June 1, 1967.

Revolution of 1917—which of course continued as a kind of civil war for a few years thereafter. What followed—whether or not blood flowed, and regardless of whether millions of people were involved—was no longer a true revolution, spontaneously set off by the masses, but what Stalin called a "revolution from above," in reality a series of administrative power plays, such as the collectivization of the peasants that was begun in 1929.

Even when Stalin attacked the Party leadership itself in the second half of the 1930s, and liquidated his rivals, Lenin's old comrades in arms, nothing changed in the structure of the leadership or the society of the U.S.S.R.—not even after his death. "Collective leadership" was exercised only at the very top of the pyramid, and only by a very few men even there. Below this level there remained a broad and entrenched layer of successful and privileged people, the functionaries and technocrats who made up what Djilas has called the "new class." These have proved their worth; an imposing rise in production, the difficult victory over Hitler, and their achievements in the space race. There is no indication whatever that changes in this system are in prospect—improvements perhaps, at most reforms, but surely not revolution.

At the beginning Mao seemed ready to follow the Soviet example here as well, and to end his revolution with the victory over Chiang Kai-shek. But ten years later, at the time of the Great Leap Forward, things had appeared that would not have been entirely surprising to anyone with a thorough grasp of his writings on contradictions. The revolution became a permanent institution. The Chinese term is *putuan koming,* literally "uninterrupted revolution." People in Peking tend to use the term "continuous revolution," in order to avoid confusion with Trotsky's "permanent revolution." But although the Chinese speak of Trotsky only with repugnance, since he was Stalin's enemy, in Moscow they themselves are damned as Trotskyists because they are seen as disciples of the idea of permanent revolution.

Mao's emphasis on the theory of contradiction can be measured by his having devoted two long essays to this subject: "On Contradiction," 1937, and "On the Correct Handling of Contradictions," 1957. There can be no doubt that the theme of contradiction is

187

central to Mao's thought, and precisely in the form set out in these early works: "The law of the inherent contradiction in things . . . is the basic law in nature . . . contradiction exists in all processes . . . and permeates all processes from beginning to end. Therein consists the generalization and absolutism of contradiction. . . . The battle of opposites is a perpetual phenomenon." [1]

Since contradiction permeates "all processes from beginning to end," it continues to exist within socialist society—and not simply in an abstract philosophical sense, but as quite concretely embodied in groups of people. For Mao, these immediately take on the aspect of opposing classes. When in 1962 he included the exhortation, "Never forget the class struggle!" in a speech at a Party meeting, he did not mean the class struggle in Latin America or in India, but within his own camp: that is, a battle not only against the Soviet Union, which in his eyes is moving towards capitalism, but also and above all against those Chinese Communists who seemingly want China to settle placidly into a new order, rather than maintain the rigorous thrust of the revolution—a battle, in other words, against a new "bourgeoisie" that is continually arising from among the ranks of his own people. The first chapter of the new Party constitution of 1969 specifically refers to the teaching of "continuing revolution" and of "class struggle."

Therefore also the ceaseless emphasis on the length of the road still to be traveled. Chapters II and III of the Little Red Book already contain warnings such as these: "the class struggle is by no means over," it "will continue to be long and tortuous"—"a long time to come," "for a long period after," "a protracted struggle," "a long historical period." Phrases such as these reach forward into the future; and what is still more important, further cultural revolutions, according to Mao, are inevitable:

The present great cultural revolution is only the first; there will inevitably be many more in the future. The issue of who will win in the revolution can only be settled over a long historical period. If things are not properly handled, it is possible for a capitalist restoration to take place at any time. It should not be thought by any Party member or any one of the people in our country that everything will be all right

[1] *Selected Works*, Volume I.

after one or two great cultural revolutions, or even three or four. We must be very much on the alert, and never lose vigilance! [2]

All this is diametrically opposed to the classical tradition of Chinese philosophy, which does not conceive of struggle as a goal or a meaningful life, but on the contrary, aims towards harmony and the reconciliation of opposites: translated into the ethical and political domain, this becomes compromise. And this is all anathema to Mao. It explains his angry attacks in 1964 on Yang Hsien-chen, the Party philosopher and longtime director of the Party school, who made the phrase "two combine into one" the central point of his teaching—as is entirely in accord with the Chinese tradition. There followed immediately a flood of articles that can only have been inspired by Mao himself (the practical politicians had neither the taste nor the time for this sort of thing) directed against Yang, accusing him of favoring foul compromises (with Moscow, for example). The basic principle, according to Mao, is exactly the contrary: "One divides into two."

These differences are still operating today—they have, as a matter of fact, become still more radical. In the past Mao maintained, as is dialectically correct, that in the struggle between force and counter-force, between thesis and antithesis, the antithesis does not simply win and annihilate the thesis, but rather a synthesis is formed in which the thesis is also contained—contained in both senses of the word. In 1959 Mao expanded on this, using the sexes as an example: "If there were only men and no women, if women were *negated*—what would happen then?" [3] The answer, clearly, is: the end of dialectic and the end of humankind. But isn't this an example of "two combining into one"? But the new philosophers of the Central Committee's Party School find the meaning of synthesis uniquely in "the old thing is set aside while the new thing wins": in other words, one thing "swallows up" [4] the other. Equally with the opposition in one's own camp—with the pragmatists among China's leaders, for example—there must

[2] *Peking Review*, 1967, #22.
[3] Stuart Schram, *China Quarterly*, #46.
[4] *Peking Review*, 1971, #17.

be no compromise; the opposition must be "swallowed up," must be annihilated.

Yet China today impresses the foreign visitor as being herself a new synthesis, a kind of harmony between Mao's revolutionaries and the representatives of the principle of law and order. The latter seem to be in no way "swallowed up," but on the contrary, to have more say in what goes on than their opponents, who have theoretically devoured them.

The philosophical deduction from the *Peking Review* quoted above can be read as a warning to them, or perhaps even an announcement of the next Cultural Revolution.

Or possibly it is a new declaration of battle aimed at Moscow. For Mao's theory (and, as has been observed, his practice as well) of contradictions is in direct negation to the Moscow thesis of the end of antagonism, or the contradictions that have supposedly been resolved once and for all as a result of the victory of the proletariat. For Mao, this victory cannot be the end of a history whose law is perpetual motion, but is a passage to something new. To put the matter dialectically: it is the new thesis which will call forth its own antithesis, and thus new tensions, that will eventually lead to the next revolution.

Peking holds firmly to this doctrine, celebrating it as Chairman Mao's historical contribution to the "treasury of Communist thought." Thus, in January, 1970, the lead editorial of the *Peking Review* once again encouraged "the study in depth of Chairman Mao's theory concerning continuing revolution under the dictatorship of the proletariat," observing that Mao, after Marx, Engels, and Lenin, has thereby established a "third shining milestone."

For the first time in the theory and practice of the international Communist movement, it is pointed out explicitly that classes and class struggle still exist after the socialist transformation of the ownership of the means of production has been in the main completed, and that the *proletariat must continue the revolution.* This is the most thoroughgoing revolutionary theory and a tremendous contribution to the international Communist movement. If this theory of Chairman Mao's is grasped, it will enable those countries where the dictatorship of the proletariat has been established to prevent, through their own struggles, the restoration of capitalism; and the people of those countries where revisionists have usurped state power will be able, through their own struggles, to overthrow revisionist rule and re-establish the dictatorship of the proletariat.

In essence, then, there will be revolution for an unlimited time toward an unforeseeable goal, to be achieved by a series of revolutionary waves. It is not conceived as a steady movement at some even speed, since dialectic theory demands that as the new contradictions emerge they must first build to a certain intensity before there can be a change for the (qualitatively) new. There are thus pauses in revolutionary activity, as there were after the Great Leap Forward and again after the Cultural Revolution. Mao wrote in 1940, "Without dams there can be no flow, without stasis there can be no motion." I tend to speak in terms of thrusts rather than leaps, since Mao's revolutions are measures directed against concrete enemies.

Who are these enemies? One must not be misled by the term bourgeoisie; it is part of the panoply of weapons of the Communist parties, although of course the remnants of the old bourgeoisie are included in the epithet. But these latter are not Mao's real concern, which is with the constant arrivals and drives of *new* bourgeoisies, who are constantly reappearing, in accordance with the dialectic of contradictions.

A summary of the lessons from the Cultural Revolution, published in 1969, contains a clear mention of the "*new* bourgeois elements that have arisen out of the apparatus of proletarian dictatorship." Thus *new* enemies have arisen within the Party and its leadership, who are different from the old, but who are to be taken even more seriously. "They work not from without but from within, not overtly but covertly . . . when they are in power they are much more dangerous than the landlords, the [old] bourgeoisie or the Kuomintang reactionaries [the followers of Chiang Kai-shek], who were open enemies." The author of this article reinforces his warning with words from Chairman Mao: "Beware of revisionism, especially when it appears in the Central Committee of our Party." [5]

So . . . once again it is revisionism, the old war-cry with which

[5] *Peking Review*, 1969, #13.

191

the lukewarm socialists in social democratic parties (especially those of Germany and Russia) were exposed as deviationists or even as traitors to the cause, and were unmasked by the true word and cast into outer darkness. And since Nikita Khrushchev represented the Soviet Union at the time of the breakup of Chinese-Soviet amity, his name was used as a new label. Khrushchevism became synonymous with revisionism, and for a long time Liu Shao-chi was never attacked by name but as "China's Khrushchev." Mao and his ideologues combat as revisionism or Khrushchevism what for them is the essence of Soviet Communism: that it is bureaucratic, bourgeois, capitalistic, and of course imperialistic (this last especially since the invasion of Czechoslovakia). Mao wants to preserve his country from such a development.

It may be that Mao criticizes the Soviet leadership with such venom because developments in the U.S.S.R. prove to him daily how easy it is for a state that restricts itself to just *one* fully defined and completed revolution to bring forth its own new class system. Mao recognized that the tendency towards a new bureaucratic-bourgeois-state under a capitalistic leadership group—or, to use a Western term, towards a new establishment—was found not only in the U.S.S.R. All around him he saw yesterday's Party and guerrilla leaders getting onto their high horses after the triumph of the revolution, to lord it over the foot soldiers and give orders to everyone around them; they would have to be hauled out of the saddle from time to time if the establishment of a new class of "riders" was to be prevented.

In addition to the theory of contradictions, with its fundamental assumption that when the temper of the nation has arrived at an internal tension it will lead to the next revolutionary thrust, there is also the psychological calculation that leads to the same conclusion: when the misdeeds of the new ruling class grow obvious to the point of public scandal that no one can overlook or contradict, then there need be only the slightest push to bring the masses to the point of clamoring for radical change; and this in turn will lead them to the next revolution. And out of all this, of course, came the realization that "permanent" revolution in the literal sense, that of a revolution without pause, might have as its result an untenable state of permanent crisis. One of the functions of the state, with its need for order and a functioning economy, is therefore to provide the disrupted and shaken country with phases of quiet and order in which to settle down and reflect. I believe that the spring of 1971, while I was in China, constituted one of these phases: the achievements of the Cultural Revolution, and above all of the revolutionary committees, had not been dissipated, but had been integrated into the new order as part of its normal organic functions. It may be wondered whether such an end to the Cultural Revolution had been foreseen as part of an overall strategic plan, or whether the force of circumstance and the power of men like Chou En-lai brought it about so as to avoid total chaos and irreparable economic damage to the country. We do not know the answer, but the facts remain.

One aspect of the Leninist revolution that has seemingly been put aside in the Soviet Union, but which Mao has certainly not given up, is the idea of creating a new man, a man such as never before existed either in the West or in the East, in Russia or in China. So far-reaching a goal cannot be achieved all at once and with one revolution, but demands a series of new revolutions whenever an entrenched or bogged-down culture threatens to block the course of progress. And were this new man to be born, then once again the old laws would surely have to be overthrown, and still newer concepts of mankind would arrive to wipe out the old. So in truth the revolution can never end—and this is really what lends to Mao's person and ideas a fascination that extends far beyond China's borders.

In his own country, however, the unchecked dynamism of Maoist thinking is surely due to its appeal to the masses. Only in them does Mao find the "correct" solutions to his problems, as was already plain from the title of his second article on contradictions. And it is here that one sees with brilliant clarity the most important difference between the political practices of Peking and of Moscow: no Soviet leader since the triumph of the revolution in 1917 has dared address the masses in any but a purely rhetorical fashion. Yet that is precisely what Mao has dared to do: no one who understands the Cultural Revolution would describe it as a "revolution from above." In fact, observers have often been inclined to believe that Mao himself might be swallowed up in the very flames he had kindled. But he seems to have risen without damage, and even with renewed strength from the testing ground of those fires—strengthened even in his already firm belief that he alone is right.

26: No More Hierarchies —Ever Again?

No nation on earth has, or ever had, a social system to equal the hierarchical structure of the Chinese extended family. We use the word "uncle," and we think the Scandinavians' differentiation between father's brother and mother's brother a bit complicated. But consider the Chinese, who have father's elder brother, father's younger brother, husband of father's sister, son of grandfather's elder brother, and then two dozen differentiations on the father's side, ending with the son of great grandfather's sister's granddaughter—a total of 262 grades within the family if you count in all the various aunts, nephews, and nieces. This is the way things were for thousands of years. But it was not some sort of bizarre game. In Confucian China, authority in the extended family or clan, which was the core of Chinese life, was strictly parceled into the slimmest differences of rank, as was the hierarchy of officialdom when it came to matters of state. So every Chinese was part of a system in which he knew who was above him and below him, and just exactly how far above or below. Of all the peoples on earth, the Chinese have the strongest sense of hierarchy.

And now we have China under Mao proposing to set up a system entirely without hierarchies! No wonder that just a few years after the Communist victory over Chiang Kai-shek, and the elimination of the old differences of rank, an entire new system of rank had sprung up. By 1956, seven years after the founding of the People's Republic, there were already thirty grades of officialdom, differentiated by a great deal more than title alone. We have no information about the salaries of the top five ranks, but we know that a sixth-rank

Minister earned 400 yuan a month, and that an employee in the thirtieth rank got 23.50 yuan. The degree of prestige and power of course followed according to rank, but it extended as far as travel accommodations and most certainly lodging: a minister and his deputy lived in villas, members of the next lower ranks lived in apartments with their own kitchen and bathroom, the next rank down had slightly worse accommodations, down to that rung of the ladder where ten families shared the same kitchen and bathroom.[1]

The Chinese feeling for rank is so strong that only a few years after the greatest revolution in history, a brand-new leadership class established a whole new system of rank, including a mandarinate, almost overnight—a system that was not far behind the imperial one in its nuances of differentiation. (The same thing might be said of developments in the Soviet Union since the 1930s.)

When Mao, in 1949, the year of his victory, came out in favor of "a more simplified administration" (see the Little Red Book, Chapter X), no one had yet heard of Parkinson's Law. And it would be almost two decades before the appearance of Anthony Downs' *Inside Bureaucracy,* with its law concerning the growth of conservatism: All organizations, as they grow older, tend to grow more conservative, unless they go through a period of very rapid growth or inner turnover.

Mao knew the dangers that threatened his goal of a nonbureaucratic society.

It was what he understood of Chinese tradition, to say nothing of his own experiences with cadres, that impelled Mao to fight against the bureaucratization of his own new class of leaders. "The core of the bourgeois world outlook is self-interest. It finds its most concentrated and glaring expression in a cadre's desire to become an official." [2]

Mao set himself the gigantic task of demolishing this entire point of view. (When I use the name Mao here, I do not mean it as a shorthand symbol for an entire group of leaders, as we say "the Kremlin" or "the White House"—I mean Mao personally, for I

[1] Doak Barnett, *Cadres, Bureaucracy and Political Power in Communist China* (New York, 1967).
[2] *Peking Review,* 1968, #45.

have come to the conclusion that essentially it is this one man who makes and executes such basic decisions.)

This demolition of categories in rank was to be accomplished by the Hsiafang, the "sending down" of officials and intellectuals to do manual labor, and by the two strongest revolutionary thrusts to date: the Great Leap Forward and the Cultural Revolution. To the West, the idea of setting up two million "backyard furnaces" throughout China, reported in the fall of 1958—thus, according to Chinese figures, putting sixty million people to work producing steel—sounded absurd. But certainly there was more behind the idea than the intention of producing primitive steel or of spiting the Soviet Union, which had stopped its deliveries of giant new furnaces. Mao also wanted to propagate the idea of small decentralized industries scattered throughout the entire country. And he especially wanted to prove to the entire population that it is possible to achieve the same result through mass initiative without institutionalized leadership, without huge plants and hierarchies encompassing everyone from the director to the man who collects the garbage. The endeavor lasted only a few months and the steel produced was inferior, but that is another matter altogether.

There can be no doubt that the Cultural Revolution was first of all a blow against hierarchy and hierarchical thinking. The first section of this book describes many instances of the campaign, at once ideological and psychological, against such attitudes—for example, in the Seventh of May School for cadres, not to mention the diminished importance, or one might even say the invisibility, of categories of rank in everyday work.

One clear impression remains fixed in my mind: the lack, in Chinese offices, of the mountainous reams of paper that are so typical of every Soviet government office. The Communist nations seem to have become "paperwork pyramids." All personal initiative is stifled, and the bureaucratic mind dominates the scene. There is not a kolkhoz, a factory, or a school in the U.S.S.R. where you don't clearly feel the leadership and control from above: the constricting sense that it is a mere cog in a centrally controlled machine. In China, on the other hand, the maxim calling for decentralization has been translated into fact; of course everyone loves Chairman Mao and the socialist fatherland, but Peking is far away and in the meantime what one lives and works for is Tachai or the tea brigade or the district of the Morning Sun. Everywhere you feel the surge of unleashed vitality and local initiative, virtually unhampered by centralized interference.

People everywhere take great pains to demonstrate to a foreign visitor that the system works—not really for political reasons, but out of justified pride in the collective achievements of the brigade, the factory, or the school. And it is my impression that the system in fact does work. One demonstration of this, as good as any, is that throughout my entire journey there were no foulups, whether in lodgings or travel accommodations or the schedule of my visit. On the other hand, how much significance can be attached to the impressions of one brief visit and to meetings with, say, three hundred people out of seven hundred fifty million? It is clearly impossible for a short-term visitor to speak with confidence about the effectiveness and stability of this new economy and this new state. All one can do is simply to round out one's own information and observation with facts from other sources.

All things considered, I think I can say with perfect candor, that the joy the Chinese appear to derive from their work and their life, the élan generated by achievements "by one's own strength," which I saw everywhere I went, were not a matter of simply following orders or of a show put on for the foreign visitor. It is the pleasure of the ordinary man at his everyday occupation, carrying out his simple tasks, and in the amazing discovery that he can do it without officials, chief engineers, head bookkeepers, and managing directors. Just how long this élan will carry him cannot be judged today, but only after a few years have passed.

A critical examination establishes, furthermore, that the Cultural Revolution has indeed produced new organizational forms that serve to foster continuity of development and social movement, as well as to prevent "the formation of new hierarchical structures." According to one of its basic documents, the famous Sixteen Points of August 8, 1966, which is attributed to Mao, these forms are to be set up after the model of the Paris Commune. What this means, according to Marxist and Maoist concepts, is well known: leaders are to be elected directly by the people, and they can be unseated by the people at any time; also, their pay must not be higher than that of the people they represent.

One essential condition for the functioning of this model is the widely applicable interchangeability of leaders. This Marx himself had recognized, and it is implicit in Lenin's well-known dictum that every cook must be able to run the state. That in China this, once again, is no mere precept set down on paper, was proved to me repeatedly at a certain point in almost every conversation. It would seem, someone would always be explaining to me how the basic principle of interchangeability had actually been applied, and would be applied still more often—how many chairmen of revolutionary committees, how many factory directors, chiefs of design departments, school principles or university presidents had been, only a short time before, ordinary workmen, employees, or just teachers or professors, and had risen to posts of leadership only through the process of the Cultural Revolution.

A further safety valve is the "three in one principle," which has been set forth in various directives. According to that principle, revolutionary committees must include three elements—i.e., representatives of the army, the cadres, and the masses. The last Party constitution, in 1969, established yet another "three in one" principle: that Party committees must consist of representatives of the older, middle, and younger generations. Even construction offices are to be made up of experienced workers, new technicians, and old engineers. All this is intended to prevent the rise of a "new [upper] class."

In 1967 and 1968, when revolutionary committees on all levels were being formed in one province after another, many observers identified them as the new Apparat for running the country, the framework of a new hierarchy. But then, in April, 1969, the Ninth Party Congress was held with enormous fanfare, and the reconstruction of the Party was announced. Every organization I visited— village brigade, factory, school, city district, hospital, or whatever— *already* had its Party organ and *still* had its revolutionary committee. Does this indicate a dualism of two parallel organizations? . . .

The first chapter of the new constitution describes the Party as "the core of leadership of the Chinese people," and states clearly that "the relation between the Party committee and the revolutionary committee is like that between leaders and led." [3]

I verified a number of points by asking the same questions again and again, and especially as a result of my conversations in the Morning Sun quarter, I arrived at the following conclusions: the purified and rejuvenated Party (as described in Article Twelve, "Shed the Old and Take up the New") is in fact to be reinstated as the "core of leadership." The revolutionary committees, which until the restructuring of the Party had carried out a double function, as at once the "core of leadership" (since there was no other) and administrative executor, in the future would concentrate on the latter.

Whenever I asked the chairman of a revolutionary committee who was the secretary of the Party committee, the answer was always, "I am." The answer was the same when I asked the same question of his deputies; it was only when I got down to the ordinary members of the revolutionary committees and of the Party committees that this unity of adherence broke down.

These structures cannot be compared with those of the U.S.S.R., because, in the first place (apart from the very highest levels) Party secretaries are not simultaneously heads of administrative offices, and also because the military element, which is so important in the Chinese revolutionary committees, is not obligatory in the Russian Soviet, i.e., the administrative office. In the Soviet Union there is little tension between the Soviet and the Party committee, because the Party committee is from the outset so very much more powerful; in China, on the other hand, the revolutionary committees are strong because among their members they must include military men, who cannot be pushed around by the Party committee.

Whether tensions between the revolutionary committees and the Party committees can be avoided under these circumstances—or whether Mao finds these tensions desirable in order to prevent the formation of new hierarchies in both institutions—cannot be discerned by a short-term visitor. And in any event, such a visitor would never be permitted to observe any such tensions.

Mao, in his persistent war against bureaucracy, is aware that he

[3] *Peking Review,* 1970, #1.

has a great reservoir of confidence among the peasants that goes back to the time of the civil war. As early as the directive of October 1, 1943, concerning the attitude of the cadres vis-à-vis the peasants in the areas that were governed at the time by the Red Army, he warned against the example of the Chiang Kai-shek regime, which tried to extract as much food as possible from the peasants "instead of helping the masses with all their might to develop their own means of production." Mao has adhered to his basic principle of burdening the peasants with relatively few taxes. They are encouraged to be as self-reliant as possible, to build their own roads, schools, and hospitals. This policy serves the double function of increasing the peasants' eagerness to achieve and of unburdening the administrative machinery, which once again is reduced rather than allowed to expand.

This spirit and these methods might be capable of curbing or at least holding down hierarchical attitudes and practices. Serious opposition on the part of the disenfranchised bureaucracy is hardly to be feared; the cadres still feel deep in their bones the humiliating experiences of the Cultural Revolution, to say nothing of their vivid memories of their stay in one of the Seventh of May schools. So one may assume that the old system of rank will not have as quick a resurgence as it did after 1949.

Or at least not among the civilians. One of the gaps in this book is that I have so little to say about the army. Knowing how sensitive great powers are when it comes to the military or to military questions, I had decided from the very beginning to omit this entire sector from my field of observation. Looking back on this decision, I believe it was the right one.

Of course, I saw a great many uniforms at the table of honor in the Great Hall of the People; I saw soldiers sitting on the revolutionary committees in the framework of the "three in one alliance"; I saw (infrequently) columns of marching soldiers and (often) officers in rumpled cotton uniforms, without insignia of rank, riding in the "soft cars" of trains. But I never asked a question that could possibly pertain in any way to a fighting army.

Is the army (insignia or no insignia) the only sector to have kept its hierarchy intact? Can it be that Mao is able to afford the extreme decentralization in the economic and administrative sectors for the reason that Lin Piao has at his disposal a highly centralized and strictly hierarchical army, to function as a strong backbone or even as a big stick? Which is the true character of the Chinese army— Mao's drive towards equality, towards grass-roots initiative, or its opposite, the drive towards order and discipline that is the inborn tendency of every army? Does Lin Piao (like Liu Shao-chi before him) permit the ageing helmsman to utter messianic "last directives" about a new society free of all hierarchy while he himself, with all power concentrated in his hands, has as his sole aim the systematic infiltration of the military, first onto the revolutionary committees, and then into the Party committees, to pave the way for a military state? And *is* Lin Piao in control of the army? I shall not venture to speculate. The entire question in fact depends on Lin Piao, the most enigmatic and least discussed of all highly placed persons in today's China.

I must admit that my imagination is insufficient for me to entertain the possibility of a society that could continue indefinitely to plow under all its elites and hierarchies every ten years in a series of revolutions, and to start again every time with a clean slate. My curiosity about how China will develop in this domain through the years ahead is one of my reasons for wanting to believe the Indian soothsayer who told me I would be still junketing about the globe in 1990.

27: The Consumer Society
—Some Day?

There was no comprehension of, or even, among the people with whom I talked in China, any interest in the rebellion of Western youth against the consumer society. One of those with whom I spoke, a man with a keen interest in world Communism, did show an interest in the youth theme, but interpreted student unrest as a minor sideshow of the class struggle among the working people, and expressed a cheerful conviction that for the students it was simply a matter of the classic aims of the worker movement—that is, higher wages, better working conditions, and the remote goal of the dictatorship of the proletariat. Quite naturally, he saw the events in Paris of May, 1968 exactly as they had been portrayed in Chinese news reports—as the inevitable uprising of the working class in which a few students also took part. I could not get it into his head that the young people in America, Japan, or Germany, and in many other countries, were concerned with other things entirely. Hippie sex, hash, and rock were all entirely unknown to him and, when I tried to explain, entirely incomprehensible.

Chinese leaders are much more concerned with the Soviet example than they are with the West. And their criticism of the Soviet Union is largely directed at the consumer mentality of the society there; Khrushchev's goulash Communism is no longer Communism at all, so far as they are concerned. They see as the lesson of the Soviet Union that once a socialist government sets out to meet or even to stimulate the population's desire for consumer goods, it is the beginning of the end for Communism. It is no accident that Liu Shao-chi, for his readiness to use material incentives as a way of getting people to work harder, was damned not as China's Nixon but as China's Khrushchev.

Does this amount to a beggars' Communism, as Khrushchev once sarcastically suggested—a state of poverty at the subsistence level elevated into a principle, with poverty defined as virtue so as to prevent any dangerous striving for consumer goods from raising its head? There is really no reason to ascribe to so thoroughgoing a Communist as Mao any such deviation from an ideology that aims at the good life for all. But a diagnosis positing a time-scheme would be dialectically possible. It would go like this: up until now, human nature has been corrupted by an emphasis on consumption and personal comforts, and we must thus first of all set about creating a new man who can no longer be corrupted in this fashion. As soon as that man has come into being, prosperity with its temptations ceases to be dangerous.

When it will be the judgment of Mao that this moment has arrived we do not know. He has always spoken of long periods of time. The Cultural Revolution of 1966 to 1968 can be assessed as an instrument in a continuing educational process; the people were tested and have been "tempered" (a favorite word among Maoists) by its fires. Other events of this sort may be in store.

It may be said, at any rate, that so far as transportation is concerned, China is still in the age of the bicycle. This was borne out by the conversation about bicycle motors in the Shanghai department store. Is it possible that China is being held down to this level by the simple expedient of cutting off the sale of gas? That bicycle motor would have been within the reach of many; it cost about as much as a television receiver, which can be bought by anyone at any department store or specialty shop (and the authorities would in no way hinder the purchase, snice the purchaser is also buying his share of propaganda at the same time). Can it be, perhaps, that the little motor would increase its owner's opportunities so enormously, as compared with the man on an ordinary bicycle, as to be looked on as a first step away from an egalitarian society and toward the setting up of status symbols?

Mao has said, or so the story goes, that men on horseback are undesirable since they immediately take on the attitudes of a cavalier (in the root meaning of the word) toward pedestrians. Would it perhaps be the same with a man who had a motor on his bicycle— that he might lord it over the people as the intellectuals and cadres once did? Very well, then—he would simply be toppled from his gas-eating high horse when the next Cultural Revolution came round. So what would be the risk of opening up the gasoline spigot just a little?

It is easy to see the lengths to which a foreign observer may be carried by speculation when he is denied all reliable information about economic policies and planning. But if he has in his baggage, as I do, not only statistics—which can lie—but experience at first hand of how China's elder brother, the Soviet Union (no matter how thoroughly disliked at the moment) went from a production economy to a consumer economy, then he must be permitted the hypothesis that China, too, may one day take a similar path.

It is Mao's determination to anchor his thought and teaching as deeply as he can in his people while he is still alive. His followers will not have an easy time of it. Each one of them will be a descendant and thus weaker than the great founder; he will, in turn, be obliged to govern more harshly and will therefore provoke unfriendly comparison with the good old days, the righteous days of Chairman Mao. If he then tries to curry favor with the people by making concessions in the realm of material things, he will run the risk of being called a "Chinese Khrushchev." Mao knows all this perfectly well.

28: " . . . to each according to his needs . . . "

Peking accuses Moscow of having betrayed the people. By this is meant that the "Soviet Revisionists," in the interests of a few "bureaucratic monopoly capitalists," have kept the people in a condition of inequality and exploitation. This is proved, according to Peking, by the failure of the Soviets, after the victory of the proletariat and the downfall of capitalism in Russia, to do away with a pay system based on "each according to his work"—which was supposed to be no more than a transitional phase of the wage system, but that in fact turned into a permanent condition. As Marx formulated it in his *Critique of the Gotha Program* (1875), the principle of "from each according to his ability, to each according to his *needs,*" was to be the ultimate aim. And as Marx had defined it, the precondition for such a transition from "socialism" (with piece-rate pay) to "communism" (with payment according to need) would occur "when productive forces have risen and all the springs of cooperative wealth flow profusely"—in other words, when the production of goods reached a level at which the needs of every citizen could be met.

In the 1930s, the Soviet Union was far from having reached this precondition. (Of course Marx had envisaged his revolution as taking place in highly industrialized nations, not in those that were underdeveloped as Russia was at that time.) So in 1931 Stalin came to the conclusion that the necessary increase in production could be achieved within a foreseeable future only with the help of "material incentives." Accordingly, he introduced a system of pay increases and premiums for superior achievement, which led to great differences in income—and thus in standards of living—among Soviet citizens. And thus the transition to communism was pushed into the future—to the year 1980 by Khrushchev, whose successors no longer even mention a date. On the one hand, the state appropriated an increasing portion of the social product for its own uses (armaments and the space race), and on the other hand the "needs" of the individual grew beyond the "reasonable limits" foreseen by the Soviet ideologues. (No society, of course, can fulfill *all* the people's wishes, including those that are unreasonable.) No one knows when production will have caught up with this rise in "needs" and expectations. So the Soviet Union is due to remain a land of wages according to work actually performed, and thus of inequality, for a long time to come.

Mao has observed these developments with his own eyes: he went to Moscow twice, once in 1950 and again in 1957. So far as his own country is concerned, he has shown by his actions that he is unwilling to tolerate either inequality or a delay in the transition to communism. He must have realized that the goal of communism would never be reached by following in the footsteps of the Soviet Union. There, every rise in production that came about must lead to a rise in demand and thus a further emphasis on inequality—in other words, it would lead further and further away from true communism.

The way out of this vicious circle is to place a clear limitation on "reasonable need." To fill even a "reasonable" demand, China would need an enormous increase in the production of consumer goods, which in turn could be brought about only by monetary rewards for labor performed. This would be difficult if, for example, "reasonable need" encompassed one car for every family; we know the far-reaching consequences of total motorization for the economy of a country, all the way from the building of highway systems to changes in the internal structure of cities to gas stations and repair shops. Filling "reasonable needs" would be quite feasible, on the other hand, if people were satisfied with a bicycle, a roof over their heads, clothing suited to the climate, and enough food for productive work. If this were to be the standard—which could be maintained on an average salary of 60 yuan in the city and 30 yuan in a village—then the supply of consumer goods as it now stands would be sufficient. The mass of the people, at least in the villages, seem to find this standard "reasonable." The Chinese are still far away from the much-discussed "revolution of rising expectations": they live like troops in a country at war, where all endure the same deprivations, and thus find them easier to bear. They are a people who do not see a privileged "new class" above them, they're all in the same boat.

In China there are no "rising expectations" such as are spurred by social ambition, by what in America amounts to "keeping up with the Joneses." If the Joneses have two cars, then the Smiths must have two cars. Since the Changs, far from owning two cars or even one, have only a bicycle, the Wangs don't need a car either, but will also be satisfied with owning a bicycle—a thing they can pay for after saving for a few months.

This modest and relatively tension-free social standard would not survive a rise in wages, and certainly not a difference in wage scales as large as the one inevitably brought about by the Russian system. In China at the time of my visit, according to the information I was able to gather, the differences in pay range from a village minimum of 20 yuan to a maximum of 100 yuan in the cities. (The few incomes that exceed this level are apparently in the process of dying out along with their recipients.) But even this relatively slight difference cannot be truly described as a system of reward for achievement. There is simply no connection between achievement and salary as in the Russian premium system: I was assured of this over and over again. It is simply taken for granted that each person is living up to his maximum achievement, and so any attempt to measure the work of hundreds of millions of peasants every day and to reward them individually would be a waste of time.

Peking has not (or not yet?) decided on the drastic measure of simply paying every working person the same amount; why, I don't know.

My description of Tachai contains a detailed account of the point system for labor on the land. In industry every worker, regardless of the kind of job he has, belongs to one of eight pay categories; and here the differences are greater than they are in the village. I discovered that in this domain the same work is not always compensated at the same rate; at various factories in various parts of the country, the categories are set differently, so that, for example, work that falls into category seven in one place might fall into category four in another. Also, the same categories are paid at varying rates in different factories and different parts of the country: category six might be compensated at 65 yuan a month in one place and at 50 in another. It was explained to me that in fact different branches of industry in various parts of the country had different pay scales, though the variations were slight. I was assured, however, that there were new directives establishing an identical pay system throughout the country. I was not able to look at these directives. (The old ones had been superseded by the Cultural Revolution—and so, unfortunately, had Charles Hoffmann's excellent study, *Work Incentive Practices and Policies in the People's Republic of China, 1953–1965.*[1])

It is true that point systems, and thus pay categories, are set everywhere according to the same three criteria: ability (for peasants, this is based first of all on manual strength; among industrial workers, the basis is professional qualifications), experience, and "consciousness." What this third category means in practice was, as the reader will recall, a question I asked at every opportunity, and the answers were always a bit vague. Ideally, the worker with the proper consciousness is a kind of "willing ox" who has no private wishes or psychological complications, and who works to the limit of his strength "for Chairman Mao and our socialist fatherland." The number of Mao portraits over his bed and the number of Mao quotations he uses when he talks are surely not unimportant in establishing the degree of his consciousness; but in fact, since the answers I got pertaining to "consciousness" and the possibility of its being measured in connection with earnings were so unconcrete, I suspect that the first two factors are what mainly enter into the

[1] Albany, New York, 1967.

evaluation. As the Tachai experience shows, consciousness is generally taken for granted.

Whenever I asked whether some defect in a person's socialist consciousness led automatically to a cut in salary, I was emphatically told that there were no such instances. It is difficult for me to believe this. Even the new constitution of the Party, an elite organization, provides (in Article Four, one of the longest) an endless catalogue of punishments for breaches of discipline, apathy, non-repentance, degeneration, and similar crimes.

Furthermore, I discovered that there were incomes above the highest salary categories. Whenever I badgered people with questions about this, the invariable answer was that these were temporary situations, that the people involved had been paid these salaries before and it was a matter of not wanting to take them away.

I wonder, also, whether it will be possible to prevent an increase in the striving after material possessions and, in the long run, a desire to be paid according to some scale of achievement. There are signs even today of opposition to Mao's egalitarian ideas. No Chinese was able to give me a convincing reason why a new edition of the Little Red Book that appeared in 1967 (with excerpts from five articles by Mao) included one of Mao's earliest works, dating to December, 1929, "On Correcting Mistaken Ideas in the Party." At that time Mao directed sharp words against "extreme egalitarianism"—in this he was even a year and a half ahead of Stalin—that were not at all in keeping with the ideas of the Cultural Revolution an its striving toward equality. In 1929 he wrote that it was not to be considered damaging to the idea of equality that an officer was on horseback, or that a few "received more" in special situations; even under socialism, as he explained it then, goods had to be distributed according to the principle of "to each according to his work."

It seems likely that those in China who regard Mao's forced march toward communism as a mistake, whoever they may be, are not inactive. To use Mao's own phrase "The battle of opposites goes on without interruption."

29: The Cult of Chairman Mao —Why and for How Long?

In airports all over the world, the waiting rooms are arranged so that whenever possible, travelers and visitors can look at the arriving and departing planes. Not so in Shanghai. Here the benches are placed with their backs to the landing field, so as to face a portrait of Mao Tse-tung.

This is one of countless, often highly original manifestations of the cult of Mao in China. Here a much quoted statement by the Chairman, from an article dealing with education, is apt: "We must resolutely carry out the instructions of Chairman Mao and his proletarian policies whether we understand them or whether for the time being we do not yet understand them." Never has a man been so devotedly, uncritically, and enthusiastically honored during his lifetime as Chairman Mao is today. Why?

According to the best knowledge available, a bitter struggle took place during the years from 1958 to 1966 between the "two ways" —that is, between the followers of Mao Tse-tung and of Liu Shao-chi. Many, in fact most, of the details of this conflict are lacking; we know only that Mao's personal comeback was dramatized to the nation by his public long-distance swim down the Yangtze in July, 1966, after which he reassumed a predominant role in China's political life. So for his followers Mao is not simply a political leader (since 1958 he has held only the office of Party Chairman, which means that he holds the same position as Brezhnev in Moscow), but he is also the embodiment of their will to build a great and united new China.

Some people have wondered about who invented and staged the grandiose Mao cult. There are those who believe it was Tao Chu, who late in June of 1966 became head of the Central Committee's propaganda section—even though he fell into disfavor before the end of the year. But no one really knows. What we do know is simply that the Mao cult is one of the greatest triumphs of publicity in a publicity-conscious century: within a very few months in 1966, Mao had been raised to such a height that any opposition could be destroyed simply by the use of his name.

The true instrument of the cult of Mao during the last few years has been the army. At a time when the Chairman's stock was low, after the failure of the Great Leap Forward, Lin Piao, as the newly appointed Defense. Minister, remained steadfastly at his side. Lin Piao trained the army in Mao's name and spirit. In 1963, long before the cult spread throughout the land, Lin told the soldiers, "Be good fighters for Chairman Mao"; he had the Little Red Book especially printed for soldiers, exhorting them in an epigraph, "Study Chairman Mao's writings, follow his teachings, and act according to his instructions." The foreword to the second edition begins, "Comrade Mao Tse-tung is the greatest Marxist-Leninist of our era." The army newspaper for June 7, 1966, carried a lead article describing Mao as the "microscope and telescope" of the revolution, praising him thirty-seven times, and finally calling him the "touchstone" for distinguishing between revolution and counter-revolution.

Then, in November of 1967, Lin Piao brushed a few words from the well-known "Song of the Helmsman" onto a sheet of paper, had them printed in facsimile by the millions and distributed throughout the land—with the result that today the idea of the helmsman and of Chairman Mao are inextricable if not identical. Whatever his real intent may have been, no one man has done more for the cult of the Chairman than Lin Piao.

The one authentic interpretation of the cult, by Mao himself, was made on December 18, 1970, in a conversation with his old friend, the American journalist Edgar Snow. According to Snow, who had last seen him in 1965, Mao told him that five years earlier—that is, before the Cultural Revolution—"a great deal of power" in China had no longer been in his hands. So at that time the cult of personality became necessary "in order to stimulate the masses to dismantle the anti-Mao Party bureaucracy."

Mao went on that "of course the personality cult had been overdone. Today, things were different. It was hard, the Chairman said, to overcome the habits of three thousand years of emperor-worshiping tradition. The so-called 'Four Greats'—those epithets applied to Mao himself: 'Great Teacher, Great Leader, Great Supreme Commander, Great Helmsman'—what a nuisance. They would all be eliminated sooner or later."

Snow then reminded Mao of the decision by the Central Committee in the year 1949, reportedly at Mao's suggestion, to forbid the naming of cities, streets, and squares after people. To this Mao replied: "Yes, . . . they had avoided that; but other forms of worship had emerged. There were so many slogans. Pictures and plaster statues. The Red Guard had insisted that if you didn't have those things around, you were being anti-Mao. In the past few years there had been need for some personality cult. Now there was no such need and there should be a cooling down."

What Mao says here about the rise of the cult of personality may be correct. He might have added that it is easier to inspire people to great, self-denying efforts, and to weld them into a nation, if they are given the sense of being led by a unique and infallible personality, instead of by some anonymous and frequently criticized Central Committee. So it would not seem exactly correct to regard Mao as no more than the reluctant object of a cult that had been forced upon him. The "four great" attributes mentioned by Snow were invented in 1966 by a man who had been close to Mao for many years, Chen Po-ta.[1]

In the spring of 1971 I saw no sign of the toning down of the cult of personality that Mao spoke of wishing would come about. I would even venture to say that the Mao cult will reach its zenith only *after* Mao; for in the ensuing struggle, his heirs will all travel under his banner, and it must be under his shadow that the quarrel for the succession will be resolved. Moreover, as Mao so accurately observed to Snow, one thing that will always exist is "the desire to be worshiped and the desire to worship."

But, it may well be asked, how can a revolution be directed against an establishment in power when that very revolution is directed by the head of that very establishment? The only possible answer must be that his presence is exalted so far above all others that it can no longer be affected by internal conflicts. This was formerly the position in China of the Son of Heaven, the Emperor

[1] Cheng Chu-yuan, *Orbis,* 1968.

himself. But in those times the Emperor remained unreachably remote, whereas Chairman Mao is omnipresent—both in image and in word, the latter as near at hand as one's own pocket. But of course he is not someone who can be addressed as an ordinary person.

It is surely no coincidence that for many years now the Chairman's voice has rarely been heard: the texts of his proclamations are read aloud by Lin Piao, while the Chairman himself stands quietly looking on—"like a bronze emperor," to use the words of Malraux—from high up on the Gate of Heavenly Peace.

30: What Do They Really Think?

What do the Chinese *really* think of Mao?

This is the question I have been asked most often since my return, and it is the one I feel least capable of answering.

We are informed daily about what Americans or Germans think by means of various public opinion polls; even the Soviet Union is beginning to have its share of these. But in China there is nothing comparable. The foreign visitor who would attempt to discern the thoughts and feelings of its people would have even a modest chance to do so only if he were able to move among them freely and talk with them as he wished. The man of the Far East has been taught by life, to a degree unknown to the European or American, not to wear his thoughts or feelings on his face or to betray them with his tongue.

That today's China does not run entirely on socialist battle cries, as press and radio, film and stage productions would have you believe, is a thing the foreigner will be able to discover for himself. But matters become a bit more complicated when an individual is encountered face to face. When a distinguished surgeon, with the Little Red Book in his hand, tells me that he has accomplished his extraordinary successes only through the help of his Mao studies; or when the patients whose severed limbs he has rejoined hold up their own Little Red Books as though they were so many miracle-working wands to which they owe their cure; when intellectuals, yet again with Little Red Book in hand, report to me on how they saw the light while in the midst of cleaning latrines—all without the least flicker of irony—what am I to make of it all? Am I to write off the whole thing as lies, tricks, and ham acting? Am I to assume that they are actually thinking, "So here's another credulous foreigner for whom we've got to put on our act!" Or are they really thinking, as their attitudes seem to indicate, "Here we have an opportunity to show a skeptical foreigner the strength of our love for Chairman Mao, and that we are on the road to a better breed of mankind"? Once again, I do not know what the answer is.

An anecdote used to be told in the Soviet Union during the 1930s of a peasant who was being shown through Radio Moscow along with a group of other visitors. "Can people outside Russia really hear the things that are being said here?" he wanted to know, and was told that they could. "You mean people all over the whole world?" he asked, and again the answer was yes. Then could he possibly try it out, and say something himself? After some discussion he was told that yes, he would be allowed to say one word. So he stepped up to the microphone and said: "Help!"

At any time during my travels, someone might have called out that word to me, or might have expressed it somehow, through some gesture of desperation, if he had been desperate enough. It would have been very risky, but on the other hand he would have been sure that such a call for help, uttered in the presence of a writer from abroad, would be heard around the world.

I can only say that if such a person exists, I did not meet him. During my travels I met with nothing but loyal devotion to Chairman Mao and his ideas. There was never an instant, never the least flicker of an eyelid that might be interpreted to mean, "I hope you understand this is all play-acting." But even this, after all, means very little; so it becomes necessary to supplement the narrow range of first-hand experience with general observations and reflection.

We must assume that the largest proportion of believing Maoists are to be found among the young. For the past five years these children and young people have heard nothing but paeans of praise to the great leader and incomparable helmsman. For those who doubt the mesmerizing effect of all this, it should be enough to recall examples elsewhere of the same phenomenon that have been experienced in the West in our time.

The people in the countryside who were hurt by the revolution —the onetime landlords and rich peasants—among whom one might expect to find opponents of the regime (however powerless), were never great in number, and of course even these must be gradually dying out. The great mass of peasants certainly have no reason to foment opposition to Mao, since their material conditions have greatly improved. There have been no official statistics in China since the time of the Great Leap Forward. But a visitor can see with his own eyes that new terraces for grain of every sort, and countless well-planned irrigation projects, are everywhere. If one is to believe the figures given by individual communes and brigades concerning their yearly production, it may be assumed that agrarian production has kept pace with increased population.

True, the income of the individual peasant, his daily and monthly wage, has not increased. But his enormous willingness to work has brought such a decided rise in the communal benefits of his labor as to produce in turn a steady increase in the wealth of the village as a whole. A greater area under cultivation; better varieties of grain; a higher yield per acre; above all, the possibilities of better irrigation—more pigs, more fruit trees, new houses, a school, their own store—these are all visible effects of their success, and every member of the brigade is proud of them and finds his life improved by them. It means very little to him if his savings account shows a rather low figure—especially since in the past he had none at all.

This visible rise in the standard of living is certainly more evident to the peasant in his working conditions and his comforts in the village than to the man in the city, who is less intimately affected by the general rise in the standard of living, or by the construction of new suburbs. But most important of all for the peasant is seeing that what is earned by the village stays there. In the Soviet Union, industrialization was accomplished at the expense of the peasant, whereas Mao, on the contrary, from the very beginning refrained from skimming off the cream of agricultural production in favor of industry. There is also an important psychological factor: the effect on the new class consciousness of a propaganda that deliberately emphasizes and honors the "poor and lower middle peasants" (a cumbersome phrase that translates the original term exactly).

It is much harder to say anything about the state of mind of the workers. Mao is a father to the entire nation, but he has remained above all a father to the peasants; whether or not the worker feels close to him in the same way is a thing I cannot be sure about. The close personal contact found among villagers is missing, of course, from any large industrial plant, and there is not the same fulfillment in work that contributes to a life experienced in common and elevates spirits with a sense of equality. That the romantic excitement and high drama of reconstruction, of which the worker is reminded all day long over the loudspeakers, have stirred his emotions, there can be no doubt. But here again there is a difference between him and his Soviet equivalent —at least if you compare his situation with the Soviet worker's during the first Five Year Plan—because he cannot feel that he occupies first place in his society and in his country. And even an intense belief in progress cannot be an equal spur toward integration, given China's much more modest degree of technological development.

I can say nothing at first hand concerning the army's loyalty to Mao, since I had no contact with soldiers and made no attempt to visit any military installation. I can only testify to the fact that the army appears to be in a very strong position and to enjoy great prestige. Soldiers occupy countless positions of importance, and there is a whole gallery of military heroes who are constantly being glorified in posters, newspaper articles, brochures, comic books, films, and plays; with very few exceptions they are all men risen from the ranks—thus making it clear to all that here is the ideal, the norm, of the new man.

It is certain that never in the long history of China has the common soldier been held in such esteem as during the last few years. Whenever I was introduced to "a comrade of the People's

Liberation Army" the tone of respect was clear and unmistakable.

The people whose prestige was most severely affected by the Cultural Revolution were the cadres—in short, bureaucrats of all kinds, intellectuals, and students. It is among them that skepticism and opposition are most likely to be found. Of those who are still in their twenties today, surely not all will have forgotten the great days when by the millions, with their Little Red Books in their hands, they were permitted to "make revolution"—and likewise what followed, beginning in 1967, when they were hauled out of the streets and finally sent, again by the millions, "down into the villages and up into the mountains." I had written about them in 1969 in a monograph, *Peking and the New Left.* On my trip two years later, I met none of them; whenever I asked, in the villages and the countryside, whether there were any "sent-down" city youth here, the answer was always no.

I suspect that whatever opposition exists is strongest, relatively speaking, among the intellectuals in their middle and later years. They, at any rate, have suffered most from the destruction of Chinese intellectual life since the mid-1950s. In the 1940s the greater part of the Chinese intelligentsia had believed in Mao Tse-tung, not Chiang Kai-shek. It is hard to imagine that the survivors can have forgotten the tragedy that overtook them.

I have no way of knowing whether all the people I saw waving the Litle Red Book also believe in its contents. And I have only one impeccable source on which to base my skepticism—Mao himself. In the previously quoted conversation with Edgar Snow, on December 18, 1970, Mao divided the people "who clamor for Mao" into three categories: the "sincere people," the conformers ("those who drift with the tide"), and the hypocrites. Mao offered no statistics for any of these groups—so how can I?

31: Are They Happy?

"Are the Russians happy?" is the question I was once asked after any lecture on the Soviet Union. Now I find myself continually being asked the same thing about China. I cannot venture a simple answer, but I can share my thoughts on the subject.

Is affluence the same as happiness? A few years ago, when the Germans had worked their way out of the rubble and began to enjoy a better life, many of them would have said yes to that question. But if this were so, the Germans—and still more, the Americans—would of necessity be the happiest nations in history. But they are not. And most particularly this is true of their youth, part of whom—and not the worst part—are turning away in disgust from the affluence of our consumer society, and are choosing, to the incredulity of their elders, poverty and risk in preference to it.

If happiness were synonymous with comfort and affluence, the Chinese would necessarily be among the unhappiest people in the word. But this has never been my impression—and never less so than in 1971, when I found them more than ever full of optimism, pride in their work and joie de vivre. How could it be otherwise? The wise men of both East and West have always believed and taught that the meaning of life and of happiness are found as one becomes absorbed in a great task, a great mission, and in a willingness to lose oneself within a force and power that carry one beyond one's separate existence.

Mao recognized and used this basic need for involvement when he spoke of man's desire "to worship"; and when he permitted to develop a cult of personality such as the world has never seen before. To seek happiness in solitary ecstasy has always been for the very few. The individual has always found life easier in the midst of a community by which he is carried, as by the force of a great stream, toward some acknowledged goal. To belong to a community, to lose oneself in it, be engulfed and carried by it, tends to give the individual a sense of security and happiness. And this sense can be heightened to a genuine selflessness that comes with a sense of being at one with the whole. In Confucian China the community was the clan, the extended family, for which one labored and which in turn took care of its own. In other times that community could be found in the secret societies, which had so strong an influence on Chinese history. And today it is "our socialist fatherland" (not the Party, which is recovering only by degrees from its humbling during the Cultural Revolution.)

People in a technological age are likely to use technical concepts. The first of many diaries attributed to the "heroes of socialism" is that of Lei Feng, whom Mao singled out by saying, "Learn from Comrade Lei Feng." The diary includes these words: "A house is made of bricks and mortar. We ourselves must be those bricks and that mortar."

Here is a Chinese poem written in the 1960s:

I would like to be a tiny bolt,
So they can put me where they want and bolt me in tightly;
Whether on the arm of a powerful crane
Or in the simplest wheel.

Put me in place and bolt me tightly.
There I shall stay firm, with my heart at rest.
Perhaps people will not know I exist.
But I know that to vibrate in the throb of a great machine
Is the life of a very small bolt.

Although I cannot be a machine all by myself,
Although I can do nothing all by myself,
Even so, I can serve my country and the people.
I know that if I stay in the background I shall soon
Be nothing but a piece of rusty metal.

I would like to be a tiny bolt
So that they can put me where I'm needed and bolt me in tightly.
I shall be happy, and in the choir of heroes
I shall tremble to hear my own exultant voice.

Never in all history has there been a more awesome machine than this nation made up of three quarters of a billion souls. It is quite possible that the consciousness of being a very small bolt in this imposing machine brings about a feeling of happiness in the face of which all else loses its importance—the hard beds, the unheated schoolrooms, the crushing burden of labor, the unending —and surely often dull—study of the works of Mao. Of course, this can be so only for someone who is happy to be a very small bolt . . .

For the rest, there is possibly another way of looking at things: they may regard what displeases them as a necessary evil. I am grateful to Chalmers Johnson of Berkeley, an outstanding student of Asian affairs, for drawing my attention to the following quotation from an article by Arthur Cohen:

It has often been demonstrated that forcing a person to express an opinion descrepant from what he privately agrees results in a change of private opinion. According to [Leon] Festinger's analysis, expressing an opinion discrepant from one's privately held position creates "dissonance", or psychological tension having drive character. The tension may be alleviated by changing one's private position to coincide more nearly with the position expressed.[1]

Such a process has surely helped many a Chinese intellectual to be, if not happy, at least not entirely unhappy.

32: Patriotism—A New Experience for the Chinese

Unless I am very much mistaken, patriotism is a very strong element in the willingness of the Chinese to work and sacrifice. Whenever I asked—of young or old, in the north or in the south—why people worked so very hard, the answer was the same: "To win honor for Chairman Mao and our socialist fatherland." Setting aside my tendency to see an essential unity in the three elements —Mao, socialism, and the fatherland—I think I would give first place to the Chinese love of country, second place to their adulation of a great leader, and third place to socialism. This last may be essential for the strengthening of the country, but it has very little effect on the individual whose personal income is low, and its visible effects on raising the national standard of living are very slight.

Nationalism is a new phenomenon for the Chinese. For thousands of years the Chinese did not think of themselves as a nation. The words "China" and "Chinese" are not used by them even today; they speak of China as the "Land under Heaven" (Tien-hsia) or the "Middle Country" (Chung-kuo), and they refer to

[1] *China Quarterly*, 1969, #39.

themselves as the people of the Middle Country. Beyond the borders of this Middle Country under Heaven lived nomadic and predatory barbarians of diverse origins, including those with white skins. From time to time, great wars were waged against then or great walls were built to keep them out; there was a certain amount of trade with them, and they were allowed to appear in the capital in order to kowtow as they brought in tribute. From time to time there was a conquest by one of them; but the great conflicts between peoples that might have fired a Chinese nationalism were regarded as too uninteresting to bother about. Occasional military actions were taken against the foreigners, of course—against the Mongols or the Manchus, the English or the French, or all those "white devils" at once—but this was usually no more than a private quarrel the emperor and his soldiers, or some fanatic sect like the Boxers, had gotten themselves into.

When the victors in the First World War turned over the old German position in the province of Shantung to Japan instead of to China, it was the students (in the Movement of the Fourth of May, 1919) who acted out of patriotic fervor. Their call for an answer to this insult to China led successfully to the withdrawal of the Chinese delegation from Paris and the refusal to sign the Treaty of Versailles.

But the dubious honor of having infected the masses with Chinese nationalism must go to the Japanese, who waged war on China from 1931 to 1945 and occupied large sections of the country. Mao's victory is due in no small measure to his success in awakening and mobilizing the patriotism of the Chinese against the Japanese and against Chiang Kai-shek, who sought alliances with the West.

Thanks to his association with Chinese patriotism and his empathy with the vast majority of the Chinese—that is, the peasants—Mao's victory in 1949 was considered a victory for China even by the intelligentsia and other sections of the patriotic bourgeoisie.

Then came the bitter confrontations with the United States (the Korean War, the stationing of the Seventh Fleet in the Straits of Taiwan, and finally Vietnam), added to the "treason of the Soviet revisionists" (and the departure of all the Soviet experts in the summer of 1960) and the 1962 war with India. All these events served to augment and nourish Chinese nationalism. When the Cultural Revolution broke out, with an intensity that startled all observers, it was directed not only against the "bosses" and bureaucrats at home, but also against foreigners, especially the Russians. Today a strong national feeling is an essential component of the Chinese mentality.

In this realm, according to my observation, there has been a drastic change. During my first visit to China, in 1929, I noticed absolutely no xenophobic sentiment. Throughout the period of the Second World War, which I spent in China, there was hostility toward the Japanese but toward no one else. By 1957 things foreign were being looked on with some suspicion; but the Chinese were then still allied with the Russians, and since I was often taken for a Russian (there were hardly any other foreigners by then), my reception was generally friendly.

During the Cultural Revolution the xenophobia reached a climax. With the end of this catharsis, it has noticeably decreased. I never once had the feeling, even in the thickest crowds, that anything unpleasant might happen. I did, however, have the feeling of being perpetually confronted by an absolutely impenetrable solidarity. In the Soviet Union during the time of Stalin, and certainly later, the foreigner might easily find himself in the situation of having a Soviet citizen encourage him to criticize the regime. I cannot imagine such a thing happening in China today.

As the reader knows from Part I of this book, whenever I inspected the achievements of a brigade or a factory I would be told that these things had been accomplished "for the state." Such expressions scarcely existed a few decades ago. The relation of the citizen to the state has also changed. For the Chinese, the very word "state" was once a dim concept, since there were also the clan, the province he lived in, and somewhere, very far away, an emperor—while nearer by, much too near, were those imperial bureaucrats the mandarins. But who thought about the state?

Today the word "state" (Kuo-chia) is one of the most frequently used words in the language. So far as I can tell, it has the same meaning in China as in the West—that is, it denotes the machinery of state and the government in power, as well as that political entity, the nation. When, for example, Mao speaks of the capitalist states that wage war against the will and the interests of their own people, he means those in control (and who according to him are usurpers) of the state machinery. But when he posits the unity of the state as a necessary precondition for socialism, what he means is the unity of the entire Chinese people.

How strong are the internationalist tendencies of the Chinese? The "foreign guest" will often encounter manifestations of some such tendency: placards on which the Chinese, together with peoples of other races, are shown storming the fortresses of imperialism; the singing of the "Internationale," which is heard more often in China today than it is in the Soviet Union, and in every theatrical production (even at the level of kindergarten) the inevitable scene in which the heroes stand with clenched fists and angry faces, declaring that they will liberate their enslaved brothers of the Third World. Or he will come on Mao quotations concerning the brotherhood of the People's Republic of China with the freedom movements of all oppressed peoples, including the American blacks. And he will be told, in the course of a visit to a factory, that production has been increased out of solidarity with the people of Vietnam in their fight against the American imperialists. But I can remember clearly the time when I would be offered the same clichés in the Soviet Union, which makes me wonder just how deep this seeming internationalism goes among the Chinese. It exists, no doubt about it. But compared with the authenticity and vitality of their nationalism, it appears very weak.

The Chinese only became conscious of themselves as a nation in the course of this century; it seems likely that this sentiment has not yet reached its apex. What Maoism will be like without Mao I can't begin to guess. But I am certain that patriotism, which Mao helped to promote, will outlive him: it may be one of his most lasting gifts to the nation.

33: Is There a "Yellow Peril?"

Among the questions I am most frequently asked since my return from China are those having to do with the "yellow peril." Is China a "peril" today? And if not, will she become one tomorrow? How the Chinese choose to pay their workers or cultivate their fields is their business; what people want to know is whether we ourselves, or our children, are endangered.

It is very unlikely that anyone can give a real answer to this question. Even if there were aggressive intentions on the part of China, we would be the last to hear of them.

I have never subscribed to the notion that China will soon have to invade other countries, such as Siberia, to make room for her growing population. And now, since my trip, I subscribe to it even less. In the Chinese People's Republic today there are, roughly speaking, just under 200 people per square mile—as compared to 55 in the United States, or 708 in Japan. True, in China there are vast areas of non-arable land; but even in Japan—statistically the most densely populated nation in the world—the bulk of the population are crowded together along the narrow coastal plains. The prosperity of the overcrowded areas in Japan and the European countries—above all West Germany, with a density of 606.1 per square mile—proves once and for all that the old bugaboo of "people without living space" has become more irrelevant than ever. It is based on fixed notions about land and territorial expansion which simply do not apply to China, with her immeasurable territorial reserves.

Of a total area of about 3,700,000 square miles (950 million hectares), something over a tenth (120 million hectares) were under cultivation in 1960. Chou En-lai said at the time that another hundred million hectares (a billion acres) were suited for cultivation. Some of this land reserve has since been brought under cultivation, but there is still more than enough space left. Also, the whole concept of what kind of land is or is not "suitable" for cultivation is extremely relative. With enough money and effort, even the Gobi Desert could be turned into fertile land. Furthermore, the yield per acre of land already under cultivation could be increased considerably.

But the visitor need not rely solely on such rather doubtful statistics; he can see the evidence with his own eyes. The average number of children per family has declined; the largest family I saw had six children, and in most there were only two or three. In the old China the number would have been anywhere from six to twelve. This impression has been confirmed by other recent observers—for example, Tilman Durdin in his report from Shanghai in *The New York Times,* April 21, 1971. The state favors late marriages and greater intervals between pregnancies. Contraceptives are available—not in large quantities, but there used to be none at all. It also seems that the traditional idea that one should have as many children as possible, especially sons (the daughters just had to be taken as part of the bargain) is becoming less widespread. It is quite possible that the next census will bring a surprise.

The visitor can also see for himself the steep mountain slopes where countless rows of new terraces can still be built. To do so would require a concentrated effort, since dams and irrigation systems would be needed. But since the project would rely mainly on human labor, at an annual cost per person of about 450 pounds of rice (which that person himself produces!), the total would be far less than the expense of a war with the Soviet Union! Even during the days in the spring of 1969 when the tensions along the Amur and the Ussuri were at their worst, I never seriously believed that the Chinese would launch a military attack against the Soviet Union. The reverse did not happen either—but that, in any event, wouldn't have fallen under the heading of the "yellow peril."

We all know that anything is possible in the realm of politics. Nevertheless, I think any military expansion by the Chinese brought on by the pressure of overpopulation is extremely unlikely, at least in this century.

A much more likely sort of expansion would be political in nature, indirect rather than overtly military. The Chinese leadership feel they have a certain mission within the Third World—or the "World Village," as Lin Piao has called it. In the summer of 1965 he called on Japan to join China in an effort to free the "World

Village" from exploitation by the "World City"—i.e., the industrial nations.

It seems reasonable to assume that China's political leaders take this mission at least as seriously as those in the Soviet Union take theirs—and probably more so. Their thinking still remains very close to the original concept of a world revolution.

On the other hand, there is plenty of evidence that Peking has no intention of risking its own interests by assisting revolutions in other countries. Just as Stalin cooperated with Chiang Kai-shek during the Chinese civil war because he needed a strong and undivided China to help him against the Japanese, so during the Pakistan civil war in 1971 Mao supported the military regime of General Yahya Khan rather than the National Liberation Movement of East Bengal, because of the need for a strong and undivided Pakistan to help him against India. In addition, he did not want to give Moscow a chance to act as a mediator in a spreading South Asian conflict, as had already happened at Tashkent in 1965.

The Chinese I met on my journey are so completely preoccupied with building up their own country that they showed almost no interest in the rest of the world at all—except perhaps for Southeast Asia, which they constantly hear and read about. But should they ever be called on to fight, they would take up arms for Mao, and endure every conceivable hardship, without the slightest hesitation. Any orders he might give would be obeyed without question. The decision does not lie with the masses, who only want peace, but with the leaders. And what do they want?

In the sacred city of Yenan I sat on the stone bench where Mao, in an interview with the American journalist Anna Louise Strong, in August, 1946, made the famous assertion that "the atom bomb is a paper tiger." Later, we read other pronouncements from him which indicated that he didn't take the possibility of a third world war very seriously. (See "Mao Speaks," Document 14 in Part IV.) Since China has begun making her own atom bombs, however, we haven't heard any more such blustering remarks. The Russians have accused Mao of wanting to needle them and the Americans into an all-out war, while China simply stood by and "watched the tiger and the lion devour each other." But if he ever had such thoughts, they must now be a thing of the past; the lion and the tiger know perfectly well that such a war would destroy them both, and they are determined not to let it happen.

As things stand today, I assume that the Peking leaders' first concern is for their own country. They want to create a new China for a new Chinese people, and it is important to them to be surrounded by friendly (or at any rate harmless) small and middle-sized countries, from Korea to Afghanistan. They are adamant only about regaining Taiwan. . . .

Whether a "Chinese peril" might eventually develop as a result of political strategy, depends not on whether China has a quarter of a billion people, more or less. The day of the Mongolian hordes is past; and nuclear weapons are less likely to be used by the world powers, China among them, than by some of the others. Mao doesn't want to conquer the world by force, but by the power of his ideology. And lately some of the steam seems to have gone out of his world revolutionary campaign. What the effect of China's foreign policy of the first months of 1971 will be within the Third World remains to be seen.

We should, however, no longer ignore another element on the scene: the economic expansion that may be expected in China in the not too distant future. Today, most of China's manpower is still at work on the land. But whoever has seen the Chinese move mountains with their bare hands, with wheelbarrows and bamboo poles, cannot but wonder what they can be expected to accomplish once their country is industrialized, provided their own frugal life style does not change. Next door, Japan has already shown what kind of production level can be reached by an Asian people—and there are already about seven or eight times as many Chinese as there are Japanese. Nobody should delude himself into believing that the Chinese are inferior to the Japanese in either industry or intelligence. China has entered the age of technology after a century's delay. But both Japan and her other neighbor, the Soviet Union, have demonstrated that the time lag can be made up very quickly indeed!

34: China and Europe

The great majority of the Chinese people have no notion of foreign policy, and Europe seems especially far away. To the adults, I was simply "our guest from West Germany"; to the children, the "uncle from West Germany." Some Chinese, mainly in Peking and the two port cities, are of course aware of such things as NATO and the Common Market, and of problems such as the partition of Berlin.

On the Common Market, my traveling companion from the Chinese Ministry of Foreign Affairs turned out to be remarkably well informed, and I had to answer many detailed questions about it. In embassy circles in Peking I heard that with China's return to world affairs, interest in the European Economic Community had risen sharply. Two revealing symptoms were reports released by Hsinhua, the Chinese news agency, on February 20 and May 24, 1971, both dealing with the European Economic Community. They were straightforward and well-informed, with no polemic against any Western European country.

Why this interest? Hsinhua itself supplied the answer. With obvious approval, it cited Western publications emphasizing that a United Europe would be "a rival to the superpowers, the U.S. and the U.S.S.R.," able to "meet the U.S. and the U.S.S.R. as an equal in world trade."

Many of Mao's political maxims are useful even for situations outside China. "In studying any complex process in which there are two or more contradictions," he has said, "we must devote every effort to finding its principal contradiction. Once this principal contradiction is grasped, all problems can be readily solved." [1] Whenever I asked what was the principal contradiction in China's foreign policy, the answer was invariably: It is the contradiction between the Chinese People's Republic and the two superpowers. This is the attitude that determines Peking's present view of Europe.

Whenever I expounded a little on the concept of a united Europe, I would get reactions like these: "We would welcome a strong

[1] Little Red Book, Chapter XXII.

227

Europe, because that would limit the hegemony that the two super-powers now exercise over Europe," or, "We Chinese are not afraid of a united Europe." Peking holds basically to the same attitude it has held for years: that it is to China's advantage for what Mao calls the "intermediary zones" (countries which, politically speaking, lie between China and the two superpowers) to be strong.

The decision in favor of the European Economic Community also explains Peking's attitude toward Bonn. Peking, for obvious reasons, is not happy about an improvement of the relations between Bonn and Moscow. But Peking is aware of the strong position of West Germany within the Common Market. While I was in China, I never heard any criticism of Chancellor Willy Brandt's policy in Eastern Europe. Also, I believe, the Chinese fully realize that of all the Communist governments in Europe, the one in East Berlin is most dependent on the Kremlin, and, thus frequently, in its attacks on China, more Russian than the Russians. All the same, the public polemics against Bonn are likely to continue.

35: The Great Triangle—the U.S.A., the U.S.S.R., and China

Over a period of less than a year, in late 1970 and early 1971, I traveled in the U.S.S.R., in China, and in the United States—in all three corners of a world triangle that emerged all the more vividly with the announcement of President Nixon's trip to China. And how does each of the three view the others?

It was my distinct impression that the Chinese believe America is in the process of disengagement on Asia. For the Russians, as the Chinese know, a disengagement from Asia is impossible; the Russia of the Communists, like that of the tsars, is an Asian power. Therefore, in the eyes of the Chinese leaders, at present and for the foreseeable future, the U.S.S.R. is far more dangerous than the U.S.A. The invasion of Czechoslovakia by the Soviet Union in August, 1968, had a profound impact on Peking. As Peking saw it, the Soviet army had occupied another Communist country simply because the U.S.S.R. did not like the, brand of Communism practiced there. The Chinese know that Moscow dislikes Maoist Communism infinitely more than it ever disliked the Communism of poor Dubcek. So the question arises, if the U.S.S.R. could attack Czechoslovakia, why should it not attack China?

The possibility that the Soviet army might move in has taken deep root in the fears of the population. In 1969 and 1970, millions of Chinese, perhaps the majority of all the adult population, were busy digging air raid shelters—not against a possible American attack but against one by the Russians. The patriotic war posters I saw in China clearly referred to the military encounter with the Russians along the Ussuri and the Amur in 1969.

People might very well forget fifty editorials criticizing the U.S.S.R. on ideological grounds, but they would surely not forget fifty hours spent digging underground shelters against a possible Russian attack.

In 1957 I was frequently taken for a Russian by the Chinese, since by then hardly any other foreigners were to be seen. At that time I encountered what seemed to be a considerable respect and gratitude toward the Russians, who had done so much to help China get on her feet. By now, it would appear, nothing remains of those feelings. I was told innumerable times over of the "treacherous behavior" of the Soviet Union, when her thousands of advisers were all withdrawn and the delivery of all goods was halted.

Unlike many Western observers, I do not have the impression that the roots of the Sino-Soviet conflict are to be found in the border dispute between the two countries. Some Chinese, of course, are alarmed by the thought of Manchuria facing Soviet border troops from three sides, and are annoyed by the boast in the name of the Soviet city of Vladivostok, which means "rule the East." But nobody ever spoke with fondness or enthusiasm for the Soviet Far East or Siberia, and I do not believe there is any sense of affinity with these regions.

But not once during my travels did I hear an expression of unfriendliness against the American people. Of course, there were the usual tirades against the imperialists, the neocolonialists, the warmongers—and these, more often than not, were symbolized by Uncle Sam's top hat and the "star-spangled banner." But I heard no accusations against the American people. To many of the Chinese, America is a paper tiger anyhow; it cannot even break the back of the North Vietnamese resistance. In 1971, as in 1957, I found what seemed to be a great reservoir of good will toward the Americans—an accumulation dating back to past decades when many Chinese considered the United States a friend standing up for them against European greed, and fighting against the Japanese occupation—and that reservoir has not been drained completely to this day. This is surely why the ping-pong players received so genuinely friendly a reception.

What were the reasons behind the Chinese decision to invite them in? Worries about Russia's intentions, of course—though these had existed for many years and no ping-pong ball or its equivalent had started rolling. For this there was at least one very simple reason: China's complete absorption for a number of years with domestic problems, above all the struggle between the "two ways" (of Maoism and the anti-Maoists), and after 1966 the Cultural Revolution. During all these years, China was practically absent from world affairs; all her ambassadors (with a single exception) were recalled, and the foreign ministry was not only under attack but at times even under siege.

China returned to the world only after quiet had returned at home. We know from Edgar Snow what Mao said in 1970 about a possible visit by Nixon to Peking. At some time before that interview, the Chinese leaders must have started thinking in terms of a new approach to world politics.

Worries concerning the U.S.S.R. probably were the most important consideration behind this new approach, but can hardly have been the only reason. There was also the desire to hasten American disengagement from Asia. That disengagement would have the same advantages for China that American disengagement from Europe has for the Russians: the reduction of tensions between the United States and the non-Communist governments of the region.

President Nixon had barely completed his television broadcast about his projected trip to Peking when other tensions began to make themselves felt, mainly from the directions of Japan and Taiwan. But they were not the only Asian countries to show uneasiness: South Korea, for example, opened talks with the North Koreans. It is obvious that the Chinese hope such tensions between Washington and its Asian allies will be to the eventual benefit of China.

There is another considerable advantage for Peking, in that many governments around the world had refrained from recognizing the People's Republic of China in order not to antagonize Washington. With the announcement of Nixon's plans, such fears were no longer of such importance. Thus there have been a whole series of recognitions. These have considerably improved Peking's international position, which in turn has given strength to her claim to the Chinese seat at the United Nations.* It may well be that a desire to find an opportune moment to press the claim for Taiwan is the single most important reason for China's new foreign policy, quite aside from her desire to see a favorable end to the war in Indochina.

China has returned to the world scene in a highly realistic and undogmatic mood. Besides supporting the government of General Yahya Khan of Pakistan against what could justifiably be called the national liberation movement in East Pakistan, she supported the ruling government against the left-wing guerrillas on the island of Ceylon. In a letter dated April 26, 1971, and made public by the Ceylonese ministry of defense and external affairs, Chou Enlai told Prime Minister Bandaranaike of Ceylon that he was pleased to know that "the chaotic situation created by a handful of persons who style themselves "Guevarists," whose ranks have been infiltrated by foreign spies, has been brought under control.[1] Peking has also greatly improved its relations with Marshal Tito, yesterday's ideological archenemy, even though Tito's own political line has not changed.

The question has been raised of how Mao could possibly agree to a Nixon visit after denouncing the U.S. president for so many years. I cannot see any serious problem for Mao, at least as far

[1] Colombo *Mirror,* May 27, 1971.

* And since the first edition of this book, China has claimed and taken that seat.

231

as the masses in China are concerned. From their point of view, all foreigners have always been barbarians, and although some of them from time to time have come to their senses for long enough to pay a visit to the capital of the Middle Country, thereby showing their respect for China, they remain barbarians just the same. A carefully worded communiqué of July 16, 1971, made it very clear that the Nixon visit had been graciously agreed to by the Chinese government after a request from Washington; it spoke of the President's pleasure in accepting the invitation, but not of any pleasure taken by China in issuing it. To the Chinese, Nixon is one more barbarian chieftain arriving to honor their great leader.

The world would do well to be equally realistic about China. In business quarters there are high hopes for trade with her. To be sure, China's needs are gigantic and the factories of all the Western world could work day and night to satisfy them. But what China has to offer in exchange is very limited. Unless I am very much mistaken, the bonanza of trade with China will remain small, as measured by the size of the country, and there will be more and more who want a piece of it. Would China buy on credit, then? Nothing is impossible, but I still recall the pride with which people in China told me about theirs being a country without foreign debts, and the wrath against the U.S.S.R. and her satellites for breaking existing trade contracts. ("Never again will we become dependent on an outside power!") So it would surprise me very much if the Chinese were to appear, hat in hand, asking other countries to industrialize China on credit.

We take it for granted that industrially underdeveloped countries want to be industrialized as rapidly as possible. Since China is one of them, we simply assume that the same applies to her. I am not so sure—in fact, I doubt very much that it does. Mao seems to be fully aware of the social and psychological implications of industrialization; a look across his northern border is all he needs to be reminded that with industrialization the U.S.S.R. has not become more but less Communist. Let it be understood that I personally am very much in favor of trade with China. I simply have my doubts that there will be any amount of it in the near future.

Among the many important questions still to be answered is

that of Mao's attitude toward the new look in China's foreign policy. Is he wholeheartedly behind this development, or did he give a reluctant assent to Chou En-lai's proposal? Does he in fact leave foreign affairs entirely to the Premier? These questions can only be asked, not answered. My own hunch is that Mao was consulted and that his consent was given without enthusiasm. His own mind is wholly on China herself.

Much has been written lately about Chinese hostility against Japan. In the interview Chou En-lai gave to James Reston on August 5, 1971,[2] Chou spoke at length about the dangers allegedly emanating from Japan. I find it a bit difficult to accept these words at their face value, for I have never encountered any such fears in China. It is my impression that the Chinese are fully aware that Japan's economic miracle rests on precarious foundations; they know, for example, that the youth and the intelligentsia of Japan are among the most radically anti-establishment in the world. Chou's words, I think, are to be taken as part of a two-pronged move. On the one hand, the Japanese are made to suspect that their big protector in Washington is making a deal with Peking, leaving them orphaned and exposed. On the other hand, they are informed that Peking is very angry with their government, which it considers a serious danger to peace in Asia. As all the Japanese want peace, and very many of the Japanese want friendship with China, it may well be that Peking's two-pronged thrust is aimed at producing among the Japanese a feeling of anxiety, such as may lead eventually to the formation of a government less pro-U.S. and more pro-China.

There is no need for me to elaborate on America's attitude toward China and Russia. But a European may perhaps be allowed a few remarks in passing. Having observed Americans in China over several decades, and having studied U.S.-Chinese relations, this observer is convinced that there is a strong pro-Chinese sentiment in the U.S., dating back to the days when American missionaries went to China by the thousands and then traveled through their own country collecting money and lecturing about the good people of China; when Pearl Buck and Lin Yu-tang wrote their best sellers;

[2] *The New York Times,* August 10, 1971.

and when the Americans and the Chinese fought on the same side in the Second World War.

For two decades this pro-China feeling was restricted to the Chinese of Taiwan, but in the long run this seemed foolish to the majority of Americans, who were ready to be friends with all the Chinese, and not just the relatively small number on that one island. This is one of the reasons, I believe, why President Nixon's announcement was followed by widespread approval rather than by a general outcry of anger. Among the politically sophisticated there is, in addition, the hope that talks between Peking and Washington may be beneficial to talks between Washington and Moscow. It will be interesting to see for which of the two great Communist nations the Americans will feel greater sympathy in the years to come.

Of the three great powers, the U.S.S.R. has had the greatest psychological difficulties in accepting the change from a bipolar to a triangular world. This is understandable: the emergence of China as the third superpower occurred at the expense of a portion of the bipolar world that had been dominated by Moscow. No wonder the Russians are unhappy; in fact, they are bewildered, since they do not really understand what is going on.

Anyone who looks into recent Russian studies of Chinese policy in the hope of discovering some insight into Maoism will be disappointed. The China specialists in the U.S.S.R. do not seem to be providing their own leaders with a useful analysis of Maoism. After reading the works of their scholars on Mao's alleged Trotskyism, anarchism, petty bourgeois chauvinism, and so on, Soviet leaders must have been no less confused than before. This confusion is not a thing to be taken lightly by the rest of us, for it brings an element of dangerous uncertainty into world affairs. It also heightens the aversion of the Russian people towards the ominous country with which they share the world's longest border.

During the Second World War, Stalin favored Chiang Kai-shek over Mao; the Soviet ambassador followed the defeated Chiang up to the very moment when the Generalissimo fled to Taiwan. Even today, the Russians would, I suspect, rather have Chiang than Mao for a neighbor.

Small wonder that the Soviet leaders were stunned by Nixon's decision to visit China. It took them a long time to react. The articles that then began appearing in a steady stream were all very critical, though at the same time cautious. Obviously the Kremlin fears that violent attacks on the Chinese might drive them still closer to America.

While Americans and Russians seemed to rule the world, the Chinese wondered where they came in. Now that Washington and Peking have opened their own lines of communication, it would seem that it is the Russians' turn to ask the same question.

Thirty-six years ago, while Mao was crossing the eastern part of the Kunlun, the central mountain range of Asia, during the Long March, he wrote a poem in praise of those mountains:

> But today
> I say to you, Kunlun,
> You do not need your great light,
> You do not need all your heavy snows.
> If I could lean on the sky,
> I would draw my sword
> And cut you into three pieces.
> I would send one to Europe,
> One to America,
> And one we would keep in China.
> Thus would a great peace reign
> Throughout the world,
> For all the world would share
> Your warmth and your cold.

36: In Retrospect

I have described the glimpse I had of life in China, a country vibrant with hard work and selfless patriotism, as it strives to bring a wholly new future into being. What I saw remains in my memory like the echo of some vast natural phenomenon, as one of the great experiences of my life. I cannot yet be sure whether what I have seen is only a moment in the history of a single nation, albeit the greatest on earth, or whether it amounts to a turning-point, which will finally bring a change of direction to the West as well.

Much of what is happening there can be explained quite simply as a function of time and place. China is now in the early phase of industrialization; she has a gigantic labor force and severely limited capital. If she wishes to reach the top, it must be largely "through our own efforts," and the population must continue to lead a life of austerity. We in the West are now in exactly the opposite situation. We are faced with problems stemming from the abundance of a highly industrialized consumer society, and we are apparently on the verge of jettisoning nationalism in favor of supranational unions.

But the goal of the new China is not simply to overtake the West. Mao has set a new direction for his people: its goal is a new man, a new society of selfless equals, which may turn out to be a model not only for the Third World but also for the rest of mankind.

Maoist China can be observed and commented on at length, but in the end each of us must decide whether or not he believes in such an ideal, and whether such a new man is in fact possible. If the answer is positive, one must be ready to accept the price that will have to be paid to reach the goal. If the answer is negative —and mine would be at least skeptical—it will be because the price seems too high. The skeptic will be appalled by some of the things he sees: the Mao cult, which is especially depressing to those who in their own lifetime have seen other cults of personality; the monotonous intellectual conformity at the level of Mao's six hundred quotations and the eight dramas of Chiang Ching; the periodic plowing under of leaders, and their treatment in the Seventh of May schools; the concept of "continuing revolution"; the enforcement of compliance via self-accusation and even self-abasement.

Some may also doubt whether China can afford to maintain her attitude of suspicion towards intellectual achievement, and her frequent changes of elite, in her transition from the status of an agrarian nation to that of an industrialized society. As industrialization proceeds, she will have an increasing need for more and more specialists. Shifts among such an elite will be continually more and more costly, and longer and longer periods of adjustment will be

236

needed to make up for the losses incurred by each revolutionary thrust. Mao appears not to believe there is any conflict between his continuous revolution and the dynamics of modernization. But I wonder. . . .

One thing is certain: the ease with which the attitudes of the Chinese can be manipulated is cause for serious concern. In 1966–67 there was revolution under the banner of the Red Guards; in 1968–69 (beginning in 1967) there was restoration by the army. There were twenty years of furious anti-American propaganda over Korea, Taiwan, and Vietnam; now suddenly there is an offer of friendship. Liu Shao-chi was second in command yesterday, but the arch-villain of today. May not everything that is praised today be damned tomorrow?

If China continues to open up towards the rest of the world, there will be a better chance to observe the country over a number of years, and thus to understand it. Now all we really know is that the Chinese are in a state of high spirits and exaltation, which has permitted them some extraordinary achievements. But this tells us very little about what the long-range developments may be.

In some ways, the Chinese are already less remote from us in the West. Like us, they are plagued with the problems of modern civilization. But they also remain strange to us, since they are meeting those problems in such a different way. Maoism is a force that can move mountains—when those mountains are Chinese.

So in the end, my feelings concerning the new China are mixed: it awakens respect, but also concern and uneasiness. What remains unequivocal is my intense curiosity concerning the outcome, and my warmest sympathy for a great people at this crucial moment in their history.

PART III: BACKGROUND

In these notes, I have limited myself to discussing a few basic issues that have received mention in earlier parts of the book, and which may be unfamiliar to some readers. This section may also serve as a brief summary of China's development since the 1958 Great Leap Forward.

37: The "Two Roads"

The standard interpretation of this phrase is to be found in a statement by Mao that was quoted by Lin Piao in his speech at the Chinese Communist Party Congress in 1969: "The struggle between the two roads—socialism and capitalism—continues."

This sentence has been included almost word for word in the first chapter of the Party constitution issued by the Congress. The expression is widely used; I heard over and over again, even in the villages and the schools, that there had been a "struggle between the two roads," but that the right one had prevailed.

It is in keeping with political tactics generally, and with the dialectical pattern of Mao's thought in particular, to reduce even the most complicated debates to a single line of argument against a single antagonist.

Before the Cultural Revolution began in earnest, the attacks of the Maoists were mostly on minor political figures. But then, in Liu Shiao-chi, they found their target—at first only vaguely hinted at, later openly mentioned by name. The whole story of Liu cannot be told here. For years he was known only as a faithful if somewhat colorless follower—Mao's first deputy Party chairman, and simultaneously president of the Republic. In 1966, when Maoist propaganda began to single him out as the villain and "secret traitor," Liu was no longer in a position to tell his version of the story. In his major pamphlet, published twenty-five years ago and entitled *How To Become a Good Communist,* very little can be found to justify his current image as the arch villain. The various statements now ascribed to him (which form the basis for the worst accusation of all, that Liu had always had hidden inclinations towards capitalism) can rarely be identified with certainty as having been made by him. But in retrospect the essence of the conflict itself is clear enough. It is the conflict of Liu the pragmatist versus Mao the ideologist. One of Liu's closest collaborators, the long-time (1954–66) secretary general of the Central Committee of the Communist Party of China, Teng Hsiao-ping, reportedly once remaked, "It doesn't matter whether a cat is black or white, so long

241

as it catches mice." This is pragmatism in its purest form: it emphasizes practical results over ideological purity, and since it will accept successful compromise, it can lead to unscrupulous opportunism.

For Mao the ideologist, the purity of the principle ("consciousness") is everything. He has not, however, offered the world a clear and systematic body of thought. The four volumes of his *Selected Works* that have so far been published cover only the years up to 1949; and of the 426 quotations in the Little Red Book, approximately three out of four are from that same period. Only twenty-one sayings date from the period after 1958, and it is during those years that Maoism developed into a form of "Marxism-Leninism" very different from Soviet Communism. Since the beginning of the Cultural Revolution, many of Mao's "Instructions" or "Directives" have been published in one form or another (see Documents 14, Part IV), and there are occasional short policy statements (for example, on the struggle of the American Negro and on the war in Indochina). But there has not been in the fourteen years since the fifty-page essay on contradictions appeared in 1957, a single coherent official statement of Mao's views. The meaning of the term "Maoism" therefore remains rather loose, though it does at least give its originator due credit as one of the founding fathers of Marxism.

The controversy over the "two roads"—as the image itself suggests—is based less on ideological than on either tactical or psychological differences. The pragmatist argues that according to Marx changes in consciousness must be preceded by changes in the material environment, and that these changes must be brought about —by whatever means—before changes in consciousness can occur.

Mao, on the other hand, believes that man and his consciousness must first of all be altered—and the sooner the better, while the revolutionary impulse is still strong—or else it will be too late, as events in Russia have already shown.

The success-oriented pragmatist takes it for granted that people are not equal, and makes full use of this fact to encourage economic progress: for instance, by stimulating people to work harder via piece-rate wages, even though this might lead to social differentiation and thus to another class society.

While pursuing his noble aims, the pragmatist has no objections to harnessing "materialistic self-interest." Mao, however, sees the slightest concession to individual ambition as a corrupting influence. He believes it was his appeal to the revolutionary will, to the selflessness of the peasants, that won the civil war; whereas Liu, during his years as an organizer of the urban workers, had learned to bargain with the ambitions of the individual and of the various social strata.

Liu Shao-chi and Teng Hsiao-ping were faced with the task of building and leading the greatest mass organization in history. The Communist Party of China, with almost twenty million members in key positions all over the country, was the world's most gigantic bureaucratic system; and so their main concern had to be with keeping things running smoothly and creating a period of stability and development after the Revolution. Mao, who had always managed to maintain an independent position within the Party hierarchy and who had never needed a large-scale organization to run his guerrillas, appealed to those forces that seemed to him pure and uncorrupted: first the peasants, and then the young, the students, and the Red Guards.

Liu Shiao-chi is reported to have said in 1961: "Chairman Mao concerns himself only with important state affairs. It is enough for him to propose to turn the whole country into one big garden and forest. He has no time to solve the problems. . . . Therefore, I have to handle it." [1]

Though this was obviously said with a degree of bitterness and irony, at the same time it originated from within the framework of close cooperation, the division of roles notwithstanding. In fact, the system had worked well over the years. It was only under the strain of the Great Leap Forward that the rift between the two temperaments and the two ways of thinking seems to have led to open conflict.

Pragmatists like Liu (and there must have been millions of them in the countless administrative offices throughout the country) had long been annoyed, one may suppose, by the moralizing sermons

[1] I am indebted for this remark, along with several other useful insights, to Tan Tsou's article in *China Quarterly*, #38, p. 75.

of the great visionary. But the prophet could no longer bear to stand by and watch his great and glorious revolution smothered by millions of small egos. Things came to a break, followed by open conflict. And it was the prophet, at least for the present, who won out.

38: The Cultural Revolution

The world first became aware of the Great Proletarian Cultural Revolution—as it is officially called—on August 18, 1966, when a million young Red Guards held their first big parade for Mao in Peking. We now know that this event on the square in front of the Gate of Heavenly Peace had been preceded by years of bitter dissension among the top leaders. Many of the grievances dated from the 1920s; but it was only after the failure of the Great Leap Forward in 1958 that the cleavage of the two roads had become inevitable. Individual power struggles and animosities were surely interwoven with profound ideological and tactical differences; much still remains unclear, though new facts are coming to light every day. Western scholars will surely turn out many volumes on the Cultural Revolution; so far, neither a complete summary of the facts nor a valid interpretation of them exists.

At the meeting of the Central Committee of the Chinese Communist Party in Lushan in mid-August, 1959, a compromise was reached between the pragmatists—who wanted to avoid any further risks—and the Maoists, who still had hopes of bringing off a second try at the Great Leap Forward. On the one hand, a group of opponents of the Mao line, led by Peng Teh-huai, the Minister of Defense, were ousted; on the other hand, there was an agreement on taking a more moderate approach in domestic policy.

In the field of literature, too, everything seemed again to be in flux. It became possible to speak critically, or even sarcastically, of the Party and its Chairman. This was done, for instance, in Teng Tao's essays entitled *Evening Talks at Yenshan.* Wu Han, the deputy mayor of Peking, wrote a play, *Hai Jui Is Dismissed,* ostensibly dealing with a sixteenth-century courtier who was dismissed by the Emperor for daring to tell him some unpalatable truths. It is easy to recognize in Hai Jui the former Defense Secretary Peng Teh-huai, and Chairman Mao Tse-tung himself in the Emperor. Mao at this time had already resigned as President of the Republic before the meeting in Lushan, and he now retreated into the background, leaving practical politics to the pragmatists, notably President Liu Shiao-chi and Premier Chou En-lai.

Beginning in the fall of 1962, and increasingly from 1963 onward, Mao's influence began to be felt once again—most strongly in cultural and ideological matters at first. The Party theoretician Yang Hsien-chen was deposed. Writers were denounced in the press for being too liberal. Mao's wife, Chiang Ching, began her campaign against the traditional opera. Mao and Lin Piao drew closer together; the people were exhorted to follow the army's example. Edgar Snow, who has given us the most intimate glimpses of what was really happening inside the Chinese leadership, reported after his latest talks that Mao's decision to break with Liu had come on January 25, 1965.[1]

The Party apparatus was still in the hands of the pragmatists. The start of Mao's counter-offensive came on November 10, 1965, when the Shanghai journalist Yao Wen-yuan sharply attacked the author of *Hai Jui Is Dismissed* and his associates within the Party. But the decisive triumph for Mao and Lin Piao came in May 1966, with the fall of almost the entire Peking Party Committee. From then on, one blow followed another. On July 25, Mao gave proof of his excellent health by swimming the Yangtze River; on August 8, a Mao-convened meeting of the Central Committee, from which some of his opponents were missing, drew up the Sixteen Points of the Cultural Revolution; on August 18, the Red Guards marched in Peking. The Cultural Revolution had begun.

The conflict, however, was not between two organized groups, two clear-cut factions within the Party. The pragmatists, led by Liu Shiao-chi, proud of their successes, had never thought of organizing against Mao. There was never a serious accusation of conspiracy —and why would there be? They were already in power. They

[1] *New Republic,* April 10, 1971.

were convinced that what they were doing was right, and that they were indispensable. They saw to it that everything ran smoothly, and simply let the old man talk; after all, his speeches made the people think their drudgery served a lofty purpose, which in turn made it much easier to control them. How little prepared the establishment under Liu was for a major battle—how little it felt itself threatened—is clear from the fact that despite of its power it could be paralyzed and defeated in a matter of months, and that almost its entire leadership has disappeared from view. Essentially only Chou En-lai remained; but he has always been a special case, and now he was indispensable for holding the political structure together.

The Maoists were still less a party within the Party than the men of the Liu faction. Mao had only a few followers among the top leaders: his longtime security chief Kang Sheng, the equally longtime head of his secretariat, Chen Po-ta, his own wife, Chiang Ching, and of course Lin Piao, the leader of the armed forces. The Red Guards entered the picture only at the very end.

Certainly the army in itself would have been powerful enough to overthrow the Party establishment and depose its leaders without the aid of the youngsters. Mao, however, is less interested in the exercise of power than he is in changing people. So he chose a different and more dangerous path, which might even have led to foreign intervention: revolution by the masses.

His success was due at least partly to the element of surprise. He did what no one had expected him to do: he turned with full force against his own Party. He mobilized the young, which probably also came as a surprise; he provided them with the Little Red Book and unlimited license to "make revolution," and covered all their violent and illegal actions with the mantle of his personal prestige, which had grown enormously through the new Mao cult. In the background, the army stood by. At the end of January, 1967 —when, as Mao himself had to admit (in an interview with Edgar Snow; see Document 14), the chaos had grown to dangerous proportions—the army was called in. By autumn, the revolution was over.

39: Revolutionary Committees

In issuing the Sixteen Points of August 8, 1966, the Central Committee of the Chinese Communist Party gave its official sanction to the Cultural Revolution. The ninth of these Sixteen Points was a directive on matters of organization: "cultural revolutionary groups, committees, and congresses" were to be set up, to serve as the "power structure" of the Cultural Revolution. But nothing came of these provisions. The Cultural Revolution developed without any organization or plan, and in a state of maximum disorder.

Even when the army was called in at the beginning of 1967, it wasn't quite clear how law and order were to be restored. Two different types or organizational setups emerged almost simultaneously: on January 31, a "revolutionary committee" became the highest authority in Heilungkiang (Amur) Province; on February 5, a million people attended the proclamation of the "Shanghai Commune," which was modeled, one learned, after the Paris Commune of 1871. Of these two possible models, the idea of the communes turned out to be short-lived; but the idea of the revolutionary committees soon spread from the far northern provinces throughout the entire country.

The characteristic feature of the revolutionary committee—the "three-in-one alliance" of army representatives, revolutionary groups such as the Red Guards, and rehabilitated pro-Maoist cadres, (i.e., Party officials,)—became the basic principle according to which, during the next eighteen months, all twenty-nine provinces were reorganized. (More precisely, there were twenty-one provinces, five autonomous regions, and the three municipalities of Peking, Tientsin, and Canton. Usually they are all grouped together as "provinces.")

It soon became clear that in the three-in-one alliance one element, the army, wielded considerably more power than the other two. This was still true in 1971.

Mao himself gave his blessing to the revolutionary committees. In a phrase he reportedly used around the end of 1967, he called the three-in-one alliances "revolutionary and representative," and declared that they possessed "proletarian authority." [1]

During 1967 and 1968, the revolutionary committees became the sole political organization in the entire country. They were generally made up of the same three components as the first three-in-one alliances in the spring of 1967 and they were to be found on every organizational level, from the humblest local group to the provincial governments. No revolutionary committee was ever established, however, on the very highest level—the Government of the People's Republic as a whole. Decisions there were made by the "Party Central" (never clearly defined after the outbreak of the Cultural Revolution), by the Politbureau, newly reconvened in 1969, and by the Council of Ministers.

40: Propaganda Teams

Though the universities no longer functioned after June, 1966, a few still served as headquarters for groups of radical students, in particular Tsinghua University in Peking, one of the largest and most respected in the country. Many of the students who in the summer of 1966 had set out, Little Red Book in hand, to join the Red Guards and "make revolution," had turned into an embarrassment as the time came to restore order—which means as early as the beginning of 1967. In the official press they were called "leftists" —always in quotes, to indicate that they presented themselves as such but were in reality nothing other than (as they were also called) "disorderly anarchists."

On July 27, 1968, workers from several Peking factories marched to the Tsinghua University campus and entered dormitories and teachers' homes to "re-educate the young Red Guard fighters." They called themselves "the workers' propaganda team for Mao Tse-tung's thought," or "propaganda team" for short. A few days later, Mao sent them a basket of fruit, indicating his approval of them having occupied the Tsinghua campus. Similar "teams"

[1] *Peking Review*, 1967, #51.

were formed in rapid succession all over the country. They still exist today; their task is to keep an eye on the ideological reliability of the school or university in question.

41: The Universities

A serious crisis between the universities and the authorities developed during the Hundred Flowers episode. On February 27, 1957, Mao made his famous speech on "Contradictions," later revised and published on June 18, 1957, under the title "On the Correct Handling of Contradictions Among the People." It was distributed on a large scale. The great importance of the speech lies in the encouragement it gave to frank criticism of the Party and the government. Much emphasis was placed on Mao's directive of May 2, 1956: "Let a hundred flowers bloom; let a hundred schools of thought contend!"

The result was that from the middle of May, 1957, onward, a rising tide of liberal criticism swept the universities. (I happened to be in China at the time of the official counterattack, which started with an article in the July 1 *People's Daily;* I later recorded my observations in an essay, "The Difficult Intellectual." [1]) But later the schools and universities in which public criticism had been voiced were penalized for months. Only very gradually did the situation return to normal, and it was a long time before the universities could function again.

The next and much more serious upheaval, which destroyed the traditional Chinese university completely (and probably for a long time to come) occurred at the time of the Cultural Revolution. On June 13, 1966, the universities were ordered not to accept any new students.[2] At it turned out, this meant that for a year all higher education came to a stop. University students and high school graduates could now be mobilized for other things; a great many of them were drawn into the whirlpool of the Cultural Revolution,

[1] See *Peking and Moscow.*
[2] *Peking Review,* 1966, #26.

joining the ranks of the Red Guards—which, according to Lin Piao, reached a peak total of thirteen million young people.

The summer of 1968 brought some important events. Propaganda teams were formed to control the universities, and soon afterwards came the "Investigative Report" on the Shanghai Machine Tools Plant #1, as well as Mao's directive setting the plant up as an example for a new system of higher education. (See Documents 5 and 6, Part IV.) Mao demanded that "students should be selected from among workers and peasants with practical experience, and they should return to production after a few years' study." A period of intensive experimentation followed.

The basic guidelines for the new university can be gathered from the development of the "Factory University" at Shanghai and also from a theoretical essay published in the summer of 1970 by the propaganda team of Tsinghua. The universities, it declared, should be led by the workers, the students should remain in close contact with all aspects of practical production; the faculty—a three-in-one alliance of sorts—should include workers, peasants, and soldiers, along with "revolutionary [i.e., Maoist] technicians" and "members of the former faculty" (only, of course, after due conversion to Maoism).[3]

The close ties between the university and the world of production are the be-all and end-all of Chinese policy on higher education in recent years. On the one hand, the propaganda teams gave the workers a voice in university affairs; on the other, the universities not only send their students to the factories, but set up factories of their own. At Tsinghua, for example, an automobile assembly plant was built; on May 28, 1970, Radio Wuhan announced that the local university had opened ten such "factories."

The difficulties in setting up these new universities along the lines of Mao's ideas must be considerable. In the spring of 1971, five years after they had been closed down, not a single university— so far as I could find out—had returned to a full schedule. Even where the new system was furthest advanced there were obviously problems; Tsinghua University, where more than twelve thousand students had once been registered, was still reported to have only

[3] *Peking Review,* 1970, #9.

three thousand students in March 1971. Also in March, **Shanghai** announced "the first registration of a large number of new students" —mostly workers, peasants, and soldiers—at the city's universities. The "large number" turned out to be twenty-six hundred, a very modest figure considering that Shanghai, with its six million inhabitants and nine universities, has always been a center of higher learning.[4]

From basic articles and conference minutes that have appeared from time to time (for example, *Peking Review,* 1970, #31, and #3, 1971, and *China Reconstructs,* January and March 1971), it is evident that the confusion has not abated. It is also significant that despite repeated requests, I was not allowed one g'impse of a university during my entire visit. Mao's often expressed doubts whether intellectuals can be "reformed" in accordance with his thought may indeed turn out to be well founded.

42: The Collectivization of the Villages

The collectivization of Chinese agriculture began only after the victory of the Communists, and even then it was tentative. In the Agrarian Reform Bill of June 28, 1950, which led to the expropriation of large and middle-sized rural estates, and their distribution among the peasants, the word "collective" was not yet to be found. It had always been clear that Mao's final goal was not the type of small-scale farming established by the Agrarian Reform Bill. From the very start, mutual farmers' aid teams were formed with active support from the Party. Since these organizations were very loose, they did not run counter to the peasant mentality; their number grew steadily and without any serious opposition from the farmers.

The second step, the formation of agricultural producers' cooperatives, was accompanied by two resolutions of the Central Committee of the Chinese Communist Party, on February 15 and

[4] *Peking Review,* 1971, #9.

December 16, 1953. Roughly speaking, these cooperatives embraced the households of one village. Every farmer who joined a cooperative would receive his share in its total output, according to (1) the amount of land, cattle, and equipment he brought in, and (2) the amount of work he did for the cooperative. These cooperatives were later categorized as those of "the lower type."

The actual collectivization of the villages began in 1954/55, with the changeover from the old "lower-type" cooperatives into those of the so-called "higher type." Here, each member is paid only according to the work he does, no matter how much property he originally brought with him.

The guidelines for the new system were given in Mao's speech of July 31, 1955, and in the Central Committee resolution of October 11, 1955. By 1957 this particular phase was all but completed. All these measures and ideas were totally new to the Chinese peasants. They were familiar enough, however, to the eye of a foreign observer: the "higher-type" cooperatives had much in common with the Soviet kolkhoz, an impression I found to be confirmed by visits to several of them in 1957.

A radical deviation from the Russian prototype came during the Great Leap Forward with the formation of the people's communes, for which there is no Soviet parallel. On April 20, 1958—as became known later—the first people's commune was set up as an experiment, consisting of twenty-seven higher-type cooperatives. This event became the starting point for one of the greatest undertakings of all time: during the late summer months of 1958, the 470,000 existing agricultural producers' cooperatives, each with an average of 160 families, were turned into "brigades," which were in their turn organized in 26,000 people's communes with an average of 4,600 families each. Within a matter of a few weeks, more than half a billion Chinese peasants found themselves living and working in ways that were totally new not only to them, but to the entire history of mankind. Their private lives were completely disrupted; in some extreme cases they were housed in barracks and fed in communal mess halls; peasants were "mobilized" and shifted about as though they were soldiers, to be used for work on all kinds of gigantic projects—such as the building of dams, often far from their own villages. The eventual failure of this enterprise, worsened but unfavorable weather conditions during the years that followed, meant that although officially the people's communes continued to exist (in somewhat smaller sizes), the also slightly smaller brigade now became the most important unit. Reliable figures are unavailable, but it has been estimated that as of late 1971 there were about seventy-five thousand Communes, with a total of around seven hundred thousand brigades, which in their turn consist of some five million production teams.

I was not satisfied with what I could discover about agricultural land taxes—either with the information I could gather myself or with the information that is officially available. In the villages I was told that there was no land tax on rice, but that there were taxes on other kinds of agricultural crops. However, a recent essay on land taxes—about which very little has been written—mentions a general tax of 6 percent.[1] Unfortunately, most of the relevant Western source material dates from before the Cultural Revolution.[2]

43: Some Official Figures on Production

The last statistics cited as authentic by Peking itself give figures for the year 1957. The Great Leap Forward of a year later has since upset all calculations. No official data have been released since then in China itself—a development that has given rise to many European, American, and Japanese studies which, though interesting, remain unsatisfactory, and differ widely in their estimates.

Only after the first signs of China's return to world affairs did Chou En-lai give at least a few verbal clues concerning the 1970 production figures. These statements were made during an inter-

[1] *Peking Review*, 1971, #22.
[2] The especially informative *Rural People's Communes in Lien-Chiang*, edited by C. S. Chen (Stanford, 1969), covers in its text and its twenty-five documents only the period up to April, 1963.

view with the American journalist Edgar Snow, who published them in the Italian periodical *Epoca* for February 28, 1971. The experts will continue to analyze them for a long time to come; many questions are raised by every figure. I shall give approximations of them here without further comment, alongside those of the last year for which statistics have been published.

Here, then, are the latest official Chinese statistics—the first in thirteen years.

	1957	1970
Grain (The Chinese include potatoes in this category; 4 tons of potatoes equal 1 ton of grain.)	185,000,000 tons	240,000,000 tons
Synthetic fertilizers	600,000 tons	14,000,000 tons
Cotton textiles	5 billion meters	8.5 billion meters
Steel (Chou: "Over the last five years, between 10 and 18 million tons a year"; steel production, he said, has decreased as a result of the Cultural Revolution.)	5,400,000 tons	10,000,000– 18,000,000 tons
Crude oil	1,500,000 tons	20,000,000 tons

I might add a rough estimate of the population, which Chou did not include. For 1957, the figure was 650,000,000; for 1970, 750,000,000.

44: The Little Red Book

The *Quotations from Chairman Mao Tse-tung*—as the English version of the Little Red Book is officially called—was originally printed, well before the Cultural Revolution, only for members of the armed forces. It was not widely distributed among civilians until the summer of 1966. The first page contains a facsimile of a statement by Lin Piao: "Study Chairman Mao's writings, follow his teachings and act according to his instructions."

For later editions, Lin Piao wrote a special five-page preface. He says that Mao "inherited, defended and developed Marxism-Leninism . . . and brought it to a higher and completely new stage." The task was now "to arm the minds of the people throughout the country with it . . . the broad masses of workers, peasants and soldiers and the broad ranks of the revolutionary cadres, and the intellectuals should really master Mao Tse-tung's thought . . . and be his good fighters." Lin Piao recommended that people "memorize important statements and study and apply them repeatedly" so that they will become "an inexhaustible source of strength and a spiritual atom bomb of infinite power."

By the end of 1967 there were reports of a new printing of 350 million copies of the Little Red Book; [1] and barely a year later the following figures were triumphantly announced, representing the total distribution for the period from the summer of 1966 to October 1968:

Little Red Book:	740,000,000 copies
Selected Works (four volumes) :	150,000,000 copies
Selected Readings:	140,000,000 copies
Mao's poems:	96,000,000 copies
Other political writings by Mao: *	2,000,000,000 copies

* *Peking Review,* 1969, #2.

That means that every person in China (not just every adult!) has a copy of the Little Red Book, and almost every family has a four-volume set of the *Selected Works*. In addition to this, ten million copies of Mao's works (probably mostly the little Red Book) were translated into a total of twenty-two languages and sent all over the world.

Never before in history have the writings of a single individual been published in such quantities. Whole forests were devoured by the paper factories. Three hundred different printing plants were needed to print the *Selected Works* alone. For the time being, the

[1] *China News Analysis,* #744.

production of all other books and magazines has all but come to a halt.

Nobody can measure the real impact of the Little Red Book on the population of China. Here I have considered only the quantitative aspect of the question—always assuming that the Peking figures are correct. In any event, a hundred million copies more or less would hardly matter.

PART IV: DOCUMENTS

Since the author's main interest lies in knowing how the storm of the Cultural Revolution affected the everyday lives of the Chinese people, rather than in the political or economic changes it brought about, the documents that follow are chiefly concerned with the ideological, sociological, and psychological aspects of Maoism, and with some phenomena and developments in China's intellectual and artistic life.

All direct quotations from Mao within these documents are in **boldface.**

Document 1: The Parable of the Foolish Old Man [1]

Mao found this legend, which expresses his own fundamental belief that the power of the human will can move mountains, in a Taoist book dating back more than two thousand years. He incorporated it into his closing speech at the Seventh National Congress of the Chinese Communist Party in Yenan on June 11, 1945, and today every child in China knows the story. Nothing else Mao has ever said expresses as clearly as this fable his firm resolve to rely on the will of the people rather than on nature or history. Mao does not think the "Foolish Old Man" is really foolish nor does he regard the "Wise Old Man" as genuinely wise.

There is an ancient Chinese fable called "The Foolish Old Man Who Removed the Mountains." It tells of an old man who lived in northern China long, long ago and was known as the Foolish Old Man of North Mountain. His house faced south, and beyond his doorway stood the two great peaks, Taihang and Wangwu, obstructing the way. With great determination, he led his sons in digging up these mountains, hoe in hand. Another graybeard, known as the Wise Old Man, saw them and said derisively, "How silly of you to do this! It is quite impossible for you few to dig up these two huge mountains." The Foolish Old Man replied: "When I die, my sons will carry on; when they die, there will be my grandsons, and then their sons and grandsons, and so on to infinity. High as they are, the mountains cannot grow any higher and with every bit we dig, they will be that much lower. Why can't we clear them away?" Having refuted the Wise Old Man's wrong view, he went on digging every day, unshaken in his conviction. God was moved by this, and he sent down two angels, who carried the mountains away on their backs. Today, two big mountains, lie like a dead weight on the Chinese people. One is imperialism, the other is feudalism. The Chinese Communist Party has long made up its mind to dig them up. We must persevere and work unceasingly, and we too will touch God's heart. Our God is none other than the masses of the Chinese people. If they stand up and dig together, with us, why can't these two mountains be cleared away?

[1] Mao Tse-tung, *Selected Works,* Volume III (Peking, 1969). From a speech given June 11, 1945.

Document 2: Consciousness Creates Matter [1]

Like Lenin, Mao wants to be not only the political but also the ideological leader of his people. He has therefore turned the parable of the Foolish Old Man, which deals with the power of will and thus with the power of the mind, into philosophical thought. He introduced it almost twenty years later in a passage he contributed to the "Draft Resolution of the Central Committee of the Chinese Communist Party Concerning Certain Current Problems of Agricultural Labor" (May 10, 1963). It is given here in its entirety.

Where do correct ideas come from? Do they drop from the skies? No. Are they innate in the mind? No. They come from social practice, and from it alone; they come from three kinds of social practice, the struggle for production, the class struggle, and scientific experiment.

It is man's social being that determines his thinking. Once the correct ideas characteristic of the advanced class are grasped by the masses, these ideas turn into a material force which changes society and changes the world.

In their social practice, men engage in various kinds of struggle and gain rich experience, both from their successes and from their failures. Countless phenomena of the objective external world are reflected in a man's brain through his five sense organs—the organs of sight, hearing, taste, smell, and touch. At first, knowledge is perceptual. The leap to conceptual knowledge, i.e., to ideas, occurs when sufficient perceptual knowledge is accumulated. This is one process in cognition. It is the first stage in the whole process of cognition, the stage leading from objective matter to subjective consciousness, from existence to ideas. Whether or not one's consciousness or ideas (including theories, policies, plans, or measures) do correctly reflect the laws of the objective external world is not yet proved at this stage, in which it is not yet possible to ascertain whether they are correct or not. Then comes the second stage in the process of cognition, the stage leading from consciousness back to matter, from ideas back to existence, in which the ideas won during the first stage are applied to social practice to ascertain whether

[1] Draft Resolution of the Central Committee, May 20, 1963.

the theories, policies, plans, or measures meet with the anticipated success.

Generally speaking, those that succeed are correct, and those that fail are incorrect, and this is especially true of man's struggle with nature. In social struggle, the forces representing the advanced class suffer defeat not because their ideas are incorrect but because, in the balance of forces engaged in struggle, they are not as powerful for the time being as the forces of reaction; they are therefore temporarily defeated, but they are bound to triumph sooner or later. Man's knowledge makes another leap through the test of practice. This leap is more important than the previous one. For it is this leap alone that can prove the correctness or incorrectness of the first leap in cognition, i.e., of the ideas, theories, policies, plans, or measures formulated in the course of reflecting the objective external world. There is no other way of testing truth.

Often, correct knowledge can be arrived at only after many repetitions of the process leading from matter to consciousness and then back to matter, that is, leading from practice to knowledge and then back to practice. Such is the Marxist theory of knowledge, the dialectical materialist theory of knowledge.

Among our comrades there are many who do not yet understand this theory of knowledge. When asked the source of their ideas, opinions, policies, methods, plans and conclusions, eloquent speeches and long articles, they consider the question strange and cannot answer it. Nor do they comprehend that matter can be transformed into consciousness and consciousness into matter, although such leaps are phenomena of everyday life. It is therefore necessary to educate our comrades in the dialectical materialist theory of knowledge, so that they can orientate their thinking correctly, become good at investigation and study and at summing up experience, overcome difficulties, commit fewer mistakes, do their work better and struggle hard so as to build China into a great and powerful socialist country, and help the broad masses of the oppressed and exploited throughout the world in fulfillment of our great internationalist duty.

Document 3: The Army: School of the Nation [1]

Mao's letter of May 7, 1966, to Minister of Defense Lin Piao (his heir apparent since 1969), was published at a moment that has since made it appear to be the manifesto of the Cultural Revolution. It appeared on August 1, 1966, immediately before the session of the Central Committee of the Chinese Communist Party at which the Cultural Revolution was officially proclaimed. It became known only later that the letter had been written three months beforehand.

At the time he wrote it, Mao was engaged in a violent struggle with hostile elements within the Party; his main objective in writing it may have been to bolster the influence and the image of the army. Later on, in connection with the Seventh of May schools mentioned in the documents that follow, the emphasis has been mainly on the second half of the letter.

The People's Liberation Army should be a great school. In this great school, our army men should learn politics, military affairs, and culture. They can also engage in agricultural production and side occupations, run some medium-sized or small factories and manufacture a number of products to meet their own needs or for exchange with the state at equal values. They can also do mass work and take part in the socialist education movement in the factories and villages. After the socialist education movement is over, they can always find mass work to do, so that the army will for ever be at one with the masses. They should also participate in the struggles of the cultural revolution to criticize the bourgeoisie whenever they occur. In this way, the army can concurrently study, engage in agriculture, run factories and do mass work. Of course, these tasks should be properly coordinated, and a distinction should be made between the primary and secondary tasks. Each army unit should engage in one or two of the three fields of activity—agriculture, industry and mass work, but not in all three at the same time. In this way, our army of several million will be able to play a very great role indeed.

[1] Editorial, *People's Daily*, August 1, 1966. The English version is from *Peking Review*, 1966, #32, pp. 6–7.

It has been Comrade Mao Tse-tung's consistent idea that the people's army should be run as a great school of revolution. We did so in the past. Now, in the light of the new conditions, Comrade Mao Tse-tung has put higher demands on the Liberation Army.

Comrade Mao Tse-tung has called on the people of the whole country to turn China's factories, rural people's communes, schools, trading undertakings, service trades and Party and government organizations into great schools for revolutionization like the Liberation Army.

Comrade Mao Tse-tung has pointed out:

While the main activity of the workers is in industry, they should at the same time also study military affairs, politics, and culture. They, too, should take part in the socialist education movement and in criticizing the bourgeoisie. Where conditions permit, they should also engage in agricultural production and side occupations, as is done at the Taching oilfield.

While the main activity of the peasants in the communes is in agriculture (including forestry, animal husbandry, side occupations and fisheries), they, too, should at the same time study military affairs, politics and culture. Where conditions permit, they should also collectively run some small factories. They should also criticize the bourgeoisie.

This holds good for students too. While their main task is to study, they should in addition to their studies, learn other things, that is, industrial work, farming and military affairs. They should also criticize the bourgeoisie. The period of schooling should be shortened, education should be revolutionized, and the domination of our schools by bourgeois intellectuals should by no means be allowed to continue.

Where conditions permit, those working in commerce, in the service trades and in Party and government organizations should also do the same.

In the following commentary, two additional points are stressed: first, that the Army is the motor force for further revolution; and second, that the gap between intellectual and manual work must be bridged.

The idea set forth by Comrade Mao Tse-tung that every field of work should be made into a great school for revolutionization, where people take part both in industry and agriculture, in military as well as civilian affairs—such is our programme. . . .

By acting in accordance with what Comrade Mao Tse-tung has said, it will be possible to promote the step-by-step narrowing of the gap between workers and peasants, town and countryside and mental and manual labour; to prevent abnormal urban and industrial development; to enable intellectuals to become at the same time manual workers and manual workers at the same time intellectuals; and to train hundreds of millions of new communist people who have a high degree of political consciousness and are developed in an all-round way. . . .

By acting in accordance with what Comrade Mao Tse-tung has said, the 700 million people of our country will all become critics of the old world as well as builders and defenders of the new world. With hammer in hand they will be able to do factory work, with hoe, plough or harrow they will be able to do farming, with the gun they will be able to fight the enemy, and with the pen they will be able to express themselves in writing.

In this way, the whole country will be a great school of Mao Tse-tung's thought, a great school of communism.

It is in accordance with this idea of Comrade Mao Tse-tung that the Chinese People's Liberation Army has worked in the last few decades and is still continuously developing and improving itself. The Liberation Army is the best great school for studying Mao Tse-tung's thought. All factories, rural people's communes, schools, shops, service trades, and Party and government organizations in the country must follow the example set by the Liberation Army and turn themselves into great schools of Mao Tse-tung's thought.

Document 4: Physical Labor for Cadres [1]

Mao's belief that civil servants, party officials, and intellectuals can be reintegrated with the masses through physical labor, dates to the period before his victory in China. It was revived during the Cultural Revolution, especially in the Seventh of May schools described in Part I of this book. Mao's directive of October 4, 1968, had a decisive influence.

CHAIRMAN MAO TSE-TUNG'S LATEST DIRECTIVE

Sending the masses of cadres to do manual work gives them an excellent opportunity to study once again; this should be done by all cadres except those who are too old, weak, ill, or disabled. Cadres at work should also go group by group to do manual work.

[1] *Peking Review,* 1968, #41.

Document 5: In the Universities: Learn from Shanghai! [1]

For a while after the universities were closed in June, 1966, on the eve of the Cultural Revolution, the question of higher education faded into the background. Only after July 21, 1968, when Mao had cited Machine Tools Plant #1 in Shanghai as a model for all future higher education in China, and after an "Investigation Report" concerning this plant had been published, the first outlines of a new system of higher education began to take shape. What follows here is the complete text of one of "Mao's Latest Directives," containing the broad generalizations and the pithy style so typical of the directives of those years.

CHAIRMAN MAO TSE-TUNG'S LATEST DIRECTIVE

It is still necessary to have universities; here I refer mainly to colleges of science and engineering. However, it is essential to shorten the length of schooling, revolutionize education, put proletarian politics in command and take the road of the Shanghai Machine Tools Plant in training technicians from among the workers. Students should be selected from among workers and peasants with practical experience, and they should return to production after a few years' study.

[1] *Peking Review,* 1968, #31.

Document 6: A Model for China's Universities [1]

On July 22, 1968, the People's Daily *published an article announced as an "Investigation Report," under the title "The Road for Training Engineering and Technical Personnel indicated by the Shanghai Machine Tools Plant." In Part I of this book (see Chapter 13) I described my visit to this plant. Its program for training its own technicians and engineers on the job became what Mao called "a model for China's Universities." In an introduction to the article, the* People's Daily *urged the replacement of the old educational system by a new one. It advises the students, "who look down on the workers and peasants, and think themselves great," to drop their "affected airs." The report itself is full of complaints about technicians of the old school: their conceit, their impracticality, their unrealistic attitude—exactly the same things I had heard during my visit to the plant. In contrast to such good-for-nothing university graduates, the workers are praised as experienced and reliable and they are hailed as the source of future technological leadership.*

The long article concludes:

The combination of the revolutionary spirit of daring to think, to act and to make a breakthrough with a strict scientific attitude is an essential prerequisite for engineering and technical personnel in scaling the heights of science and technology. A person's world outlook as well as his practical experience is of vital importance in achieving this combination. Many technicians of worker origin, free from the spiritual fetters of working for personal fame or gain and rich in practical experience, dare to do away with fetishes and superstitions and break through all unnecessary restrictions and are the least conservative in their thinking. Take, for instance, the recently successfully trial-produced precision grinder which has reached advanced international standards. Because the technicians of worker origin courageously broke through long-standing restrictions, they cut the time needed to make the prototype from the usual eighteen months to six. The surface finish was advanced four

[1] *People's Daily,* July 22, 1968. Quoted in the *Peking Review,* 1968, #31.

grades, and the number of parts and the total weight were both reduced by one-third. It cost only 15.5 percent of the price of an imported precision grinder of the same type. Some technicians trained in schools do not pay attention to their own ideological remolding. They are prone to be concerned with their own gains and losses, and fear to lose face or give up their airs. At the same time, because they have accommodated themselves to many regulations and restrictions, it is not easy for them to do away with old fetishes and superstitions and evolve new technologies. Some of them say: "The more books one reads, the heavier the yoke becomes. And, as a result, one loses the spirit of a path-breaker."

If faced with a choice between graduates from colleges or graduates from secondary technical schools, the workers in the Shanghai Machine Tools Plant prefer the latter because the technical school students put on less airs, have more practical experience and are less bound by foreign conventions though they may have less book knowledge. Quite a number of students in this category have made much more rapid progress than students from colleges. For example, the current designing of two highly efficient automatic production lines is led by a couple of 1956 graduates from secondary technical schools.

The Orientation for the Revolution in Education as Shown by the Plant

An analysis of the different types of engineering and technical personnel at the Shanghai Machine Tools Plant and the roads they have traversed shows us the orientation for the revolution in education.

From practical experience, the veteran workers and many of the young technical personnel of the plant have come to realize more deeply the wisdom and correctness of Chairman Mao's teaching: **"The domination of our schools by bourgeois intellectuals should by no means be allowed to continue."** They find that the carrying out of the proletarian revolution in education in accordance with Chairman Mao's thinking on education is a matter of great importance which brooks no delay. Chairman Mao's series of instructions on the revolution in education have shown us the way forward. The question now is to act unswervingly and faithfully in line with Chairman Mao's teachings.

In accordance with Chairman Mao's thinking on education and in view of the actual conditions in the plant, the workers and technical personnel put forward the following opinions and ideas in respect to the revolution in education:

First, schools must train up **"workers with both socialist consciousness and culture"** as pointed out by Chairman Mao and not "intellectual aristocrats" who are divorced from proletarian politics, from the worker and peasant masses and from production, as the revisionist educational line advocated. This is a cardinal question which concerns whether or not revisionism will emerge. Comrades at the Shanghai Machine Tools Plant are of the opinion that the past practice of college graduates working as cadres in factories or in the countryside right after leaving college was irrational. Integrating themselves with the workers and peasants and participating in productive labor is the important way for young students to remould their world outlook and gain practical technical knowledge. Therefore, they propose that college graduates should first take part in manual labour in factories or in the countryside and work as ordinary labourers. They should get "qualification certificates" from the workers and peasants, and then, according to the needs of the practical struggle, some may take up technical work while participating in labor for a certain amount of time. The others will remain workers or peasants.

Second, school education must be combined with productive labor. Chairman Mao teaches: **"Our chief method is to learn warfare through warfare."** As was seen from the case of some technical personnel at the Shanghai Machine Tools Plant, one serious drawback of the old educational system was that theory was divorced from practice and scholasticism was vigorously established so that the students became bookworms and the more they read the more foolish they became. Only by taking part in practice, can one grasp theory quickly, understand it profoundly and apply it creatively. Workers and technical personnel at this plant suggest that schools should have experienced workers as teachers, so that workers appear on the classroom platform. Some courses can be given by workers in the workshops. There was a young technician who worked in a research institute right after he had graduated from college. All day long, he immersed himself in books, trying to digest theory and learn foreign languages. Since he was divorced from practice, he felt more and more frustrated. In the initial stage of the great cultural revolution, he went to learn from some veteran workers with rich experience in the machine tools plant where he worked at the bench. As a result, things were quite different. Recently he and some workers made a significant creation in the field of mirror surface grinding. He is particularly impressed by the fact that he must have the workers as his teachers.

Third, as to the source of engineering and technical personnel, they maintain that, apart from continuing to promote technical personnel from among the workers, junior and senior middle school graduates who are good politically and ideologically and have two to three or four to five years of practical experience in production, should be picked from grass-roots units and sent to colleges to study. All conditions now exist for this to be done. Take the Shanghai Machine Tools Plant for example. Most of its workers have acquired a level equivalent to or above junior middle school education. The advantages in selecting such young people to go to college are as follows: first, they have a fairly solid political and ideological foundation; second, they have a certain competence in practical work and are experienced in productive labor; and third, junior and senior middle school graduates average about 20 years of age after they have taken part in labour for a few years. A few years of higher education then fits them for independent work at the age of 23 to 24. But as it is now, after being assigned to their work posts, college graduates generally have to undertake two to three years of practical work before they are gradually able to work independently. Therefore, the selection of young intellectuals with practical experience for college training is in conformity with the principle of achieving greater, faster, better and more economical results.

Fourth, on the question of reforming the present technical force in factories and raising its level, they point out that large numbers of school-trained technical personnel have for a long time been poisoned by the revisionist educational line and the revisionist line in running enterprises. There is also a group of technical personnel trained before liberation. Though some of them are patriotic and hard-working, do not oppose the Party and socialism and maintain no illicit relations with any foreign country, yet there are many unsolved problems in their world outlook and style of work. Factories should hold aloft the great revolutionary banner of criticism in line with Mao Tse-tung's thought and organize them to participate actively in revolutionary mass criticism and repudiation in accordance with the policies laid down in the Decision of the Central Committee of the Chinese Communist Party Concerning the Great Proletarian Cultural Revolution. This will enable them to repudiate thoroughly the fallacies that "experts should run the factories" and "technique comes first" as well as the "philosophies of going-slow" and of "servility to things foreign" which China's Khrushchev trumpeted. It will also enable them to repudiate thoroughly bourgeois ideas of chasing after fame and fortune. Factories should, at the same time, help them take the road of integrating themselves with the workers and linking theory with practice by organizing them to work, by stages and by groups, as rank-and-file workers, or by arranging more time for them to work in the workshops.

Document 7: He Swam for Mao[1]

Very often, the new heroes who are held up to the people as examples are soldiers. In the course of the Cultural Revolution, however, the "re-education" of the young intellectuals became an important issue, and some popular heroes came from that group as well. Chin Hsün-hua from Shanghai is one of them. Born in 1949, the year of Communist victory, he graduated from high school, and his twelve years of schooling made him one of the "educated young." At the beginning of the Cultural Revolution, he joined the Red Guards; at twenty, he volunteered for manual labor in Manchuria.

His diary was published after his death in the summer of 1969. It shows how he gradually came to the conclusion that the ostensibly uneducated peasants with whom he worked were really more intelligent than he—in spite of all his "years of book learning." Here are some of the entries:

JULY 7

I weeded the land with a hoe today. I thought that weeding wouldn't be difficult for me who had had many years of schooling. Hoe all the weeds and leave the maize plants behind; the more plants left standing, the bigger the harvest.

The poor and lower-middle peasants pointed out that the way I was hoeing would not bring about a bumper crop this year. I thought that I had been right! I didn't know that the maize would be stunted when too many plants were left. This would certainly lead to a poor yield. I came to understand this later. It's thus clear that what I have learnt in the past is divorced from practice. I must earnestly accept re-education from the poor and lower-middle peasants so as to remold my thinking and integrate theory with practice.

JULY 17

I had a stomach-ache this afternoon. At first I didn't want to go to work.

[1] *Peking Review*, 1970, #4.

But as I thought of the amount of work to be done and the shortage of hands, I became aware that, though my absence wouldn't matter much, the effect on others would be bad. So I decided to go. As I worked, my stomach-ache somewhat eased. This shows that as far as we young people, especially the educated youths, are concerned, labor helps relieve some of our aches and pains. While our thinking is being remolded we can also rid ourselves of some of our physical ailments. I'm determined to improve my physical health while painstakingly remolding my ideology.

JULY 28

I must learn from the unsung heroes, honestly be a willing "ox" for the people, diligently and conscientiously serve the poor and lower-middle peasants all my life.

AUGUST 4

We must strengthen our preparations against war and be in battle array to hit hard at the wolfish social-imperialists [i.e., the Soviet Union].

AUGUST 14 [*the day before his death*]

Today I was angry beyond words when I heard over the radio the note of our Foreign Ministry. [In a note dated August 13, 1969, the Chinese Foreign Ministry lodged a protest with the Soviet Government against the incidents on the Russian-Chinese border in Central Asia.] We warn the imperialists, revisionists and other reactionaries throughout the world that the revolutionary young people living in the era of Mao Tse-tung Thought are not to be bullied. Should U.S. imperialism and Soviet revisionist social-imperialism dare to come for a trial of strength with us, we will certainly give them a taste of the iron fists of the third and fourth generations of China!

We are young people of the new generation of socialist China. U.S. imperialism and Soviet revisionism pin their hopes for "restoration" on us. What daydreams! Corrosion by bourgeois ideas will be wiped out. Fully-armed paper-tigers are nothing to be afraid of! . . .

Down with social-imperialism!

We will defend our fatherland's territory, no matter what happens!

We will defend Chairman Mao even at the cost of our lives!

Chin's death is reported to having taken place in this way:
One day as Chin was at work in a field near a river, some
poles that were to be used in the construction of an electricity
network were swept away by the high tide. Without hesitation
Chin jumped into the torrent, which was racing along at speeds
of "seven or eight meters" per second, and tried to save the
poles, though they shot through the waters "fast as arrows."
The account continues:

Someone from the river bank called out, trying to stop him: "The current is too swift. It's too dangerous!" But Hsiao Chin shouted back: **"When we die for the people it is a worthy death."**

The production team leader, knowing that Hsiao Chin had a stomach ailment, cried out: "You can't catch up with the poles. Come back at once!" He was afraid that Hsiao Chin couldn't hold out and an accident might occur. But Hsiao Chin shouted in a firm voice: "Don't worry about me. After the poles, quick!"

He battled the tempestuous waves bravely. One big wave dashed him into a whirlpool, but he raised his head again and made for the nearby pole. Another wave whipped him back into the whirlpool, but again he emerged and rushed ahead for the pole. A third big wave descended upon him, with tenacity he pushed his head to the surface again and dashed towards the pole.

To Chin Hsün-hua, the floating poles were not merely two pieces of wood. They were part of the transmission and telecomumnication lines which stand upright on the vast expanse of our motherland's frontiers. They were the means through which Chairman Mao's words and the news of victories in struggles were transmitted.

The tests Hsiao Chin experienced in battling the three wave onslaughts involving a life-and-death struggle are a powerful criticism of the revisionist "philosophy of survival." Hsiao Chin's strength began to fail with each struggle, and he was carried deeper and deeper into the water and farther and farther away from the shore, but, on the other hand, he was climbing nearer and nearer to the ideological peak of **"fearing neither hardship nor death."**

Charge forward, charge forward! Seizing the pole means victory! Only one meter separated Hsiao Chin from the pole. But just then, another torrential wave rushed in and roared over Hsaio Chin. . . .

Comrade Chin Hsün-hua died a martyr's death.

Document 8: Fresh Tomatoes Thanks to Mao's Thought [1]

"Life study" of the teachings of Chairman Mao is the first rule in every aspect of daily life. One result is the appearance of articles such as the following, written by the "Scientific Research Group for Experimental Vegetable Farming of the Agency for Alimentary Supplements" in Peking.

Once during a scientific experiment, while checking over tomatoes which had been stored for over a month, we found three still in good condition. Why hadn't these three turned bad when all the others had? With this problem in mind, we made a thorough study of Chairman Mao's philosophical works. Chairman Mao teaches: **"In particularity there is universality."** If these three tomatoes could be kept fresh, we reasoned, why not others? Provided similar conditions were created, other tomatoes could also be preserved. Accordingly, we engaged in extensive research on three factors involved in good storage—temperature, ventilation and humidity—and finally succeeded in keeping large quantities of stored tomatoes in good condition.

Soon afterwards, in line with Chairman Mao's teaching, **"Practice, knowledge, again practice, and again knowledge,"** we summed up our experience in storing tomatoes: If the temperature in the store room is too high and the humidity too great, the tomatoes will spoil more readily. If the temperature is too low, they will get chilled, while if the room is too drafty, they will lose their freshness through dehydration and shrinking. It is therefore important to handle properly the contradictory relations between temperature, humidity and ventilation. How could this be done best?

Chairman Mao teaches us: **"In studying any complex process in which there are two or more contradictions, we must devote every effort to finding its principal contradiction. Once this principal contradiction is grasped, all problems can be readily solved."** Accordingly, we carried out one experiment after another, analyzing the results each time specifically with regard to these three basic factors. In the end we found out that the

---

[1] *China Pictorial,* February, 1971.

principal contradiction is one between temperature and ventilation and that the principal aspect in this contradiction is temperature. Thus various effective measures were first taken to keep the temperature at the correct level in the storage cellar, and after that humidity and ventilation were properly dealt with. As it turned out, in July we succeeded in storing more than 800,000 *jin* of tomatoes and sending them to market steadily throughout August and September. This basically solved the contradiction between the seasonal nature of tomato growing and the steady demand of the market.

Although initial success had been scored through the experiments on tomato storage, we were not entirely clear as to the laws governing the contradictoriness within the tomato. [!] Chairman Mao teaches us: "It [materialist dialectics] **holds that external causes are the condition of change and internal causes are the basis of change, and that external causes become operative through internal causes.**" In line with this teaching, we continued to experiment and investigate, eventually grasping the laws governing the inner changes of the tomato.

Metabolism of the tomato still goes on after it is separated from the plant. It gives off carbon dioxide and takes in oxygen, completing what is known in botany as "post ripening" as it gradually uses up its nutrient.

According to this law, we did more experiments and adopted a new method for more effectively depressing the respiration of the tomato and lowering its metabolism, in order to enable it to remain fresh over a long period of storage. The results proved satisfactory. Since then, Peking residents have been able to enjoy fresh tomatoes in winter. The tomato, formerly known as an "overnight headache" because of quick spoilage, is now praised for its "hundred-day freshness."

Document 9: Redeemed by Mao [1]

*The following confession from a Chinese physicist, Tang
Ao-ching, a professor at the university of Kirin in Manchuria,
is psychologically quite illuminating; it describes in a relatively
articulate way—instead of the usual wooden prose—how he
was converted to Maoism and was "integrated with the
masses."*

Before liberation [i.e., before 1949] I was studying abroad. I returned to
China early in 1950 with a strong desire to contribute to the development of science in my country. Educated by the Party and Mao Tse-tung.
Though, my political level became higher and in 1958 I became a member of the Communist Party.

But I had received a bourgeois education. I worked in higher institutions where Liu Shao-chi's revisionist line in education kept me away
from the worker and peasant masses, away from class struggle and
actual work in production. This prevented me from conscientiously trying to change my thinking in a working-class direction.

The Great Proletarian Cultural Revolution started and led by Chairman Mao shook me up and made me see that I was far from solving the
fundamental problem of integrating myself with the workers, peasants
and soldiers and serving the people of China and the world, a principle
Chairman Mao has always insisted on.

Last year I went with a group of young teachers to work in a chemical
plant where we joined the workers in experiments to find a non-mercury
catalyst. The workers asked me many technical and theoretical questions.
But I always answered, "I'm only here as a pupil. Let me learn from
you first." It was not that I was being modest. I was afraid to give the
wrong answer and lose the "dignity" of a professor.

As time went on the workers saw that some kind of fear lay behind
my "modesty." Many of them came to me to talk warmly and honestly.
They told me that under Liu Shao-chi's revisionist line the plant had
continued to use a mercury catalyst in some processes. It was a capitalist
technology which seriously impaired the health of many workers. To free
them from this menace and save mercury for more urgent uses, the plant

---

[1] *China Reconstructs,* April, 1971.

began experimenting in 1958 to find a non-mercury catalyst. But the capitalist-roaders in the plant ignored the health problem and tried to stop the experiments. An experimental shop was set up only after the working class took over power in production during the cultural revolution.

"We hope you will make our hopes and worries your hopes and worries," said the workers. "We hope you will shift your stand completely to the side of the working class and firmly take the road of integration with the workers, peasants and soldiers."

I opened Chairman Mao's *Talks at the Yenan Forum on Literature and Art* [1942] and read the passage where he said that if the intellectuals wish to serve the proletariat, **"They must change and remold their thinking and their feelings. Without such a change, without such remolding, they can do nothing well and will be misfits."**

The words seemed pointed straight at me. I remembered visiting this plant when the revisionist line still held sway. I had seen only the plant director, the chief engineer and a few of the shops. Now I realized that it was Liu Shao-chi who had separated me from the working class. Having come into direct contact with the workers, I saw how vastly different our thoughts and feelings were. What the working class had in mind was the health of their class brothers, the interests of the revolution. What I had in mind was a professor's "dignity" and my own interests. Though I had put on worker's clothes, I was not thinking like a worker. . . .

I lived and worked with the men in the plant. In our experiments I offered my views and discussed them with the workers. When there were problems, we studied Chairman Mao's works together to look for guidelines. Several times the equipment for the experiments stalled. Worried, I proposed changes and climbed the two-story steel frame with the workers to make the alterations. We not only quickly eliminated the cause of the stalling but increased the efficiency of the experiments.

"The professor has thrown off his airs," said the workers. "His heart has moved closer to ours."

While the experiments were still going on, I went back to the university to attend a Mao Tse-tung Thought study class. When I returned to the plant I was eager to really make something of the experiments. The first day, someone told me that the workers had launched a mass criticism of the revisionist idea of blind worship of everything foreign and trailing behind others at a snail's pace. He added that the slogans

279

"Break away from foreign conventions" and "Throw away foreign crutches" were aimed at me. I was shocked. Had I become a "foreign crutch"?

The next morning I went to the shop rather apprehensive. A master worker greeted me warmly and told me that the plant was learning from the advanced experience of other plants and taking the road of **"maintaining independence and keeping the initiative in our own hands and relying on our own efforts."** He said that because Liu Shao-chi's revisionist line blocked scientific experiment, the workers were criticizing the line and had raised the slogans, "Break away from foreign conventions! Throw away foreign crutches! Produce a non-mercury catalyst!"

I breathed a sigh of relief. I was not the "foreign crutch" after all. But then I thought of the words of a member of the workers' propaganda team in our university who was working with us: "You should take a correct attitude toward mass criticism and stand on the side of the working class." I took a real good look at my thoughts during the previous two days. The first day I had stood with the bourgeoisie when I thought I had become a "foreign crutch." The second day when I realized I had nothing to do with "foreign crutches," I had made myself an onlooker of the mass criticism—revealing the fact that I actually did have "foreign crutches" in my mind. In those two days I did not stand on the side of the working class. . . .

I looked up at Chairman Mao's portrait on the wall and thought of July 31, 1966, the day I had met Chairman Mao with scientists from Asia, Africa, Latin America and Oceania attending a physics symposium in Peking. Chairman Mao was expressing his concern and encouragement, hoping the scientists would stand together with the revolutionary people of the world who oppose imperialism, revisionism and reaction, and make greater contributions to this struggle. Yet here I was, standing on the opposite side of the working class. The more I thought about it, the more I felt I had not lived up to the expectations of Chairman Mao and the working class. . . .

In the past I always chose my subject for experiment from foreign literature. They were of little practical value. Now I began to see that any research we do must fit the needs of the workers, peasants and soldiers, the needs of production, the needs of the revolution. . . .

Chairman Mao has said that a **"change in world outlook is something fundamental."** This change involves a man's entire outlook on life, not just the solving of one or another ideological problem that comes up for a time. The proletarian outlook on life centers around public interest. The bourgeois outlook on life centers around self-interest. . . .

I will never forget an incident. During the experiment the workers suggested that if we could find an active center in the non-mercury catalyst system, we could raise output by a big margin. I pored over a great amount of literature and data and worked out a plan which I felt was theoretically rational. I expected it to produce unusual catalytic activity. The workers were also saying to each other, "The professor has not committed himself for several months now. He's not the type to take the lid off the pot before his stuff is well cooked. You can expect something great."

I was full of self-satisfaction myself. I worked at the experiment practically around the clock. When the time came, there was no activity at all! I was stunned and chagrined. I couldn't keep my mind off the formulas and elements, not even when I was eating and sleeping. The workers knew how I felt. "Draw your lessons," they said, "not from the technical side of the experiment, but from the ideological side."

What was my ideological problem? I turned to Chairman Mao's teaching, **"These comrades have their feet planted on the side of the petty-bourgeois intellectuals; or, to put it more elegantly, their innermost soul is still a kingdom of the petty-bourgeois intelligentsia."**

This unlocked my ideological problem. . . . I discovered that my innermost soul was still a kingdom of the bourgeois intellectual—I had thought that if the experiment was successful, I would have solved an important problem in chemical production, done something outstanding in integrating myself with the workers and won new fame.

Fame for myself, the center of my outlook on life, coiled around me like a poisonous snake. . . .

I went among the workers and asked for their opinions about the experiment, combining my book knowledge with their practical experience in our experiments. A worker suggested, "This stuff very possibly has catalytic activity. The question is that we haven't found out the conditions for producing it." His words gave me ideas. I put the stuff back into the original intermediate and right away activity was evident. Productivity was ten times higher.

This success helped me to a deeper understanding of Chairman Mao's words, **"Until an intellectual's book knowledge is integrated with practice, it is not complete, and it may be very incomplete indeed."** It was not enough to accept political re-education from the working class, I had

281

also to learn from them in production and research. I stayed close to them and after a year of effort we succeeded in producing a catalyst without mercury. It was an important achievement.

Thus the facts have shown me that the revisionist way of scientific research is a blind alley. It not only poisoned the intellectuals' minds, but let their talents go to waste. By integrating with the workers, peasants and soldiers an intellectual can find plenty of room for his abilities. This is the only way to serve the people.

Document 10: Chiang Ching and the Arts [1]

In both of Mao's speeches on arts and literature given at Yenan in May, 1942 (Selected Works, Volume III), and after that in briefer declarations (Peking Review, 1967, #23), he placed great emphasis—as Lenin had done before him—on the class character of the arts. But it has been his wife, Chiang Ching, who even more than Mao himself has dedicated her efforts towards bringing Maoism to the arts. Her campaign to replace traditional art forms with new and revolutionary ones, a campaign she had been waging almost without interruption since around 1950, finally scored a complete success during the Cultural Revolution.

Her views are most clearly expressed in her speech of July 1964,[2] and in the proceedings of the Forum on Literature of February, 1966, at which she presided.

The following excerpts from the minutes of the Forum also give some information about Chiang Ching herself.

At the beginning of the forum and in the course of the exchange of views, Comrade Chiang Ching said time and again that she had not studied Chairman Mao's works well enough and that her comprehension of Chairman Mao's thought was not profound, but that whatever points she had grasped she would act upon resolutely. She said that during the last four years she had largely concentrated on reading a number of literary works and had formed certain ideas, not all of which were necessarily correct. She said that we were all Party members and that for the cause of the Party we should discuss things together on an equal footing. This discussion should have been held last year but had been postponed because she had not been in good health. As her health had recently improved, she had invited the comrades to join in discussions according to Comrade Lin Piao's instructions.

Comrade Chiang Ching suggested that we read and see a number of

[1] *Important Documents of the Great Proletarian Cultural Revolution,* Peking, 1970.
[2] *Peking Review,* 1967, #21.

items first and then study relevant documents and material before discussing them. She advised us to read Chairman Mao's relevant writings, had eight private discussions with comrades from the army and attended four group discussions, thirteen film shows and three theatrical performances—watching the films and the theatrical performances. And she advised us to see twenty-one other films. During this period, Comrade Chiang Ching saw the rushes of the film *The Great Wall Along the South China Sea,* received the directors, cameramen and part of the cast and talked with them three times, which was a great education and inspiration to them. From our contacts with Comrade Chiang Ching we realize that her understanding of Chairman Mao's thought is quite profound and that she has made a prolonged and fairly full investigation and study of current problems in the field of literature and art and has gained rich practical experience through her personal exertions in carrying on experiments in this field. Taking up her work while she was still in poor health, she held discussions and saw films and theatrical performances together with us and was always modest, warm and sincere. All this has enlightened and helped us a great deal.

In the course of about twenty days, we read two of Chairman Mao's essays and other relevant material, listened to Comrade Chiang Ching's many highly important opinions and saw more than thirty films, including good and bad ones and others with shortcomings and mistakes of varying degrees. We also saw two comparatively successful Peking operas on contemporary revolutionary themes, namely, *Raid on the White Tiger Regiment* and *Taking Tiger Mountain by Strategy.* All this helped to deepen our comprehension of Chairman Mao's thought on literature and art and raise the level of our understanding of the socialist cultural revolution.

The last three years have seen a new situation in the great socialist [3] cultural revolution. The most outstanding example is the rise of Peking operas on contemporary revolutionary themes. Led by the Central Committee of the Party, headed by Chairman Mao, and armed with Marxism-Leninism, Mao Tse-tung Thought, literary and art workers engaged in revolutionizing Peking opera have launched a heroic and tenacious offensive against the literature and art of the feudal class, the bourgeoisie and the modern revisionists. Under the irresistible impact of this offensive,

[3] The "Great Proletarian Cultural Revolution" was so called only after 1966.

Peking opera, formerly the most stubborn of strongholds, has been radically revolutionized, both in ideology and in form, which has started a revolutionary change in literary and art circles. Peking operas on contemporary revolutionary themes like *The Red Lantern, Shachiapang, Taking Tiger Mountain by Strategy* and *Raid on the White Tiger Regiment,* the ballet *Red Detachment of Women,* the symphony *Shachiapang* and the group of clay sculptures *Rent Collection Courtyard* have been approved by the broad masses of workers, peasants and soldiers and acclaimed by Chinese and foreign audiences. They are pioneer efforts which will exert a profound and far-reaching influence on the socialist cultural revolution. They effectively prove that even that most stubborn of strongholds, Peking opera, can be taken by storm and revolutionized and that foreign classical art forms such as the ballet and symphonic music can also be remolded to serve our purpose. This should give us still greater confidence in revolutionizing other art forms. Some people say that Peking operas on contemporary revolutionary themes have discarded the traditions and basic skills of Peking opera. On the contrary, the fact is that Peking operas on contemporary revolutionary themes have inherited the Peking opera traditions in a critical way and have really weeded through the old to bring forth the new. The fact is not that the basic skills of Peking opera have been discarded but that they are no longer adequate. Those which cannot be used to reflect present-day life should and must be discarded. In order to reflect present-day life we urgently need to refine, create, and gradually develop and enrich the basic skills of Peking opera through our experience of real life. At the same time, these successes deal a powerful blow at conservatives of various descriptions and such views as the "box-office earning" theory, the "foreign exchange earnings" theory and the theory that "revolutionary works can't travel abroad."

We must destroy the blind faith in what is known as the literature and art of the 1930s. At that time, the Left-wing movement in literature and art followed Wang Ming's [4] "Left" opportunist line politically; organizationally it practiced closed-doorism and sectarianism; and its ideas on literature and art were virtually those of Russian bourgeois literary critics such as Belinsky, Chernyshevsky and Dobrolyubov and of Stanislavsky in the theatrical field, all of whom were bourgeois democrats in tsarist Russia with bourgeois ideas and not Marxist ones. The bourgeois-democratic revolution is a revolution in which one exploiting class replaces another. It is only the proletarian socialist revolution that finally

[4] A one-time rival of Mao, now living in Moscow.

285

destroys all exploiting classes. Therefore, we must not take the ideas of any bourgeois revolutionary as guiding principles for our proletarian movement in ideology or in literature and art.

We must destroy blind faith in Chinese and foreign classical literature. Stalin was a great Marxist-Leninist. His criticism of the modernist literature and art of the bourgeoisie was very sharp. But he uncritically took over what are known as the classics of Russia and Europe and the consequences were bad. The classical literature and art of China and of Europe (including Russia) and even American films have exercised a considerable influence on our literary and art circles, and some people have regarded them as holy writ and accepted them in their entirety. We should draw a lesson from Stalin's experience. Old and foreign works should be studied too, and refusal to study them would be wrong; but we must study them critically, making the past serve the present and foreign things serve China.

As for the relatively good Soviet revolutionary works of literature and art which appeared after the October Revolution, they too must be analyzed and not blindly worshiped or, still less, blindly imitated. Blind imitation can never become art. Literature and art can only spring from the life of the people which is their sole source. This is borne out by the whole history of literature and art, past and present, Chinese and foreign.

It has always been the case in the world that the rising forces defeat the forces of decay. Our People's Liberation Army was weak and small at the beginning, but it eventually became strong and defeated the U.S.–Chiang Kai-shek reactionaries. Confronted with the excellent revolutionary situation at home and abroad and our glorious tasks, we should be proud to be thoroughgoing revolutionaries. We must have the confidence and courage to do things never previously attempted, because ours is a revolution to eliminate all exploiting classes and systems of exploitation once and for all and to root out all exploiting-class ideologies, which poison the minds of the people. Under the leadership of the Central Committee of the Party and Chairman Mao and under the guidance of Marxism-Leninism, Mao Tse-tung Thought, we must create a new socialist revolutionary literature and art worthy of our great country, our great Party, our great people and our great army. This will be a most brilliant new Literature and art opening up a new era in human history.

We should give the fullest attention to the themes of socialist revolution and socialist construction, and it would be entirely wrong to ignore them.

A serious effort should now be made to create works of literature and art about the three great military campaigns [5] . . . while the comrades who led and directed them are still alive. There are many important revolutionary themes, historical and contemporary, on which work urgently needs to be done in a planned and systematic way.

. . . We must not mind being accused of "brandishing the stick." When some people charge us with over-simplification and crudeness, we must analyze these charges. Some of our criticisms are basically correct but are not sufficiently convincing because our analysis and evidence adduced are inadequate. This state of affairs must be improved.

. . . But when the enemy condemns our correct criticisms as over-simplified and crude, we must stand firm. Literary and art criticism should become one of our day-to-day tasks, an important method both in the struggle in the field of literature and art and in Party leadership in this field of work. Without correct literary and art criticism it is impossible for creative work to flourish.

In the struggle against foreign revisionism in the field of literature and art, we must not only catch small figures like Chukhrai.[6] We should catch the big ones, catch Sholokhov and dare to tackle him. He is the father of revisionist literature and art. His *And Quiet Flows the Don, Virgin Soil Upturned* and *The Fate of a Man* have exercised a big influence on a number of Chinese writers and readers. Shouldn't the army organize people to study his works and write convincing critical articles containing well-documented analysis? This will have a profound influence in China and the rest of the world. The same thing should be done with similar works by Chinese writers.

As for method, we must combine revolutionary realism with revolutionary romanticism in our creative work, and must not adopt bourgeois critical realism or bourgeois romanticism.

The fine qualities of the worker, peasant and soldier heroes who have emerged under the guidance of the correct line of the Party are the concentrated expression of the class character of the proletariat. We must work with wholehearted enthusiasm and do everything possible to create heroic models of workers, peasants and soldiers.

. . . Ours is the side of justice and the enemy's is the side of injustice. Our works must show our arduous struggle and heroic sacrifices, but

[5] Here follow some famous battles of the civil war.
[6] A character in *Quiet Flows the Don*.

287

must also express revolutionary heroism and revolutionary optimism. . . .

Regarding the selection of subject matter, only when we plunge into the thick of life and do a good job of investigation and study can we make the selection properly and correctly. Playwrights should unreservedly plunge into the heat of the struggle for a long period. Directors, actors and actresses, cameramen, painters and composers should also go into the thick of life and make serious investigations and studies. In the past, some works distorted the historical facts, concentrating on the portrayal of erroneous lines instead of the correct line; some described heroic characters who nevertheless invariably violate discipline, or created heroes only to have them die in a contrived tragic ending; other works do not present heroic characters but only "middle" characters who are actually backward people, or caricatures of workers, peasants or soldiers; in depicting the enemy, they fail to expose his class nature as an exploiter and oppressor of the people, and even glamorize him; still others are concerned only with love and romance, pandering to philistine tastes and claiming that love and death are the eternal themes. All such bourgeois and revisionist trash must be resolutely opposed. . . . For historical reasons, before the whole country was liberated it was rather difficult for us proletarians to train our own workers in literature and art in the areas under enemy rule. Our cultural level was relatively low and our experience limited. Many of our workers in literature and art had received a bourgeois education. In the course of their revolutionary activities in literature and art, some failed to pass the test of enemy persecution and turned traitor, while others failed to resist the corrosive influence of bourgeois ideas and became rotten. . . . We must plunge into the thick of life for a long period of time, integrate ourselves with the workers, peasants and soldiers to raise the level of our class consciousness, remold our ideology and wholeheartedly serve the people without any regard for personal fame or gain. It is necessary to teach our comrades to study Marxism-Leninism and Chairman Mao's works and to remain revolutionary all their lives, and pay special attention to the maintenance of proletarian integrity in later life, which is not at all easy.

Document 11: Arias from "Tiger Mountain" [1]

Taking Tiger Mountain by Strategy *is the title of an endlessly revised and, in the opinion of the leaders, most important and successful "Peking opera." The original version was completely reworked in 1963, at the request of Mao's wife, Chiang Ching. A few years later the mise-en-scène was again revised. The commentaries on this newest version hail it as the perfect model for all operas. They also list the following criteria for all successful modern opera:*

The principal hero—the "good guy"—must dominate every scene. (In the 1967 version, one scene still focused on Shao, a minor hero, instead of on Yang, the protagonist.)

In all his actions, the hero must be guided by Mao Tse-tung Thought. (In the 1963 version, this was not mentioned at all.)

The villains (such as the enemy Commandant, known as The Vulture, in Tiger Mountain) *must not, as they still did in earlier performances, possess any good qualities at all.*

The heroic nature of the main character must be emphasized by the stage settings. On his way to Tiger Mountain, for example, Yang used to travel through a forest "with low-hanging branches and twisted tree trunks"; now, "tall, straight pines reach to the sky. Sunshine filters down through the trees. The whole scene is ringing with the majestic strains of 'Through the snowy forest, spirits soaring,' to express meaningfully and effectively the brave, resolute, steadfast, and fearless nature of the hero."

The figure of Yang is praised as "the shining prototype of the Great Hero, the like of which has never been created in the arts of all mankind."

The arias that follow were written for the two male leads and the young heroine, Pao. The first aria is sung by Shao, the regimental Chief of Staff, at his headquarters—"against a backdrop showing majestic mountains."

[1] October 1969 script; *Peking Review*, 1969, #51–52.

SHAO.

Icy wind howls through the woods,
Rustling branches shake the deep gully.

[*A gust blows the door open. He goes to door and looks out.*]

Snowflakes dance in a hazy mist,
The mountains are mantled in silver;
What a magnificent scene of the north!
Beautiful our land, majestic and grand,
How can we let ravening beasts again lay it waste?
The Party Central Committee points the way,
Revolutionary flames cannot be quenched.
Bearing the hopes of the people, the P.L.A. [People's Liberation Army]
    fight north and south
And plant the red flag all over our country.
Let the Yanks and Chiang [Kai-Shek] gang up,
Prating about peace while making attacks,
Fighting openly and sniping in the dark.
Let them resort to a hundred tricks,
With justice in our hands; class hatred in our hearts,
One against ten, we'll still wipe them out. . . .
We've had the enemy sized up in the last few days,
We've analyzed carefully and pondered over our plan.
Tiger Mountain has a system of bunkers and tunnels,
So the better course is to take it by strategy.
Select a capable comrade to disguise as one of their kind,
Then penetrate into the enemy's lair,
And strike from without and within.
Who should we choose for this critical task?—
Yang has all the qualifications to shoulder this load.
Born of a hired-hand peasant family,
From childhood he struggled on the brink of death;
Burning with hatred, he found his salvation
In the Communist Party and took the revolutionary road.
He joined the army, vowing to uproot exploitation,
A veteran in battle, he's distinguished himself many times.
By wits, he blew up many an enemy fort,
He's entered enemy territory, killed traitors
And rescued many comrades and villagers,

He's fought many a battle with bandits here in the forest,
Caught Luan Ping and Hu Piao and took Howling Wolf as well.
If I send him on this dangerous mission alone,
I'm sure, with his heart red as fire,
A will strong as steel,
He'll surely overcome Vulture.

[*Shao gives Yang his orders. Yang sings:*]

YANG.

A Communist always heeds the Party's call,
He takes the heaviest burden on himself;
I'm set on smashing the chains of a thousand years
To open a freshet of endless happiness for the people.
Well I know that there's danger ahead,
But I'm all the more set on driving forward;
No matter how thickly troubled clouds may gather,
Revolutionary wisdom is bound to win.
Like the Foolish Old Man who removed the mountains,
I shall break through every obstacle;
The flames that blaze in my red heart
Shall forge a sharp blade to kill the foe.

[*A few days after the previous scene. In the foothills of Tiger
Mountain. A deep snowy forest. Tall, straight pines reach to
the sky. Sunshine filters down through the trees.*]

YANG.

[*Sings offstage vigorously.*]

I press through the snowy forest, spirit soaring!

[*Yang enters in disguise. He pantomimes a horseback ride. He
executes dances depicting his journey through the dense forest,
leaping across a stream, mounting a ridge, dashing down a
steep slope, galloping across a distance and then looking all
around.*]

To express my determination the mountains I staunchly face.
Let the red flag fly all over the world,

Be there seas of fire and a forest of knives. I'll charge ahead.
How I wish I could order the snow to melt,
And welcome in spring to change the world of men.
The Party gives me wisdom and courage,
Risks and hardships are as naught;
To wipe out the bandits I must dress as a bandit,
And pierce into their stronghold like a dagger.
I'll bury Vulture in these hills, I swear,
Shake the heights with my will.
With my courage the valleys fill,
At the Hundred Chickens Feast [on Tiger Mountain] my comrades and I
Will make a shambles of the bandits' lair.

> [*A tiger roars in the distance. The horse is startled, stumbles. Yang reins in, makes it rear, turns and halts it. Leaps from the horse. The tiger's roar draws nearer. Yang quickly leads his horse off. Re-enters, throws off his overcoat, pulls out pistol and fires at tiger. The beast screams and falls dead. Other shots are heard in the distance.*]

> [*The brotherhood of the army and the people is clearly expressed in the arias of Shao, the railroad worker Li, and the young hunter's daughter Pao.*]

SHAO.

We're worker and peasant soldiers, come
To destroy the reactionaries and change the world.
We've fought for years north and south for the revolution,
With the Party and Chairman Mao leading the way,
A red star on our army caps,
Two red flags of the revolution on our collars,
Where the red flag goes dark clouds disperse,
Liberated people overthrow the landlords,
The people's army shares the people's hardships,
We've come to sweep clean Tiger Mountain.

YUNG-CHI.

> [*His feelings bursting out like spring thunder.*]

Our eyes are nearly worn out, looking for you day and night.
Who would have thought that here in the mountains today

You've come, fighting the bandits and saving the poor—
Here before us our own army!
Our own army,
I shouldn't have confounded right and wrong,
I shouldn't have taken friend for foe.
I am ashamed beyond words.

[*Pushes down the dagger stabbed into the table.*]

For thirty years I've been sweating like a slave.
Feeling these lashes and bruises I can hardly suppress my rage,
I struggle in a bottomless pit.
We have untold misery and wrath to pour out,
Those bandits we all hate to the core.
Some said our suffering would go on and on.
Who would have believed an iron tree could blossom,
That we would at last live to see this day.
I'll go with the Party to drive out those beasts,
Whatever the sacrifice and danger, be it fire or water,
When Tiger Mountain is being swept clean and free,
I, Yung-chi, in the front ranks will be.

PAO.

. . . How I long for the day
When the bandits are slain and a blood debt repaid.
With deep hatred, morning and evening
I sharpen my sword and oil my gun.
On the high cliff the blizzard may blow,
Storm the tiger's den—that I dare.
Why then pick on me to guard the village?
I must see the Chief of Staff at once
And tell him again what's on my mind.
My resolve is to fight on the battlefield,
For I've pledged to kill them all.

YANG.

Hacking through thorns and thistles,
I battle in the heart of the enemy.
When I look into the distance and think of my

Comrades-in-arms, the army and the people, awaiting the signal
To attack these wolves, my spirits soar.
The Party places great hopes on me,
Comrades at the Party branch committee meeting offer weighty advice,
Their many exhortations give me strength,
Their flaming hearts warm my breast.
I must never forget to be bold yet cautious,
And succeed through courage and wits.
The Party's every word is victory's guarantee,
Mao Tse-tung Thought shines for ever.
Tiger Mountain is indeed heavily fortified
With forts above and tunnels below.
The leadership's decision to use strategy is right,
A direct attack would mean heavy losses.
After seven days here I know the disposition well,
I have the secret report concealed on my person.
Now at daybreak, pretending to take a stroll, I'll send it out. . . .

[*Notices something.*]

Why have the guards suddenly been increased?
Something's up.
This message—
If I don't get this message out,
I'll miss the opportunity and ruin our attack plan,
And let the people and Party down.
Lunar New Year's Eve is fast approaching.
I mustn't hesitate, I must push on,
Though the grass be knives and the trees swords,
Down to the foot of the slope.
What though the mountain be tall?
Standing in the cold and melting
The ice and snow, I've the morning sun in my heart.

[*The sun rises filling the sky with red clouds which tinge the
sharp crags.*]

[END]

294

Document 12: The Fidelity of Peking and the Treachery of Moscow [1]

The one hundredth anniversary of the Paris Commune in 1971, like the one hundredth anniversary of the birth of Lenin in 1970, was used as an occasion for renewed pledges of allegiance to Lenin and the Commune—and at the same time to denounce Moscow for betraying those ideals.

In the last two chapters of a long article, published simultaneously in the three leading newspapers of the country (People's Daily, Red Flag and Liberation Army Daily)—an indication that it must be regarded as particularly important—both themes are strongly emphasized. The article also expresses the fundamental schism between Moscow and Peking on the issue of a "single" versus a "continuous" revolution.

V. The Modern Revisionists Are Renegades From the Revolutionary Principles of the Paris Commune

At the time when the proletariat and the revolutionary people of the world are marking the grand centenary of the Paris Commune, the Soviet revisionist renegade clique is putting on an act, talking glibly about "loyalty to the principles of the Commune" [2] and making itself up as the successor to the Paris Commune. It has no sense of shame at all.

What right have the Soviet revisionist renegades to talk about the Paris Commune? It is these renegades who have usurped the leadership of the Soviet Party and state, and as a result the Soviet state founded by Lenin and defended by Stalin has changed its political colour. It is they who have turned the dictatorship of the proletariat into the dictatorship of the bourgeoisie and put social-imperialism and social-fascism into force. This is gross betrayal of the revolutionary principles of the Paris Commune.

From Khrushchev to Brezhnev, all have tried to mask their dictator-

[1] *Peking Review*, 1971, #12.

[2] "The Paris Commune and the Present," article in Soviet revisionist *Kommunist*, No. 2, 1971.

ship of the bourgeoisie as the "state of the whole people." Khrushchev used to say that the Soviet Union had been "transformed . . . into a state of the whole people." [3] Now Brezhnev and his ilk say that theirs is a "Soviet socialist state of the whole people" [4] and that what they practise is "Soviet democracy." All this is humbug.

The Soviet, a great creation of the Russian proletariat, embodied the fact that the working people were masters in their own house, and it was a glorious title. However, the name "Soviet," like the name "Communist Party," can be used by Bolsheviks or Mensheviks, by Marxist-Leninists or revisionists. What is decisive is not the name but the essence, not the form but the content. In the Soviet Union today, the name "Soviet" has not changed, nor has the name of the state, but the class content has changed completely. With its leadership usurped by the Soviet revisionist renegade clique, the Soviet state is no longer an instrument with which the proletariat suppresses the bourgeoisie, but has become a tool with which the restored bourgeoisie suppresses the proletariat. The Soviet revisionist renegades have turned the Soviet Union into a paradise for a handful of bureaucrat-monopoly-capitalists of a new type, a prison for the millions of working people. This is the whole content of what they call a "Soviet socialist state of the whole people" and "Soviet democracy." It is by no means the fact that "the state of the whole people is a direct continuation of the state of the dictatorship of the proletariat," [5] but rather that Brezhnev's line is a "direct continuation" of Khrushchev's line. This is essentially why Brezhnev and his like are clinging desperately to the slogan of the "state of the whole people."

Their frenzied opposition to violent proletarian revolution is another concentrated expression of the betrayal of the revolutionary principles of the Paris Commune by the Soviet revisionist renegade clique. Brezhnev and his company clamorously demand of "the leaders of the proletariat to reduce violence to the minimum at every stage of the struggle and employ milder forms of compulsion"; they bleat that "armed struggle and civil war are accompanied by colossal sacrifices and sufferings on

[3] N. S. Khrushchev's report on the "Programme of the C.P.S.U." at the Soviet revisionist "22nd Congress," October 18, 1961.

[4] L. I. Brezhnev's report at the meeting in "commemoration" of the centenary of Lenin's birth, April 21, 1970.

[5] "The State of the Whole People and Democracy," article in the Soviet revisionist *Pravda,* June 7, 1970.

the part of the masses of the people, by destruction of the productive forces, and by the annihilation of the best revolutionary cadres." To find a pretext for their fallacy of "peaceful transition," this group of renegades wantonly distort history, even preaching that the Paris Commune was "initially" an "almost completely bloodless revolution." [6]

The revolution of the Paris Commune was from beginning to end a life-and-death fight between the proletariat and the bourgeoisie, a struggle of violence between revolution and counterrevolution. In less than six months before the Paris Commune uprising, the people of Paris had staged two armed uprisings, and both were bloodily suppressed by the reactionaries. And in the battles following the uprising, tens of thousands of workers and other working people laid down their lives. How can this revolution be described as an "initially" "almost completely bloodless revolution"? Marx pointed out: "Working men's Paris, with its Commune, will be for ever celebrated as the glorious harbinger of a new society. Its martyrs are enshrined in the great heart of the working class. Its exterminators history has already nailed to that eternal pillory from which all the prayers of their priests will not avail to redeem them." [7] The Soviet revisionist renegade clique has now come out into the open and is playing the part of the priests saying prayers for the exterminators. This is a monstrous insult to the martyrs of the Paris Commune!

The Soviet revisionist renegades try in a hundred and one ways to justify counterrevolutionary violence, but they curse revolutionary violence with clenched teeth. Under the rule of violence by imperialism and the reactionaries, the working people suffer unending pain and large numbers of them die every day, every hour. It is precisely to put an end to this man-eating system so as to free the people from exploitation and enslavement that the oppressed people carry out violent revolution. But the Soviet revisionist renegades level so many criminal charges against the revolutionary armed forces and their revolutionary wars, making allegations about the "sufferings of the people," the "annihilation of cadres" and "destruction of the productive forces," and so on and so forth. Doesn't this logic of theirs mean that the first law

[6] Sinister anti-China book compiled by F. Konstantinov and others, Russian ed., the "Mysl" Publishing House, U.S.S.R., published in August 1970, pp. 119–20.

[7] Marx, "The Civil War in France," *Marx and Engels, Collected Works,* Chinese ed., Vol. 17, . 384.

under heaven is for the imperialists and reactionaries to oppress and massacre the people, whereas it is a hellish crime for the revolutionary people to take up arms and rise in resistance?

The Soviet revisionist renegades want the people of all countries to reduce revolutionary violence "to the minimum," but they themselves keep on increasing counter-revolutionary violence to the maximum. Indifferent to the life or death of Soviet people, Brezhnev and his gang are going all out for militarism and the arms race, spending more and more rubles on more and more planes, guns, warships, guided missiles and nuclear weapons. It is by means of this monstrous apparatus of violence that these new tsars oppress the broad masses at home and maintain their colonial rule abroad, trying to bring a number of countries under their control. It is this apparatus of violence that they are using as capital for bargaining with U.S. imperialism, pushing power politics and dividing spheres of influence.

The Soviet revisionist renegades want the revolutionary people to employ "milder forms of compulsion" against counter-revolution, while they themselves use the most savage and brutal means to deal with the revolutionary people.

May we ask:

Is it a "milder" form when you send large numbers of armed troops and police to suppress the people of different nationalities in your country?

Is it a "milder" form when you station large numbers of troops in some East European countries and the Mongolian People's Republic to impose a tight control over them, and even carry out the military occupation in Czechoslovakia, driving tanks into Prague?

And is it a "milder" form when you engage in military expansion everywhere and insidiously conduct all manner of subversive activities against other countries?

What the Soviet revisionist renegades have done fully shows that they not only oppose violent revolution but use violence to oppose revolution. They put on benevolent airs, but actually they are **"the worst enemies of the workers—wolves in sheep's clothing."** [8] . . . Khrushchev, the arch-representative of modern revisionism, has long been swept into the rubbish heap of history. Novotny and Gomulka, who followed Khrushchev's revisionist line, have also toppled in their turn. There can be no

[8] Engels, "Preface to the Second German Edition of 'The Condition of the Working Class in England,' 1892," *Marx and Engels, Collected Works,* Chinese ed., Vol. 22, p. 373.

doubt that whoever runs counter to the laws of history, betrays the revolutionary principles of the Paris Commune and turns traitor to the proletarian revolution and the dictatorship of the proletariat will come to no good end.

VI. Persist in Continuing the Revolution Under the Dictatorship of the Proletariat and Strive for Still Greater Victories

Historical experience since the Paris Commune, and especially since the October Revolution, shows that the capture of political power by the proletariat is not the end but the beginning of the socialist revolution. To consolidate the dictatorship of the proletariat and prevent the restoration of capitalism, it is necessary to carry the socialist revolution through to the end.

The world proletarian revolutionary movement has gone through twists and turns on its road forward. When capitalism was being restored in the homeland of the October Revolution, for a time it seemed doubtful whether the revolutionary principles of the Paris Commune, the October Revolution and the dictatorship of the proletariat were still valid. The imperialists and reactionaries were beside themselves with joy. They thought: Since the Soviet Union has changed through "peaceful evolution," won't it be possible to overthrow the dictatorship of the proletariat in China in the same way? But, the salvoes of the Great Proletarian Cultural Revolution initiated and led by Chairman Mao himself have destroyed the bourgeois headquarters headed by the renegade, hidden traitor and scab Liu Shao-chi and exploded the imperialists' and modern revisionists' fond dream of restoring capitalism in China.

Chairman Mao has comprehensively summed up the positive and negative aspects of the historical experience of the dictatorship of the proletariat, inherited, defended and developed the Marxist-Leninist theory of the proletarian revolution and the dictatorship of the proletariat, advanced the great theory of continuing the revolution under the dictatorship of the proletariat and solved, in theory and practice, the most important question of our time—the question of consolidating the dictatorship of the proletariat and preventing the restoration of capitalism. Thus he has made a great new contribution to Marxism-Leninism and charted our course for carrying the proletarian revolution triumphantly to the end. In China's Great Proletarian Cultural Revolution, Mao Tse-tung Thought and Chairman Mao's revolutionary line are being integrated more and more deeply with the revolutionary practice of the people in their hundreds of millions to become the greatest force in consolidating the dictatorship of the proletariat.

Socialist society covers a considerably long historical period. Throughout this period, there are still classes, class contradictions and class struggle. The struggle still focuses on the question of political power. The defeated class will struggle; these people are still around and this class still exists. They will invariably seek their agents within the Communist Party for the purpose of restoring capitaism. Therefore, the proletariat must not only guard against enemies like Thiers and Bismarck who overthrew the revolutionary political power by force of arms; it must in particular guard against such careerists and schemers as Khrushchev and Brezhnev who usurped party and state leadership from within. In order to consolidate the dictatorship of the proletariat and prevent the restoration of capitalism, the proletariat must carry out the socialist revolution not only on the economic front, but also on the political front and ideological and cultural front and exercise all-round dictatorship over the bourgeoisie in the superstructure, including all spheres of culture. It is essential to enable the Party members, the cadres and the masses to grasp the sharpest weapon, Marxism-Leninism, and to distinguish between the correct and erroneous lines between genuine and sham Marxism, and between materialism and idealism, so as to ensure that our Party and state will always advance along Chairman Mao's proletarian revolutionary line.

Document 13: Songs [1]

Apart from the music of the operas and ballets, two songs are heard endlessly all over China. They are played on every public-address system, and they blare from loudspeakers everywhere; they are sung by every group on the march. The third I heard less often, though it is described as "one of the best loved revolutionary songs in praise of our Great Leader."

LONG LIVE CHAIRMAN MAO! *

The golden sun rises in the east; its radiance spreads.

The East wind sweeps over the land; flowers bloom; red flags wave like a vast ocean.

Our great teacher and great leader, our respected and beloved Chairman Mao!

You are the sun in the hearts of the revolutionary people, the red sun in their hearts!

The mist has lifted; the dark clouds are blown away; the sky grows bright.

The sails of revolution brave winds and waves, bound for the glorious future.

Our great supreme commander, great helmsman, our respected and beloved Chairman Mao!

With you as their guide, the revolutionary people will never lose their bearings.

Storms roaring over the Five Continents and the Four Seas bring freedom and liberation.

The evil society shall be smashed, leaving no place for monsters to hide.

[1] The English text of "Long Live Chairman Mao," (described as "a literal translation") is from *Peking Review,* 1968, #18. The two others, "The East Is Red" and "Song of the Helmsman," are from a supplement to *China Reconstructs* date 1968.

* This is one of the best loved Chinese revolutionary songs in praise of our great leader Chairman Mao.

We are for the bright future and happiness! We are for Chairman Mao!
The revolutionary people follow you towards the goal of communism!

Long live Chairman Mao! Long live Chairman Mao!
A long, long, long, long life to Chairman Mao!
(Hei) A long, long life to Chairman Mao!

THE EAST IS RED

The East is red
There the sun rises
China has brought forth
Mao Tse-tung
He works for the people
He will free the nation

Chairman Mao
Loves his people
He will lead us
To build a new China
He leads us on

SONG OF THE HELMSMAN

To sail the seas
You need a helmsman.
Life and growth
Are dependent on sun.
Rain and dew
Nourish the crops.
To make a revolution
You need Mao Tse-tung.
Fish can't live without water
And a melon needs roots,
The revolutionary masses
Need the Communist Party.
Mao Tse-tung's thought
Is the sun ever shining.

Document 14: Mao Speaks

In addition to the 426 quotations in the Little Red Book, about 150 other Mao sayings are frequently quoted. They appear either as "Latest Directives" or "Words of Chairman Mao Tse-tung" in newspapers and periodicals, or in the texts of articles and printed speeches, where they are always recognizable as Mao sayings by the boldface type in which they are set, usually without any indication of the original source. Among the quotations that follow are those I heard most often during my visit, together with others that might contribute to an understanding of China after the Cultural Revolution.

The headings and italics are generally mine. The year the quotation originally appeared—when that is known—is given in brackets along with the source (LRB stands for Little Red Book, *PRe for* Peking Review) *All page numbers refer to the Peking edition of the Little Red Book.*

AGAINST THE FORMING OF A NEW CLASS

Every Communist working in the mass movements should be a friend of the masses and *not a boss* over them, an indefatigable teacher and *not a bureacratic politician.* [1938. LRB, p. 272]

Any specialized skill may be capitalized on and so may lead to *arrogance* and contempt of others. [1944. LRB, p. 239]

A dangerous tendency has shown itself of late among many of our personnel—an unwillingness to share the joys and hardships of the masses, a concern for *personal fame and gain.* This is very bad. [1957. LRB, p. 190]

With victory, certain moods may grow within the Party—*arrogance,* the *airs* of a self-styled hero, *inertia* and *unwillingness to make progress, love of pleasure* and *distaste for continued hard living.* [PRe 1967/43, p. 25]

It is necessary to maintain the system of cadre participation in collective productive labor. The cadres of our Party and state are ordinary workers and not *overlords sitting on the backs of the people*. [1964. PRe 1968/47, p. 2]

Some of our comrades are allergic to . . . criticism. . . . They appear frightful like the backside of a tiger which cannot be touched. Ten out of ten people who adopt this attitude will fail. People *will* talk. Is the backside of a tiger really untouchable? We *will* touch it! [1962. Jerome Chen, ed., *Mao Papers* (London, 1970), p. 38]

ALWAYS: THE CLASS STRUGGLE

How should we judge whether a youth is a revolutionary? How can we tell? There can be only one criterion, namely, whether or not he is willing to integrate himself with the broad masses of workers and peasants and does so in practice. If he is willing to do so and actually does so, he is a revolutionary; otherwise he is a non-revolutionary or a *counter-revolutionary*. If today he integrates himself with the masses of workers and peasants, then today he is a revolutionary; if tomorrow he ceases to do so or turns round to oppress the common people, then he becomes a non-revolutionary or a *counter-revolutionary*. [1939. LRB, p. 291]

[If] our cadres were to shut their eyes to all this and in many cases fail even to differentiate between the enemy and ourselves but were to collaborate with the enemy and were *corrupted, divided, and demoralized* by him, if our cadres were thus pulled out or *the enemy* were able to sneak in, and if many of our workers, peasants, and intellectuals were left defenceless against both the soft and the hard tactics of *the enemy*, then it would not take long, perhaps only several years or a decade, or several decades at most, before a *counter-revolutionary restoration* on a national scale inevitably occurred, the Marxist-Leninist party would undoubtedly become a *revisionist party or a fascist party*, and the whole of China would change its color. [1963. LRB, p. 41]

The revisionists deny the difference between socialism and capitalism, between the dictatorship of the proletariat and the *dictatorship of the bourgeoisie*. What they advocate is in fact not the socialist line but *the capitalist line*. [1957. LRB, pp. 20–21]

We must heighten our vigilance. We must conduct socialist education. We must correctly understand and handle *class contradictions and class struggle,* distinguish the contradictions between ourselves and the enemy from those among the people and handle them correctly. Otherwise a socialist country like ours will *turn into its opposite* and *degenerate,* and a *capitalist restoration* will take place. From now on we must remind ourselves of this *every year, every month, and every day.* [1969. Quoted in Lin Piao's Speech at the Ninth Congress.]

Those representatives of the bourgeoisie who have sneaked into the Party, the Government, the Army, and various spheres of culture are a bunch of *counter-revolutionary revisionists.* Once conditions are ripe, they will seize political power and turn the dictatorship of the proletariat into a *dictatorship of the* bourgeoisie. Some of them we have already seen through, others not. *Some are still trusted by us and are being trained as our successors.* [1966. PRe 1967, 7 21, p. 9]

CHANGES IN LEADERSHIP

In the process of a great struggle, the composition of the leading group in most cases should not and cannot remain entirely unchanged throughout the initial, middle and final stages; the activists who come forward in the course of the struggle must constantly be promoted *to replace those original members of the leading group* who are inferior by comparison or who have degenerated. [1943. LRB, p. 285]

A human being has arteries and veins through which the heart makes the blood circulate, and he breathes with his lungs, exhaling carbon dioxide and inhaling fresh oxygen, that is, *getting rid of the stale and taking in the fresh.* A proletarian party must also get rid of the stale and take in the fresh for only thus can it be full of vitality. Without *eliminating waste matter* and *absorbing fresh blood* the Party has no vigor. [PRe 1968, 2, p. 2]

NO LIFE WITHOUT CONTRADICTIONS

If there were no *contradictions,* there would be no world. [1956. Schram, *China Quarterly* No. 46, April–June 1971, p. 237]

If there were no *contradictions* in the Party and no ideological struggles to resolve them, the Party's life would come to an end. [1937. PRe, 1969, 39, p. 3]

THE TWO ROADS

Socialist society covers *a fairly long historical period.* Throughout this historical period there are classes, *class contradictions and class struggle,* there is the struggle between the socialist road and the capitalist road, there is the danger of *capitalist restoration. . . .* These contradictions can be resolved only by depending on the Marxist theory of *continued revolution.* [Party Constitution of 1969, Chapter I]

The fundamental contradiction to be solved by the Great Proletarian Cultural Revolution is the contradiction between the two classes, the proletariat and the bourgeoisie, and between *the two roads,* the socialist and the capitalist. The main targets of the present movement are those *Party persons in power* taking the capitalist road. [PRe 1969, 39, p. 6]

THE BELIEF IN THE MASSES

To talk about "arousing the masses of the people" day in and day out and then to be scared to death when the masses do rise—what difference is there between this and Lord Sheh's love of dragons? (Lord Sheh loved pictures of dragons, but was frightened out of his wits when he encountered a real dragon.) [1927. *Selected Works,* Vol. I, p. 56]

The masses are the real heroes, while we ourselves are often childish and ignorant. [1941. LRB, p. 118]

The people, and *the people alone,* are the motive force in the making of world history. [1945. LRB, p. 118]

The masses have *boundless creative power.* [1955. LRB, p. 118]

SELF-RELIANCE

On what basis should our policy rest? It should rest on *our own strength,* and that means regeneration *through one's own efforts.* . . . We stress regeneration through our own efforts. [1945. LRB, 194.]

. . . maintaining independence and keeping the initiative in our own hands, relying on *our own efforts.* [Quoted by Lin Piao in his report to the Ninth Party Congress, 1969, p. 46]

MIND AND MATTER

While we recognize that in the general development of history the material determines the mental and social being determines social consciousness, we also—and indeed must—recognize *the reaction of mental on material things,* of social consciousness on social being and of *the superstructure on the economic base.* [1937. LRB, p. 222]

THE TEST OF PRACTICE

Practice, knowledge, again *practice,* and again knowledge. This pattern repeats itself in endless cycles, and with each cycle the content of practice and knowledge rises to a higher level. [PRe, 1968, 10, p. 8]

. . . it is often not a matter of first learning and then doing, but of *doing and then learning,* for doing is in itself learning. [1936. LRB, p. 309]

CHINA—A CLEAN SHEET

Apart from their other characteristics, the outstanding thing about China's 600 million people is that they are *"poor and blank."* This may seem a bad thing, but in reality it is a good thing. Poverty gives rise to the desire for change, the desire for action and the desire for revolution. On *a blank sheet of paper free from any mark,* the freshest and most beautiful characters can be written, the freshest and most beautiful pictures can be painted. [1958. LRB, p. 36]

THE CULTURAL REVOLUTION

The current Great Proletarian Cultural Revolution is absolutely necessary and most timely for consolidating the dictatorship of the proletariat, *preventing capitalist restoration* and building socialism. [PRe, 1969, 39, p. 8]

The Great Proletarian Cultural Revolution is in essence a great political revolution carried out *under the conditions of socialism by the proletariat, against the bourgeoisie* and all the exploiting classes . . . a *continuation of the class struggle.* [PRe, 1969, 39, p. 8]

Hold high the great banner of the proletarian cultural revolution, thoroughly expose the reactionary bourgeois stand of those so-called *academic authorities* who oppose the Party and socialism; thoroughly criticize and repudiate reactionary bourgeois ideas in the sphere of academic work, education, journalism, literature, art, and publishing, and seize the leadership in these cultural spheres. [PRe, 1969, 39, p. 7]

There is no construction without destruction. *Destruction* means criticism and repudiation; *it means revolution.* [1966. PRe, 1967 21, p. 8]

Marxism consists of thousands of truths, but they all boil down to the one sentence: *"It is right to rebel."* [1939. PRe, 1969 39, p. 7]

SCHOOLS AND UNIVERSITIES

The length of *schooling should be shortened,* education should be revolutionized, and the domination of our schools and colleges by bourgeois intellectuals should not be tolerated any longer. [1966. PRe, 1969, 39, p. 9]

To accomplish the proletarian revolution in education, it is essential to have *working class leadership*; the masses of workers must take part in this revolution and, in cooperation with the *Liberation Army fighters*, form a revolutionary triumvirate [three-in-one combination] with the activists among the students, teachers and workers in schools and colleges, who are determined to carry the proletarian revolution in education through to the end. [PRe, 1969, 39, p. 9]

NOT AT A SNAIL'S PACE!

We cannot just take the beaten track traversed by other countries in the development of technology and *trail behind them at a snail's pace*. We must break away from convention and adopt as many advanced techniques as possible in order to build our country into *a powerful modern socialist state* in not too long a historical period. [PRe, 1969 25, p. 2]

U.S.A. AND U.S.S.R.: HAND IN GLOVE

Working hand in glove, Soviet revisionism and U.S. imperialism have done so many foul and evil things that the revolutionary people the world over will not let them go unpunished. The people of all countries are rising. A new historical period of struggle *against U.S. imperialism and Soviet revisionism* has begun. [PRe, 1969, 30, p. 2]

WAR AND THE USE OF FORCE

The seizure of power by armed force, *the settlement of the issue by war*, is the central task and the highest form of revolution. [1938, LRB, p. 61] We Communists oppose all unjust wars that impede progress, but we do not oppose progressive, just wars. Not only do we Communists not oppose just wars, *we actively participate in them*. [1938, LRB, pp. 59-60]

Political power grows out of *the barrel of a gun*. [1938, LRB, p. 61]

If the imperialists insist on launching *a third world war*, it is certain that several hundred million more will turn to socialism, and then there will not be much room left on earth for the imperialists; it is also likely that the whole structure of imperialism will utterly collapse. [1957, LRB, p. 68]

The atom bomb is a paper tiger. . . . It looks terrible, but in fact it isn't. Of course, the atom bomb is the weapon of mass slaughter, but the outcome of a war is determined by the people, not by one or two new types of weapon. [1946, LRB, p. 140]

"I debated this question (of a third world war) with a foreign statesman. He believed that if an atomic war was fought, the whole of mankind would be annihilated. I said that *if the worst came to the worst and half of mankind died,* the other half would remain while imperialism would be razed to the ground and *the whole world would become socialist;* in a number of years there would be 2,700 million people again and definitely more." [1957, in Moscow, PRe, 1963, 36, p. 10]

With regard to the question of world war, there are but two possibilities: one is that *the war will give rise to revolution,* and the other is that revolution will prevent the war. [Quoted by Lin Piao in his speech to the Ninth Congress, 1969]

Be prepared against war, be prepared against natural disasters, and do everything for the people. [Quoted by Lin Piao in his speech to the Ninth Congress, 1969]

NO FEAR OF DEATH

I am for the slogan: "fear neither hardship nor death." [PRe, 1969, 32, p. 3]

MAO TO EDGAR SNOW, DECEMBER 18, 1970

Later the conflict during the Cultural Revolution developed into war between factions—first with spears, then rifles, then mortars. When foreigners reported that *China was in great chaos,* they were not telling lies. It had been true. . . . The other thing [Mao] was most unhappy about was the maltreatment [during the Cultural Revolution] of "captives"—Party members and others removed from power and subjected to re-education. . . . *Maltreatment of captives* now had slowed the rebuilding and transformation of the party.

. . . He was, he said, only *a lone monk* walking the world with a leaky umbrella. [*Life,* April 30, 1971]

Index

Ceylon, 231
Chang Hsüeh-liang, 154
Chang Tso-lin, 154
Changsha, 22
Chao Hsiao-ho, 163-164
Chen Chung-wei, 122
Chen Po-ta, 11, 30-31, 211, 246
Chen Yung-kui, 45, 46, 52, 163, 185
Chenpao Island, 162
Chi Teng-kuei, 34
Chiang Ching, 125, 138, 145-149, 180, 236, 245, 246, 283-288 *passim*, 289
Chiang Kai-shek, 154-156, 161, 182, 187, 200, 216, 220; defeat of, 194, 286, 290; Stalin and, 225, 234; troops of, 106, 120, 123, 141
Chin dynasty, 181
Chin Hsün-hua, 272-274
Chinese Travel Service, 16, 17, 20, 38, 39, 40
Chiu Hui-tso, 33
Chou En-lai, 5, 31-32, 35, 127, 148, 168, 193, 223, 231, 233, 245; banquet given by, 29-30, 43, 167; home at Yenan, 124-125; indispensability of, 246; production figures given by, 253, 254
Christianity, 151
Chufu, 126, 179
civil war: Chinese, 120, 147, 200, 225, 243; in Russia, 187
clans, 58, 186, 194, 217
class struggle, 181, 188, 190, 201, 260, 278, 290, 300; Mao on, 304-305, 306
clothing, prices of, 25, 26, 37, 73
coal, 45; conservation of, 64
Cohen, Arthur, 219
collectives, agrarian, 45. *See also* cooperatives; people's communes
Common Market. *See* European Economic Community
communes: Canton, 161; prehistoric, 154; Shanghai, 247. *See also* Paris Commune; people's communes
Communist Manifesto, 70
Communist Party: activists in, 185-186, 305; Central Committee, 30, 33, 47, 124, 125, 189, 209, 211, 244, 245, 247, 251-252, 260, 262, 284, 290; Congresses, 32, 96, 98, 118, 125, 149, 198, 259, 307; constitution, 198, 208, 241; and Cultural Revolution, 180, 198, 218, 246, 247; founding of, 100, 128; and Kuomintang, 127; leadership, 199, 209; organization, 85-86, 91, 198, 243; Soviet, 118, 167, 199; triumph of, 186. *See also* Politburo; revolutionary committees
Communist Youth League, 63, 103-104
conformity, 216
Confucianism, 151, 153, 186, 217
Confucius, 126, 152-153, 180-181, 182; temples of, 27, 127, 151, 179
consciousness, Maoist view of, 117, 185, 242, 260-261
consumer products, 174, 176, 202, 205; prices, 27; sale of in villages, 51, 73
contraceptives, 224. *See also* birth control
contradictions, Mao on, 117-118, 185, 187-188, 190, 191, 192, 193, 208, 242, 249, 276, 305-306
cooperatives, 88, 251-252
corn, production of, 51, 56
cotton: clothing, 25, 26; rationing of, 25; textile production figures, 254
counterrevolutionaries, 147, 297, 298, 304
crude oil, production of, 254
Cuba, 43
cucumbers, growing of, 72-73
Cultural Revolution, 43, 180, 183, 186, 190, 193, 196-201, 203, 208, 230, 244-246, 254, 299; captives, maltreatment of, 310-311; documents of, 60, 146, 180, 262; and education, 105, 111-116, 248-251; effects of, 42, 80, 81, 83, 149, 174, 177; and Great Leap Forward, 173; leaders, 146, 148; Mao on, 308; name of, 284; onset of, 221, 244; and Party organization, 85; Red Guards and, 157, 158, 244; restrictions on visitors during, 27, 159; Sixteen Points, 197, 245; and "two ways," 46. *See also* cadres; Communist Party; intellectuals; universities
Culture, Ministry of, 146
currency, 18, 54; rates of exchange, 26, 27

Great Leap Forward, 15, 31, 50, 76, 104, 133, 134, 163, 173, 187, 191, 196, 214, 252, 253; failure of, 210; and split between Mao and Liu, 243, 244

Great Proletarian Cultural Revolution. See Cultural Revolution

Great Wall, 29

Grove of Steles, 151

guerrillas: Cambodian, 35; Chinese, 120, 127, 163, 192, 243; Laotian, 166; in theatrical productions, 67, 138, 139, 141

gymnastics, 74, 99

Hainan Island, 138

Hangchow, 77, 80, 119, 129, 161

happiness, nature of, 217

Harbin, 36

Hegel, G. W. F., 117, 123

Heilungkiang Province, 61, 62, 247

"Helmsman, Song of the," 57, 60, 121, 129, 143, 210, 302

heroes, 161-164; Mao on masses as, 306; military, 215-216; in opera, 289

hierarchies: army, 200-201; Confucian, 186, 194; Party, 32; Soviet, 177

highways, 28, 29, 60, 205

history, 83, 150, 151, 183; Mao and, 181, 182, 306; Russian, 179; study of, 101, 180

Ho Lung, 125

Hoffmann, Charles, 207

Honan, 34, 71

Hong Kong, 9, 16, 17, 145, 175

horses, 28, 29, 49; in sculpture, 152, 183

hospitals, 50, 73, 93, 122, 200

hotels, 23, 38-39, 43, 44

housing, 27, 50, 206; in industrial suburb, 92, 94-95

Hsiafang ("sending down"), 174, 196

Hsiang, county of, 59

Hsinhua, 227

Hsuan-tsang, 151, 152

Huang Ho, 144

Huang Pu, 36

Huang-ti (the Yellow Emperor), 150-151, 179-180

Huang Yung-sheng, 33

Hunan Province, 22

Hundred Flowers episode, 15, 173-174, 249

ideology, 84, 177; Maoist, 185, 202, 241-242, 260-261

Imperial Palace, Peking, 23, 24

imperialism, 94, 102, 104, 110, 114, 131, 152, 222, 229, 273, 297, 298; Mao on, 118, 259, 309

India, 151, 188, 220, 225

Indochina, 88, 166, 231

industrialization, 110, 176, 226, 232, 236; early stages of, 137, 236; small-scale, 134, 196; Soviet, 214

infirmaries, 65, 72, 93. See also hospitals

"Intellectual Youth to the Countryside," 22, 97, 98

intellectuals, 102-103, 173-174; and Cultural Revolution, 122, 196, 216, 264, 278; and Little Red Book, 213; Mao on, 268, 281, 308; "re-education" of, 64, 68-69, 70, 251, 272, 281

interest rates, 55, 93

"Internationale," 121, 139, 222

internationalism, 222

irrigation, 19, 49, 55, 62, 75, 214, 224

Ivan the Terrible, 179

Ivanov, W. W., 178

Japan, 43, 159, 220, 223, 224, 226, 231, 233; occupation by, 45, 67, 69, 120, 123, 138, 154, 182, 230; in Second World War, 160, 221

Johnson, Chalmers, 219

Johnson, Eldridge, 152

journalists, 34, 43, 178

Kang Mao-chao, 31

Kang Sheng, 11, 31, 125, 246

"keeping up with the Joneses," 206

Khrushchev, Nikita, 44, 192, 202, 205, 295, 296, 300

Kiangsi, 34

Kiangsu Province, 147

kindergartens, 57, 65, 92, 93, 222

Kirin, University of, 122, 278

kolkhoz, Soviet, 52, 55, 175, 196, 252

Korea, 31, 43, 226, 231, 237

Korean War, 127, 220

Kosygin, Alexei, 165, 177

Kunlun range, 235

Kuo clan, 58

dice against, 68, 272; rich, 45, 92, 214; Russian, 187; at Yenan, 125-126

Peitaiho, resort at, 128

Peking, 23-28, 41, 247; Academy of Sciences, 33; foreign colony, 16, 18-19, 42, 43, 115; legation quarter, 159-160; Morrison Street, 24; railway station, 23; schools, 98-104; setting, 28-29; "Street of Anti-Revisionism," 43; theater, 137-144; tourist attractions, 156-158, 179. *See also* East Peking; Gate of Heavenly Peace

Peking opera, 48, 107, 141-142, 145, 147, 289; revolutionizing of, 285

Peking Review, 44, 116, 128, 149n, 167, 190-191, 251, 266, 267, 283, 303-311 *passim*

Pen Nouth, 165

Peng Teh-huai, 244, 245

pensions, 86, 94

people's communes, 45-46, 62, 71-77, 253; financing of, 75; relation to production brigades, 90-91

People's Daily, 24, 31, 61, 64, 186n, 240, 262, 267, 295

People's Democracies, 173; architecture, 20

People's Liberation Army, 103, 141, 163, 215-216, 286, 290; and Cultural Revolution, 262-264

Peter the Great, 179

pharmacies, 65, 73

Philharmonic Orchestra of Peking, 148

philosophy: classical, 189; Maoist, 117-118, 123. *See also* Confucianism

Phnom Penh, 15, 31, 34, 165

piano, popularity of, 143, 148-149

pigs, production of, 46, 56, 66, 77, 214

ping-pong, 34, 134; visiting teams, 27, 174, 230

"ping-pong politics," 9, 16, 160, 177, 183

planning, economic, 203

Poland, 175

Politbureau, 30, 31-33, 116, 248

"political consciousness," 98, 100, 111; and pay scales, 53, 84-85, 207-208; teaching of, 102, 105

population figures, 88, 95-96, 223-224, 254

poverty, Mao on, 202, 307-308

practice, Mao on, 115, 122, 276, 307

pragmatism, 177, 189-190, 241-243, 244, 245

Pravda, 31, 296n

prices, 26-27, 37, 93; bicycle motors, 37-38; clothing, 25, 26, 37, 73; grain, 56, rice, 93; tea, 72

private property, 50, 51, 153

processions, 57, 120, 184-185. *See also* marching production brigades, 45-46, 72, 76, 87-92, 197, 214, 253; economics of, 56

productivity, increase in, 78-79, 174, 205, 214

proletariat, 122, 137, 287; Russian, 296; victory forecast, 117, 190. *See also* dictatorship; masses

propaganda teams, 105, 108-109, 248-249, 250

Quiet Flows the Don (Sholokhov), 287

quotas, 115

radio broadcasting, 29, 43-44, 126, 144, 167, 168, 250

railways, 28, 132; travel accommodations, 16, 21, 200

rationing, 25, 93

Red Detachment of Women, The, 138-140, 285

Red Guards, 98, 104, 144, 157, 158, 211, 237, 244, 245, 247, 248, 272

Red Lantern, The, 108, 147-148, 285

re-education. *See* intellectuals; Seventh of May schools

religion, 151, 152. *See also* Buddhism

Rent Collection, The, 180, 285

rents, 27, 94

reservoirs, 22

restaurants, 26-27; on trains, 21

Reston, James, 233

revisionism, 190-192; in literature, 284, 287, 288; Liu Shao-chi and, 278; in opera, 147; remedies for, 68; and scientific research, 282; Soviet, 102, 104, 114, 131, 132, 135, 136, 162, 183, 204, 220, 273, 295, 297-298, 309; and work incentives, 81 revolution, 86, 98, 106, 185, 186-194, 211, 236, 237, 242, 244, 287-288, 308; support of in other countries, 224; war and, 310

revolutionary committees, 47, 69, 85-86, 105, 186, 198-199, 247-248; in industrial suburb, 95, 96-98; at Machine Tools Plant #1, 110; in production brigades, 87, 90-91; role in setting wages, 80

rice: cultivation, 22, 62, 66; export, 133; increased production, 88; prices, 93; rationing, 93; tax-free status, 253

Russia, tsarist, 228, 285

Russian Orthodox church, 43

salaries, 27, 56, 63, 75, 76, 94, 176, 177, 206; of officials, 195; of propaganda teams, 108. *See also* pay categories; wages

sandstorms, precautions against, 75

sanitary facilities, 65, 94. *See also* latrines

Sanlitun, suburb of, 42, 44

savings, 55, 93, 214

Scandinavia, 194

schools, 122, 180; building of, 56, 75; elementary, 104-109; in industrial suburb, 92; middle, 74, 98-104; in villages, 56-57

science, 181

sculpture, 152, 285

Second World War, 9, 160, 178, 179, 221, 234

secret societies, 217

self-criticism, 70, 71, 82, 115, 236

self-interest, 195, 243, 281. *See also* egotism

self-reliance, 100, 184, 197, 200; Mao on, 116-117, 280, 307; national, 102, 133, 135

Seventh of May schools, 34, 60-71, 196, 200, 236, 262

Shamian Island, 20

Shanghai, 9, 32, 36-39, 44, 209, 245, 251; administration, 95-96; foreign colony, 36; industrial exhibition, 132-133. *See also* Machine Tools Plant #1; Tsaoyang

Shansi Province, 45

Shantung, 220

Shaoshan, 128

Shensi Province, 120, 123

shoes, price of, 37

Sholokhov, Mikhail, 288

Sian, 27, 116, 123, 150, 156, 167; museum at, 151, 182

Siberia, 179, 223, 229

Sihanouk, Prince Norodom, 15, 29, 33; government of, 29, 31, 164-165; relations with China, 35, 77, 166; and Soviet Union, 165-166

silk industry, 77, 94, 129

slavery, 152-153

Snow, Edgar, 210, 211, 216, 230, 246, 254, 310

social democratic parties, 192

socialism, 56, 60, 68, 190, 219, 222; contradictions within, 118, 188; enemies of, 180; transition to communism, 204-205

Songs, 301-302. *See also* "East Is Red"; "Helmsman"; "Internationale"

Souphanouvong, Prince, 166

Soviet Union, 9-10, 227-229, 234-235; alliance with China, 22, 221; border dispute with China, 229, 273; bureaucracy, 196; compared with China, 137, 175-178, 179, 226; demonstrations against, 43, 59; education, 104; embassy in Peking, 43; enmity with China, 174, 224, 229, 230; painting, 128; Party organization, 199; philosophical errors, 117, 118; possible Chinese attack on, 224; withdrawal of aid by, 114, 131, 132, 135, 232. *See also* October Revolution

specialization: mockery of, 176; need for, 236; "old" universities and, 110-111; Seventh of May edict against, 60-61; Soviet, 175, 177

Stalin, Josef, 44, 56, 77, 84, 102, 104, 128, 132, 175, 179, 187, 208, 221, 286

Stanislavsky, Constantin, 285

state, 94; appropriation of social product by, 205; Chinese concept of, 221-222; and education, 114; as holder of common property, 94; and individual, 98, 103; relations of silk industry to, 78; and tea brigade, 78

steel production, 196; figures, 254

Steles, Grove of, 151, 153

320